Black Bonanza

Black Bonanza

*Alberta's Oil Sands and the
Race to Secure North America's
Energy Future*

Alastair Sweeny

John Wiley & Sons Canada, Ltd.

Library and Archives Canada Cataloguing in Publication

Sweeny, Alastair
   Black bonanza : Alberta's oil sands and the race to secure North America's energy future / Alastair Sweeny.

Includes index.
ISBN 978-0-470-16138-8

   1. Oil sands—Government policy—Alberta.   2. Oil sands—Economic aspects—Alberta.   3. Oil sands—Environmental aspects—Alberta.   4. Oil sands industry—Technological innovations—Alberta.   5. Athabasca Tar Sands (Alta.).   I.   Title.

HD9574.C23A54 2010   333.8'232097123   C2009-906379-4

Production Credits
Cover design: Natalia Burobina
Interior design: Adrian So
Typesetter: Thomson Digital
Cover Printing: Lehigh Phoenix
Printing and Binding: Friesens Printing Ltd.

Editorial Credits
Executive Editor: Karen Milner
Project Coordinator: Pauline Ricablanca

John Wiley & Sons Canada, Ltd.
6045 Freemont Blvd.
Mississauga, Ontario
L5R 4J3

Printed in Canada
1 2 3 4 5 FP 14 13 12 11 10

ENVIRONMENTAL BENEFITS STATEMENT

John Wiley & Sons - Canada saved the following resources by printing the pages of this book on chlorine free paper made with 100% post-consumer waste.

TREES	WATER	SOLID WASTE	GREENHOUSE GASES
70 FULLY GROWN	32,260 GALLONS	1,959 POUNDS	6,698 POUNDS

Calculations based on research by Environmental Defense and the Paper Task Force. Manufactured at Friesens Corporation

Dedication

For Ewan Sweeny, Albertan, on his thirtieth birthday.

Contents

Preface

Welcome to *Black Bonanza*, the story of Canada's Athabasca Sands, one of the greatest reservoirs of fossil fuels on the planet.

I started to write this book during a growing attack on the Sands by global warming alarmists. The whole movement seemed unreal to me, and not entirely about the environment, and I wanted to do some due diligence to see what was really behind these attacks. I did some research in the 1980s for Alberta Energy Company, one of the original investors in Syncrude, and have been tracking the history of the Sands ever since. I was particularly struck by former Alberta Premier Peter Lougheed's recent concerns about runaway Sands development, and other worries about water and air pollution. So, I felt it was time to dig deeper into the issues and share my findings with people interested in a wider perspective on our energy future. As I got further into the research, I realized that the story of the early days of the Sands and the huge engineering challenges faced was fascinating as well.

The first part of *Black Bonanza* tells how the Sands were formed millions of years ago, and the one-hundred-year quest to crack the code of removing usable oil from what is essentially tarry dirt. Reminiscent of the Klondike gold rush days, only in slow motion, the quest for oil from the Sands attracted a parade of dreamers, adventurers and explorers, pulled by the lure of the frontier. All of them went broke. However, the rise in oil prices in the 1970s and 1980s attracted major investors, and finally, in the 1990s, a marvelous new below-ground technology emerged, to transform the industry from a backwater resource to the global giant it is today. There is spectacular wealth in the Sands, far more than we originally believed, and this story must be told as well.

In the second part of the book, I explore the new role of the Sands as the "whipping boy" of radical green activists and as "the worst project on earth." Just as the Sands emerged to help us deal with a growing oil supply emergency, a massive campaign by global warming crusaders has staked a claim against Canada's oilsands developers. In an effort to demonize the Sands, an army of public relations activists were unleashed to turn the Sands from what should be a treasure chest of wealth and energy security, into what Al Gore calls "a threat to our survival as a species."

Some of my green-leaning friends would disagree, but I'm afraid that, for the past decade, the Anthropogenic Global Warming (AGW) crusaders have sucked all the oxygen out of most other environmental campaigns, and many far more serious concerns have been set aside to placate these U.N.-backed agitators. Even the oilsands producers seem like deer caught in the headlights, unable to flee from this onrushing army of warmists.

The book becomes a a bit of a detective story, as I go behind the public relations spin of AGW and try to unravel the people and players behind the crusade. I wanted to find out why they are so bent on painting Canada black and even trying to shut down the Sands, especially when the country is really only a bit player in the global emissions game. This is a legitimate question, when the U.S. and Chinese coal industries have a far more serious environmental footprint.

• • •

> *Sherlock Holmes: I have no data yet. It is a capital mistake to theorize before one has data. Insensibly one begins to twist facts to suit theories, instead of theories to suit facts . . .*
> —*Arthur Conan Doyle,* A Scandal in Bohemia (1891)

There clearly is far more going on with this AGW circus than meets the eye. First, why are millions of people obsessing about carbon dioxide (CO_2), a trace gas in the atmosphere, 3 percent of which is due to human emissions? And why are government officials demanding that billions of dollars be spent to control this gas that is so essential to plant growth, while real pollution concerns cry out for solutions and scores of our fellow citizens starve to death or die from preventable diseases? Frankly I am baffled. This seems like something out of Orwell's novel, *1984*.

Where does the truth stand? Why have scores of scientists bought into climate models that still don't stand up to scrutiny? Physicist Richard Feynman called this "cargo cult science," where flawed research produces useless results and scientists fool themselves. And why did prominent climate experts take the risk of fudging data to support the United Nations Intergovernmental Panel on Climate Change (IPCC), when they knew they would be found out eventually? Who has been paying for all this folly if not the taxpayer? Clive Crooks said it best in *The Atlantic*: "The stink of intellectual corruption is overpowering. This scandal is not at the margins of the politicized IPCC process. It goes to the core of that process."

Another question that intrigued me as I researched this book was this: Why are the leaders of AGW blaming "Big Oil" for the problems of the planet when most of them have worked for, taken grant money from, or even partnered with the oil majors? Even the lead environmental sled dogs, Greenpeace and WWF, have taken funding from Big Oil. So who is co-opting whom?

For the sake of understanding this issue, I believe it is crucial for people to set aside their very real environmental concerns and question what is really going on behind AGW and the stigmatizing of the Sands. Is it just hypocrisy we are dealing with? Is the whole campaign over AGW just a fund raising scam, or is it more? This whole advocacy issue, while painful for some, is just too important to ignore. There are serious economic interests at stake here and some major economic repercussions.

I know that public relations professionals have little interest in that quaint concept called truth. They have a job to do and clients to satisfy. And, obviously, the major oil companies in the Sands have their own public relations departments, as well as hiring outside consultants, but what amazed me is how big a public relations exercise AGW and the "carbon jihad" has become, and what a colossal amount of money has been spent on dirtying the reputation of the Sands. I wanted to drill down and find out who profits and who pays.

Behind the scenes, that whole AGW crusade is being stage managed by a number of well-paid advocacy consultants. These people are experts at using the complete arsenal of modern public relations, including on-line campaigns, viral interactive media, rapid response, securing placement for opinion pieces, issues branding, political rhetoric, and persuasion.

A lot of the divide seems politically driven. Al Gore himself doesn't dare cross the street without his trusty public relations lady, Kalee Kreider, formerly a senior vice president and Washington manager of Fenton Communications, and a veteran activist and publicist who has worked closely with Greenpeace and the WWF. The *Washington Post* says that Fenton founder David Fenton, a senior hippy who's the public relations guru of the U.S. left, is "not just the poster child of liberal causes; he's the designer, producer and distributor of the posters." New York-based Fenton is the guy who single-handedly changed the tired old terminology "left wing" into a shining new brand: "progressive." He also edits Al Gore's speeches.

Jim Hoggan, who runs Canada's David Suzuki Foundation, is a very smooth public relations pro as well. His blog, desmogblog, pretty much recycles the Al Gore carbon chastity mantra developed by Fenton.

But then again, in this house of mirrors, we find that not all left-wingers are warmists. In that great lobby bazaar called Washington, home of almost 40,000 registered lobbyists, and hundreds of thousands of policy promoters, both the Democrats and the Republicans happily accept donations from pretty much the same large corporations, with few exceptions.[1]

So we have to drill down further. I find it fascinating that several of the major players have extensive ties to the oil industry. Al Gore's father, a U.S. senator, boosted the family fortune sitting on the board of Armand Hammer's Occidental Petroleum (Oxy), and helped Oxy get into Libya. Today, Oxy is the world's largest user of CO_2 for enhanced oil recovery (EOR), a technique used to increase production from mature wells. The current Oxy Canada is primarily a gas reseller, but the original Occidental Petroleum Canada Ltd. has morphed into Nexen Inc., a respected and innovative oilsands operator.

Rajendra Kumar Pachauri, head of the UN IPCC, was lead author on the IPCC's second report, which paved the way to Kyoto—which, in turn, ushered in the world's first carbon trading schemes. Pachauri is closely involved with India's biggest company, Tata Industries, who have bankrolled his TERI Energy Research Institute for thirty years. Pachauri has served as a director of the Indian Oil Corporation and is a director of Oil and Natural Gas Corp. In 2005, he founded his own oil company, GloriOil Limited, of Houston, Texas, to exploit patented processes developed by TERI. In 2007, Kleiner Perkins, the Silicon Valley venture capital firm that has Al Gore as a partner, invested $10 million in the company. Pachauri sits on the advisory board of the Chicago Climate Exchange.

I also wanted to explore the contribution to the movement by Canadian Maurice Strong, the godfather of global warming, who is the spider at the center of a very impressively woven web. A grade eleven dropout and former fur trader who once worked as a security guard at the United Nations, Strong now has oodles of honorary degrees for his work on the environment. After a business career in the energy and international development business,

---

[1] For a chart showing a recent huge rise in the number of "Climate Change Lobbyists," please see the Web support site, *Black Bonanza* Maps & Charts—Climate Change. < * >

Strong founded the UN Environmental Program (UNEP), was a member of the Club of Rome, ran the 1992 Earth Summit at Rio, founded the UN IPCC, the heart of the AGW movement, and is also vice-chair of the advisory board of the Chicago Climate Exchange. But Strong also knows the energy business as an insider—he was founding president of Petro-Canada, recently absorbed by major oilsands player Suncor Energy.

Moving beyond all the public relations issues, we have to look at who benefits from the AGW crusade and the demonization of the Sands. We have to question whether the Chicago Carbon Exchange and other emissions markets and carbon credit schemes really work, and whether there are better ways to promote renewable energy, such as simple taxes at the pump and tax breaks for energy conservation and innovation.

It appears that we are starting to reach "Warmageddon," the last battle in the AGW crusade. At the time of writing, I feel these AGW spin doctors, however bright and persuasive they may be, are flogging a dying horse. Even before the "Climategate" release of incriminating e-mails, the real science was dragging them down and the recession was making it worse. Now polls show that climate fatigue is setting in, and people are increasingly yawning and changing the channel in face of the most brutal apocalyptic statements by Al Gore and others. Why do they keep up the pretense and keep repeating the same tired mantra—Canada's oil sands are evil? They are not, and it's time to move on.

Finally, I wanted to explore the concept put forward by a number of experts, from inventor Kay Kurzweil to financier Warren Buffett, that we are very close to some amazing breakthroughs in solar power, and twenty years from now most short-haul vehicles on the road will be electric. In the final section of the book, I explore what this will do to the oil industry, and what transitional role the Athabasca Sands can play in the race to real energy security.

• • •

I hope you enjoy *Black Bonanza*. If you want to learn more about the Sands and the issues I discuss in the book, I invite you to visit my Web Support Site at: www.alastairsweeny.com/blackbonanza/index.php .

I have added chapter-related images and videos, and a full resourcebase of Sands-related images and videos, documents, useful Web links, and a bookstore with direct links to order pages at on-line retailers.

The Web Support Site also has clickable Web-linked references that connect you right to the original article that I've cited in each chapter. These are indicated at the end of appropriate footnotes in the book with the symbol < * > . I have also built a gallery of images you can refer to while you read each chapter of the book.

While I have tried making material about oilsands technology as reader-friendly as possible, if you need help with technical terms and want to understand the oilsands universe better, I invite you to use the glossary on the Web Support Site.

A note on spelling and definition: The Athabasca Sands are not properly "tar sands" because tar is a by-product of coal oil. They used to be called "the tar sands," and the "dirty" oil attackers insist on using the term for spin. Oilsands pioneer, Karl Clark, was the first to argue that they should more properly be called "oil sands" or "oilsands." In this book, I have used all three terms, and generally prefer to call them "the Sands."

● ● ●

Before and after publication, I will also be adding material on the Web Support Site, twittering @alastairsweeny and posting, from time to time on the *Black Bonanza* Weblog at: http://blackbonanzablog.blogspot.com/ .

Thanks for reading *Black Bonanza*. I hope you enjoy this book and find that it provides you with insight, context, and understanding about the amazing saga of Canada's oil sands and their role in our energy security.

I welcome your feedback, questions, and comments.

Alastair Sweeny
Ottawa, Canada
blackbonanzabook@gmail.com
December 15, 2009

Acknowledgments

Scores of people gave me input and wise counsel with this book. In particular, I'd like to thank Pierre Alvarez, Neil Camarta, Angela Crocker, Travis Davies, Earle Gray, Vincent Lauerman, Steve McIntyre, Dave Mitchell, Gwyn Morgan, Stephen Rodrigues, Kelli Stevens, as well as a number of energy company employees, association spokespeople and environmental consultants who spoke on the condition of anonymity. My research load was made easier by staff at Library and Archives Canada, the Calgary Public Library, the universities of Alberta and Calgary, the Provincial Archives of Alberta and Natural Resources Canada, particularly Lexie Lewis. At Wiley Canada, I would like to thank Karen Milner and her splendid crew: Deborah Guichelaar, Liz Mccurdy, Pauline Ricablanca, Lucas Wilk and Brian Will, as well as my amazingly astute editor Carol Bonnett. To all, many thanks.

Finally, no, I am not an "oil company shill" and the opinions expressed in this book are entirely my own.

1

All About the Oil Sands

He that will not apply new remedies must expect new evils,
for time is the greatest innovator.

—Francis Bacon

Hard-hatted, I'm standing in the middle of a reeking moonscape of black bitumen-coated sand. Around me are enormous diesel haulers and an old electric shovel that has had its day. It's a hot afternoon and the stuff the engineers refer to as "dirt" stinks like the fresh asphalt I poured in my driveway last June. I pick up a bit of the dirt—it's soft, moist, and a bit sticky. My feet even sink gently into the stuff. Later, I find the leather soles of my shoes are spotted with oil.

Everything is big in the Athabasca Sands. Landing in the main Syncrude site is like being inside a giant crater on another planet. The colossal yellow Caterpillar 797Bs that can each haul 400 tons of oil sands from the shovels to the separation plant, are the biggest trucks money can buy. Each one has the horsepower of a hundred pickup trucks. They're monster versions of the yellow Tonkas my sons had in their sandbox. Fully loaded, they weigh more than two Boeing 747s. Each 400-ton run delivers enough dirt to make about 200 barrels of oil, or 1,000 U.S. gallons (3,785 liters) of gasoline.

To get up into the cab, I have to climb fifty feet (15.24 meters) up a welded steel staircase of twenty steps. From the top, the landscape appears lunar—a lumpy black asphalt field stretching to the horizon—and over to the east, the greasy sludge ponds kept in by a monstrous tailing dam—the largest in the world by volume—standing as high as a house. Beside the plant, the eye is drawn to the neatly stepped pyramid of shocking yellow sulphur, a by-product of synthetic crude, to be shipped out to make fertilizer.

Like the tar that pools out of road asphalt on a blistering hot day, liquid bitumen has always oozed out of the high banks of the Athabasca River for as long as native people can remember. In summer, it can stick to your boots; in winter, you can burn it like coal. Also called pitch, bitumen is the heaviest of the naturally occurring crude oils, a hydrocarbon with most of the hydrogen missing.

The driver says it's a lot different here in the winter when blizzards roar up the valley from the Arctic Circle. Take some molasses and put it in the fridge for a few hours. Then try to pour it. Nothing much happens. That's raw bitumen, as thick and sticky as cold blackstrap molasses. But try and take it out of the ground when the temperature is 58 degrees below 0 Fahrenheit (negative 50 Celsius), and it is as hard as rock.

On a hot June day, with sweat trickling down from under my Syncrude hardhat, I try to imagine working here in January, on a windswept landscape where it's so cold that diesel fuel freezes to the consistency of Vaseline, and light engine oil becomes as hard as grease. In the worst days of winter whiteout, you have to keep the engines of these heavy haulers running twenty-four hours a day. If you let the engine stop when it's that cold, you might not be able to start it again until the spring thaw three months later.

The black gold rush currently taking place in the Sands of the Athabasca is the biggest industrial project on the planet. The Sands are not pretty and the climate can be brutal, but for the people who

2

work here mining the Sands, steaming the oil off underground deposits or just servicing the big operators, it's a chance to strike it rich in a modern-day Klondike.

• • •

If energy is supposed to be the master resource of the human race, then Canadians are truly blessed. Beneath the boreal forest of Saskatchewan and Alberta, halfway between Edmonton and the border of the Northwest Territories, lies a black bonanza of oil-soaked sand, with more petroleum than the entire Middle East.

It's hard for people to grasp this simple fact—the bitumen and heavy oil of the Canadian provinces of Alberta and Saskatchewan are the largest known petroleum assets on the planet. Covering an area larger than England, this belt of oil-soaked silicon dwarfs the light oil reserves of the entire Middle East. According to Clive Mather, former head of Shell Canada, "We know there's much, much more there. The total estimates could be two trillion or even higher. This is a very, very big resource."

However, this treasure chest lies in rich moist layers that are not ideal for extraction. Over the past twenty-five years, a posse of chemists, geologists, and drilling service companies have spent millions on research to come up with new underground wizardry that will eventually allow us to extract at least one trillion barrels from the 80 percent of the Sands which are too deep to be mined.

On the surface, the strip miners have also refined their technology, cutting their costs, and squeezing out synthetic crude by using less and less heat and water. Over the next few years, they are being forced to apply themselves to drying out and reclaiming the giant tailing ponds that have so disfigured the landscape and caused so much hand-wringing from green activists around the globe.

The below-ground producers have a much smaller footprint, using an amazing new process—steam assisted gravity drainage or SAGD—invented by Calgary chemist, Roger Butler, to gently coax the oil from the sand. These producers use less energy and, in some cases, are completely recycling heat and water. Some of them use underground combustion or electricity rather than steam to warm the bitumen underground. Others are using solvent to reduce the need for both water and energy for steam. Some are working out completely closed-loop systems, making their own steam from the energy below. Underground extraction uses a great deal of steam and natural gas is still the major fuel source, but massive new discoveries of gas are coming onstream in North America and these will keep the costs in line.

In fact, most production and "lifting" costs in the Sands are not out of line compared to conventional oil and far cheaper than offshore drilling, plus there is no exploration cost to pay.[1]

It's a huge undertaking. Companies that want to tap into the bonanza of the Sands are forking over billions of dollars every year in capital costs and have spent over $1 trillion to date. In the past twenty-five years, the Sands have generated an economic impact in GDP terms of more than $3.5 trillion across Canada.

Apart from conventional crude and natural gas, the Sands alone have paid federal taxes of over $200 billion, and provincial taxes and royalties of more than $300 billion.

• • •

We need this oil, but with all the media reports about global warming and peak oil, we're stricken with a strange kind of neurosis. While we sing along with Joni Mitchell when she complains that we "pave paradise and put up a parking lot," most of us have no

---

[1] Crude Oil Production Costs and Crude Oil Production (U.S. Energy Information Administration); Web Support Site, *Black Bonanza* Footnotes—Chapter 1. < * >

intention of returning to a medieval lifestyle or taking up hunting and gathering in the boreal forest or some other "Garden of Eden." Clearly there is little popular support for shutting the Sands down, and yet there is a strong demand for more environmental steward-ship in the Sands, an issue that is finally being addressed.

Our way of life requires fossil fuel and we will need it for at least another half century, or until we develop alternative sources for powering our lifestyle. The Sands are bountiful. They offer a stable and secure supply for North America that no other country in the world can match. After fifty years of tinkering and innova-tion, operators can produce synthetic crude out of the Sands at a price that is getting comparable to conventional crude and less than offshore oil.

The U.S., in particular, needs this oil—imports from Canada have doubled over the past decade. Canada now fills about a quarter of the U.S. oil needs, exporting over 80 million barrels a month, almost as much as Saudi Arabia, Venezuela, and Nigeria combined.[2]

Let's be realistic. In spite of all the protests and complaints, we will never summon the political will to shut down oil operations like the Sands, because we want to secure and maintain our stan-dard of living. So where does this black bonanza leave us in terms of our energy future and security?

First of all, the price of oil is one of the governors of the world economy, and, perhaps, the most important price of all. The more oil we can deliver, the more able we are to keep the price stable or at least reasonable. No one wants to go back to 2008 when the oil market went mad, whipped by speculators and out-of-control hedge fund trading. Panic drove the price of crude up to a strato-spheric $148 a barrel at the peak. The crash, when it came, was severe and the price landed with a sickening thud at $38 a barrel.

---

[2] U.S. Imports by Country of Origin; Web Support Site, *Black Bonanza* Footnotes—Chapter 1. < * >

Today, unless there are any foolish speculators around who want to get burned all over again, the price seems to have stabilized in the mid $70s. It shouldn't go too crazy again until the lead bulls can generate another crude stampede.

• • •

Some people describe the Sands as dirty and nasty, but I would like to make a pitch for bitumen, because it is one of the true markers of our civilization. Neanderthal cave people first used it to glue flint tips onto their spears. Three thousand years ago, the Mesopotamians valued it highly for waterproofing boats, bricks, cisterns, water pipes, and pottery, and it was a sought after trade good throughout the Middle East. Indeed, it was essential for their way of life and very survival, as their climate warmed and dried.

Bitumen played a big part in early human religion as well, from caulking Noah's Ark, to building the Tower of Babel, to the fire and brimstone that destroyed Sodom and Gomorrah. I find it fascinating that some of this religious sentiment was inspired by a kind of guilt and envy about power that persists even today.

Ancient priestly complaints from the Bible are eerily similar to the moralistic essence of today's environmental creed—that our oil-fueled civilization is an affront against nature. Today's climate crusade is based solidly on the age-old attack by priests and religion on the follies of human civilization, technology, and pride. Back in the time of Babylon, it was the Tower of Babel that was the enemy; today, it's technology, overpopulation, industry, America, the human race, and now the tar sands of the Athabasca.

• • •

At about the same time as the Klondike gold rush lured prospectors to the Yukon, the Sands became a magnet for seekers of black gold.

In fact, for the first half of the twentieth century, the Athabasca Sands were like the Klondike, except in slow motion. Very slow motion.

In the case of the Athabasca Sands, there was no stampede and no panic to get at the treasure. No more than fifty prospectors and drillers came to the remote Athabasca frontier over a forty-year period before World War II. All of these starry-eyed dreamers went broke, including a dashing German aristocrat named Alfred von Hammerstein. But they believed they had the chance to strike it very rich by finding a large pool of crude oil, or at least make a modest buck by producing barrels of tar or by mining the Sands to pave the muddy roads of the Canadian Prairies with Athabasca asphalt. And they made some progress in understanding the riddle of the Sands. The Athabasca River was not Bonanza Creek, and bitumen-soaked sand was not gold dust. At least not at that time.

The main problem faced by early pioneers was the huge extent of the boreal forest that surrounded the Athabasca River and tributaries. The Canadian portion amounts to 1.4 billion acres (5.7 billion square km), but the Athabasca Sands underlays only 35 million acres (142,000 square km) or one-fortieth of the total. The mineable portion is under 0.1 percent of the whole boreal ecosystem. So, Canada's boreal forest is, at its heart, huge and indestructible. It's a deep green desert that will never be populated to any extent, and the Sands are only a surface scratch that will ultimately heal.

While most critics of oilsands development focus on its impact on the natural environment, and some decry the "destruction of the boreal forest," I don't buy the argument that the industry will destroy this ecosystem. Believe me, there is an almost endless supply of boreal forest up there, and a friend of mine almost died in its vastness.

Years ago, some friends and I were on a prospecting job in the Northwest Territories to pay our university fees. We were doing geophysical exploration south of Great Slave Lake, a three-day walk from any other human life. Flying over it, the Boreal Forest is an enormous green ocean. Down on the ground, it was an endless landscape of short, scrubby spruce, peaty muskeg, grey green reindeer moss, swamp, and shallow lakes, some of them with springs of warm sulfur-smelling water. One of my friends got lost, and it took a day to find him. He was smart. He stayed still until he could hear us shouting.

My friends and I got there in mid-June, when there was twenty-four hours of daylight and the forest was alive. We heard moose crashing through the spruce, and saw countless songbirds, sandhill cranes, and great horned owls. We kept our meat in a hole in the ground. Five feet down there was frosty soil, as cold as a beer fridge.

It was truly the kingdom of the mosquito. We worked with head nets and went through cases of insect repellent. Even the Dene guys we worked with, who claimed their blood was 5 percent mosquito venom, said the modern stuff was a hell of a lot better than bear grease. We prayed for a breeze off Great Slave Lake to chase away the flies. Most nights I drove the Bombardier muskeg tractor down to the lake for an icy cold swim and to fill the water barrel.

Suddenly, we had a frost in August and the bugs were gone. Then we had deepening darkness at night as our part of the planet shifted its gaze away from the sun, and then the shimmering green curtains of the aurora borealis lit up the sky, as cosmic rays, directed by the earth's magnetic field, slammed into the atmosphere above us.

• • •

The earliest oilsands development started after World War I, when Canadian government surveyor, Sidney Ells, mapped the richest Sands deposits, and Karl Clark of the University of Alberta worked on extracting 100 percent clean bitumen and building the first pilot plants.

The need for oil and asphalt exploded in the twenties, as the automobile came of age and the Sands soon lured in various wealth seekers, including a group of New York City policemen who were convinced the Athabasca forest hid an enormous oil field. They lost their shirts. The North West Company Ltd., an Imperial Oil subsidiary, drilled a few wells in the Sands and found nothing. A Prince Edward Island promoter named Robert Fitzsimmons set up a small bitumen plant and sold barrels of the stuff to hardware stores as roof tar.

The first serious investor in the Sands was an enigmatic American geologist named Max Ball, who had advised Shell, Esso, and the White House, and was author of a lively bestseller called *This Fascinating Oil Business*. With some partners from Toronto, he built a small plant that actually produced diesel fuel and gasoline. The Canadian government took it over as a wartime reserve to supply U.S. troops in Alaska. Interest lagged after World War II, but with U.S. reserves starting to decline and "peak oil" worries rising, it took a Philadelphia oilman named J. Howard Pew, head of the Sun Oil Company, to make the final leap to large-scale production. His Great Canadian Oil Sands (GCOS) mine, which opened on September 30, 1967, burned through over $250 million before it started making a profit. Today run by Suncor Energy, the GCOS was the world's first complex dedicated to mining oil sands and upgrading bitumen into synthetic crude oil.

• • •

In the 1970s, OPEC and the oil crisis caused prices to balloon, and suddenly the Sands made a lot more sense. The governments of Alberta and Canada also wanted a bite of the bonanza, and started an escalating ten-year war for control that saw the creation of government oil companies—Alberta Energy Company and

Petro-Canada—and then a terrible collapse of business when the world price for oil plunged.

But the crisis pushed the companies in the Sands to innovate in order to get costs down, and when the happy days returned, their profits mushroomed.

The riches of the Sands also brought the U.S. to the free-trade table, something Canada had been urging for a century. The Canada-U.S. Free Trade Agreement gave the U.S. the petroleum price and supply security it needed, and the two countries agreed not to bring in any tax or duty that would favor one country over the other. Either party could bring in energy supply restrictions or price hikes as long as it kept the same price or percentage of supply for the other party. The 1994 North American Free Trade Agreement (NAFTA) went even further, limiting export/import restrictions, keeping the proportion of energy exports relative to total supply, and avoiding dual pricing.

The Sands came of age in the early 1990s, when the new Alberta Premier, Ralph Klein, took most of the brakes off oilsands development. Canada soon had three major mines in operation, and suddenly the country had joined the exclusive club of energy superpowers.

• • •

A former newspaper reporter and Liberal mayor of Calgary, Ralph Klein was no green groupie, and under his fourteen-year reign the oilsands business barreled ahead. Generous write-offs and a new tax and royalty rate led to the spending of billions of dollars a year. It was, perhaps, the biggest industrial boom in Canadian history. In a part of the country used to boom and bust, the governing mantra was "make hay while the sun shines."

While oilsands mining went flat out, Klein and the companies also directed a whole whack of money toward oilsands research, mainly at the universities of Calgary and Alberta, but also on site, where oilsands operators invested in automating production, and in improving water recycling and heat exchange bit by bit. All this research cash soon gave birth to a raft of new technology start-ups that tried to exploit promising patents and innovations. The greatest of all of these new inventions was SAGD (pronounced SAG-D), which is turning into one of the key breakthroughs in energy history.

But the good times had a downside. The tailing ponds of the mines grew wider, and the companies slacked off on their promises to reclaim the mined land, so that today, the governments are forcing the oil companies to play an expensive game of catch up. The tailing ponds also alarmed many environmental groups, including Alberta's Pembina Institute, who expressed concern about leakage into the Athabasca River or even the breaching of a dyke, which could seriously damage the entire Athabasca-Mackenzie River watercourse. A doctor downriver at Fort Chipewyan found rare cancers that he suggested could be caused by toxic compounds leaking from the ponds. While an Alberta enquiry absolved the Sands' operators, the issue is still a "he said–she said" battle. The issue needs further research, and matters are complicated by the fact that there are also four pulp mills upstream from the mines as well.

What really changed the attitude of many citizens toward the Sands was the rapid growth of a movement against global warming caused by the burning of fossil fuels, which releases carbon dioxide (CO_2). The fascinating thing, and one I devote a chapter to in this book, is why the Sands, a bit player among emitters, became such a symbol for the environmentalists, when other CO_2 sources are far more significant. The story has many twists and turns, but inevitably comes down to money and power. A lot of individuals and groups directly benefit by focusing on the Sands, and ignoring other global warming villains.

So suddenly, it was "Tar Wars" time, as the Sands morphed into something akin to the kingdom of Mordor in Tolkein's *Lord of the Rings*, and a talisman for sophisticated attacks on the energy business as a whole.

• • •

We're being asked to wager trillions of dollars and substantially curtail freedom on climate models that are imperfect and unproven.

—George Will, *Washington Post*

The world's biggest industrial project started to attract world-class attention in about 2005. At one end of the spectrum, Bill Gates and Warren Buffett jetted up to the Athabasca in the summer of 2008 to check on their investments. At the other end, the Sands were visited regularly by Greenpeace eco-warriors, eager to hang their banners on heavy haulers. Soon, a succession of green groups were making the pilgrimage to Fort McMurray and flying over the Sands, so they could report back on the devastation done by the world's ugliest mines.

The mainstream green groups were determined to portray the extraction of oil from the Sands as bad for the environment, and some went as far as to demonize the Sands as a modern day Mordor for questing green hobbits. Why? Because in reality, trashing the tar patch shored up their fundraising activities and helped their bottom line. The Sands are monumentally ugly, and they are far enough away from big population centers so donors can't look too closely at the message. Besides, "Blame Canada" is a tried and true slogan in the U.S.

All this attention led Al Gore and others to ramp up the demonization of the Sands even further. In a speech in Toronto in the fall of 2009, Gore pulled out all the stops saying that, "the oil sands threaten our survival as a species."

So what's with the apocalyptic language? Who is benefiting from these over-the-top attacks? And what are the oilsands companies doing to combat the counter the demonization?

In this book I argue that the oilsands companies are ill prepared to fight what has turned out to be the mother of all pubic relations battles. The Sands have become the poster child for "environmental Armageddon," but the companies have little response. They take a reactive rational approach when what they are facing is nothing less than a new religion determined to defeat them in a last battle, a "Tarmageddon" if you will.

Apart from the young hearts and rich foundations arrayed against them, the Sands operators are also facing a growing and formidable phalanx of new companies determined to tithe the energy industry and use tax breaks to build alternative and sustainable energy projects.

In some ways, global warming is just a sideshow. Paleoclimatologists show convincingly that Earth's climate has been changing naturally for millennia before the Medieval Warm Period (800 to 1300 AD), when temperatures where higher than today, and the Little Ice Age (1500 to 1850 AD), when temperatures were lower, and no climate prediction models can infallibly map the distant future. Indeed, as the recent release of the "Climategate" e-mails and documents from the influential Climatic Research Unit (CRU) at the University of East Anglia show, the current models are enormously crude.

Climate "deniers," or as they like to call themselves, "climate realists," are clearly in the ascendant, even though the global warming crusaders endlessly taunt them as being "shills for big oil." Ironically, the "Climategate" e-mails show that the CRU fundraisers had no problem with big oil, and actually met with Shell Oil environmental officials to enlist them as strategic partners, while getting them to bankroll pro man-made global warming research. The e-mails also reveal that the CRU was trying to get research grants from oil giants British Petroleum and

Exxon-Mobil. All three companies are enthusiastic operators in the Athabasca Sands.

Even the famous "hockey stick" graph used by the United Nations' Intergovernmental Panel on Climate Change (IPCC), and heavily featured in Al Gore's movie, *An Inconvenient Truth*, has been thoroughly debunked by retired Toronto mining engineer and statistician Steve McIntyre.

But the demonization continues, and now it is Canada that is under the spotlight. The country "is the dirty old man of the climate world," according to a recent *Guardian* article. The most pious of the global warming pundits, George Monbiot, wrings his hands when he thinks of what a nasty country Canada has become:

> When you think of Canada, which qualities come to mind? The world's peace-keeper, the friendly nation, a liberal counterweight to the harsher pieties of its southern neighbor, decent, civilized, fair, well-governed? Think again. This country's government is now behaving with all the sophistication of a chimpanzee's tea party.
>
> I am watching the astonishing spectacle of a beautiful, cultured nation turning itself into a corrupt petrostate ... Canada is slipping down the development ladder, retreating from a complex, diverse economy towards dependence on a single primary resource, which happens to be the dirtiest commodity known to man.
>
> Until now I believed that the nation which has done most to sabotage a new climate change agreement was the United States. I was wrong. The real villain is Canada. Unless we can stop it, the harm done by Canada in December 2009 will outweigh a century of good works ...

Various diplomats have taken up Monbiot's moaning cry, calling for Canada's expulsion from organizations like the Commonwealth because it failed to meet its commitments under the 1997 Kyoto Cimate Change Treaty. But neither have the Europeans, in spite of some creative climate accounting, emissions trading, land-use changes, and carbon offsets.

All of this is happening while the emerging problem may, in fact, be global cooling. Ecologist Peter Taylor has shown that the jet stream shifts south as the magnetic field of the sun falls, and this was characteristic of the Little Ice Age. In 2007, the sun's magnetic field fell to an all-time low and this repeated through 2008 and 2009. So, we may need the energy from the Sands more then we realize.

Polls still show that most people in Canada don't buy the demonization and support continuing to work the Sands. U.S. and British pollsters are also finding out that "climate fatigue" and the recession have combined to cause the global warming scare to retreat down to the very bottom of peoples' concerns.

Stepping back from the spin, it struck me that perhaps all these attacks and the demonization of Canada and its oilsands bonanza are one way of distracting Americans and Europeans from the problems in their own back yard. U.S. coal-fired electricity (some of which is sold to Ontario) is immensely more polluting, and produces forty-four times more CO_2 than the Athabasca projects. Mountaintop removal in the Appalachians does far more damage than tailings ponds in the Athabascsa.

I have also come to the conclusion that genuine environmentalism went into the ditch when the pollution debate was gradually reframed along one obsessive line—global warming. An eager Al Gore, together with market makers who want to build a global climate exchange using cap-and-trade systems, have ended up monopolizing the green agenda. But after a decade of intense lobbying, they too are starting to fail, and *Financial Post* editor, Terence Corcoran, suggests a reason why: "Carbon trading is an economic black hole, a high-risk pseudo market set up around an orchestrated shortage for a largely unmeasurable, naturally occurring thing called carbon dioxide." It's also clear that a market that is not based on rational needs, but rather government policy is ripe for exploitation. According to Europol, the perils of making a market on hot air are very real—carbon trading fraudsters may have accounted for up to 90 percent of all market activity in some European countries, and criminals have got away with an estimated €5 billion, mainly in Britain, France, Spain, Denmark, and Holland.

The shame of it is, we have real pollution, starvation, and public health issues that desperately need to be solved, and we may have just wasted fifteen or twenty years and billions of dollars that could have been used to attack these problems.

Instead, we have green evangelists urging us to accept carbon taxation as a real solution, when we should be changing to hybrid vehicles, demanding higher mileage, teleconferencing instead of using jet planes, and saving energy rather than wasting it. We have been programmed to obsess about global warming and spend fortunes on controlling minuscule temperature variations, when we should be making simple lifestyle choices to reduce pollution in general.

In spite of all the spin people are exposed to today, and growing climate fatigue, there is still a definite will to improve the environmental footprint of Canada's oilsands industry, diminish the tailings problem, and restore a scarred landscape. And this is finally being dealt with, as I detail later in this book.

Global warming has been a lucrative crisis for certain sectors for the past twenty years, and nourished whole generations of policy-makers, interest groups, and organizations that thrive through public fundraising. For many people, the argument mirrors the debate in their own souls between the green of the earth and the bonanza of wealth we enjoy from using fossil fuels. But now we're seeing an entirely new energy scare emerging to take the focus off pollution and global warming. It's another issue that its devotees say threatens human civilization itself—the phenomenon of peak oil.

• • •

Extraordinary claims require extraordinary proof.
—Carl Sagan

Back in the 1980s, I was told by a prominent Alberta oilman that there was more oil in Alberta than in the entire Middle East. It turns out we have quite a bit more – over 1 trillion barrels that is recoverable, 3.3 trillion barrels in total. So why are we wringing our hands about peak oil?[3]

The peak oil theory was first put forward in the 1950s by Shell's lead geologist, King Hubbert, who made the shocking prediction that U.S. conventional oil output would peak in the early 1970s, and thereafter decline, making the U.S. increasingly dependent on foreign oil. Hubbert was right on the money about America, formerly the world's number-one oil exporter, but he was wrong in his other prediction—global oil production would taper off after 2000. But only because he lacked clear statistics and did not factor in Canada's Athabasca Sands. He also did not factor in 3 billion new players—the Chinese and the Indians—who were not in the market until the year 2000.

It all depends on what you mean by "peak." Outside fortress North America, the oil business is still a "Mad Max" kind of world, with supply scrambling to meet demand, with bullies, dictators, and thugs holding sway over cowering citizens, and with national oil companies (NOCs) used as personal banks by the local ruling kleptocracy. At the same time, oil-poor nations like China and India are thumbing their noses at UN-mandated emissions targets and enthusiastically adopting a fossil-fuel-based lifestyle.

Some petro-pessimists, including those who also buy into global warming, tell us with the utmost confidence that the crunch is already here, and we're entering a real age of scarcity on the road to ruin. They say our fossil fuel civilization is toast, because

---

[3] For an excellent summary of the peak oil debate, see the video, "A Crude Awakening"; Web Support Site, *Black Bonanza* Video—Peak Oil < * >

world crude oil production has passed its peak, and we're not finding enough oil to replace what we're consuming.

Even most oil analysts still maintain the strange fiction that the Athabasca Sands are second only to Saudi Arabia in recoverable oil reserves. This fiction persists in the face of growing evidence that the Athabasca Sands are far larger. A trillion barrels of synthetic crude is four times greater than Saudi Arabia's 250 billion-odd barrels of conventional oil, and the 175 billion barrels that the International Energy Agency estimates for Canada as a whole.

For many Americans, Hubbert's peak oil theory is a terrifying prospect and one that could rock their whole way of life. For others, the scenario is pleasing, because our seemingly insatiable demand for fossil fuel is morally wrong and scarcity will force us to switch to windmills and biomass for fuel.

Suddenly, new horizontal drilling technology has ridden to the rescue, giving the world a gas glut and an elegant new way to exploit heavy oil and oilsands deposits. Roger Butler's SAGD means another hundred or so years of energy security that we never thought we had.

Now, many people attracted to the peak oil crusade are lowering their placards and going home. The apocalypse has been put off for at least another century. Energy economists have suddenly discovered that Hubbert's Peak is just a ragged plateau—that scary-looking downward roller-coaster slope of Hubbert's bell curve has significantly flattened out.

The Sands of the Athabasca will help insulate us from the shock of temporarily higher prices. The Sands are also a lifeline for North America and the rest of the world, until we engineer technology that can tap the powerful radiation of the sun.

Still, the threat that one day the planet's oil resources will run dry is very real, and it's obvious we have to work toward true energy independence. But the rewards of getting there are great—we'll finally be free of the peak oil threat, price manipulation by dictators and scoundrels, soaring and crashing oil prices and the roller-coaster ride of booms and recessions, and the risks of famine and petro-conflict. The U.S., in particular, will free itself of having to spend up to $2 billion each and every working day to buy imported crude.

The blessing of the Sands is that they give us the luxury of time. After the oil shocks of the past thirty years, the Sands give us the chance to plan what I describe as the "Blue Shift," to adopt new power technologies and get to the other side of any energy security minefield the world may have to cross.

So what are the best ways to make the Blue Shift, and how do we get there?

Smart investors like Warren Buffett, the Oracle of Omaha, are already preparing their portfolios for the Blue Shift. Buffett, who believes all cars on the road in 2030 will be electric, has already invested in a Chinese company working on the technology to make it happen.

●　●　●

"Blue is the new green," and blue is where the future lies.

We're a race that runs on oil. A cheap supply of energy, first wood and wind, then coal, and now oil and gas, has given humanity a whole new way of life. With some exceptions, the Age of Oil has given us countless blessings, but the wells of fossil fuel will one day run dry. We have probably a fifty-year window of security made possible by reserves like Canada's oilsands. But even before that time, even in the next decade or two, we should be able to make what I call the Blue Shift into an abundant new energy future.

U.S. futurist Ray Kurzweil has a theory that innovation proceeds on an exponentially rising curve and that we are well into the curve for getting economical energy from the sun. Applying his Law of Accelerating Returns, Kurzweil calmly predicts that solar nanotechnology will produce all the energy needs of Earth's people in just twenty years. "If we could convert .03 percent of the sunlight that falls on the earth into energy," he says, "we would meet all of our projected needs for 2030."

Many people are now getting the point that solar energy freedom is just around the corner. Blue post-environmental activism is now emerging and it's not just a word shift from green to blue. Tens of billions of dollars are being invested in blue research and development, in a race to come up with the cheap and scalable clean energy that we need. You can see it in California where most of the world's trends start—savvy venture capital companies in Silicon Valley are shifting their focus from computing to renewable energy, the cheap generation of electric power, and, of course, super cool battery-powered vehicles like the Tesla. That's where the future is, and that's where the fun can be found.

The emerging Blue Shift should take us gracefully out of the age of oil, and usher in an era of super abundance right out of a science fiction novel. It's perhaps ironic that solar energy will eventually replace crude oil and natural gas as the fuel that powers the world, but we should be thankful that plentiful hydrocarbon resources like those found in the Sands will let us make the transition without stress and violence, without the risk of apocalypse, or the collapse of liberal democracy.

The major danger in the shift to blue is having enough petroleum to keep fueling the global agricultural revolution so that we can avoid the specter of large-scale famine. World food production today is heavily linked to fossil fuels and inorganic fertilizer. The biggest risk right now is not peak oil; it's maintaining the equilibrium, and we must do it by ensuring the production of secure energy supplies and food at a reasonable price, and by ramping up solar technology. This is no time to be taxing carbon and shoving people into poverty. That issue should wait until climate science is more settled.

You would think that the arrival of nanosolar and other blue technologies could put Canada's synthetic crude on the road to obsolescence. But things never happen that quickly. Synthetic crude from the Sands is just a great insurance policy for North Americans and an immense future resource for petrochemicals and other uses of fossil energy.

Even if you're the most dedicated of climate lemmings, ready to follow Al Gore anywhere, you'll have to agree with me that we need to make a smooth transition from the Age of Oil to the new Solar Era. The Sands will help us get there.

One hundred years ago, as the Age of Oil was just beginning, Canadian drillers working for the Anglo-Persian Oil Company (today's BP), struck the first oil in the Middle East at Masjid-e-Soleiman in present-day Iran. One hundred years ago, an Ontario driller named Eugene Coste spudded the first gas well in Alberta. And one hundred years ago, a passionate young Canadian government geologist named Sidney Ells arrived in the Athabasca Valley to do an inventory of the Sands and bring out samples for study. Today, a century later, we are poised to enter another more permanent energy era, the Solar Age, and we'll get there easily, with the help of an ocean of bitumen laid down 100 million years ago.

2

Origins

All Hell for a Basement

How did the largest known oil resource on the planet—3.3 trillion barrels—come to be formed?

The story begins over 200 million years ago, as the Farallon and Pacific tectonic plates jammed into the westward-moving North American landmass. As the plates slid under North America, they set off chains of volcanoes and levered up the Cascade, Coast, and Rocky mountain ranges. This action trapped a huge pool of hydrocarbons, already created by marine and swamp organisms, that had seeped into the porous limestone and shale of ancient seabeds and marshes from deep beneath the Gulf of Mexico, through Texas, up to Alberta, all the way to Tuktoyaktuk, Northwest Territories, and under the Arctic Ocean.

At the same time, a succession of swift rivers poured from the Precambrian granite domes along what is now Hudson Bay, carving through the hard rock and depositing huge quantities of pure quartz sand and clay on the east coast of the ancient seabed. As the land in the West tipped upwards even further 100 million years ago, gravity and pressure laid some of these hydrocarbons down as coal to the west, and pushed the remaining hydrocarbons east through the permeable stone strata, where some pooled as crude oil and some got trapped as natural gas. The rest seeped further east into the old river-borne debris, losing the lighter gases, until coming to rest in a sea of bitumen-soaked silica—the fabulous Sands of the Athabasca.

Over time, these precious Sands were buried and reburied by glaciers, clay, and gravel debris, and by spruce bog and muskeg. One hundred years ago, the only sign that they existed at all were deep tarry banks along the Athabasca and Peace rivers, and springs of soft bitumen flowing out of the silent forest.

• • •

The word "bitumen" is of Celtic origin and comes from the Latin word meaning "pitch" or "tar." The first people to use bitumen were the Neanderthals, in between the last two ice ages in what is now the Middle East.

It likely happened that a family group of hunters were moving up a river valley when they came upon a black tarry substance oozing out of the rocks by a stream and collecting in globs under the water. It grew sticky in the heat and hard to rub off their feet and hands, but they could poke a stick into it and the stick would stay upright, or they could roll it into a ball with some sand and grass. One of the hunters may have had a loose spear point. He put a small ball of the black stuff into the notch at the end of his wooden weapon, set the sharp stone spearhead into the goo, and bound it up tighter onto the shaft. It was a cool night, and the next morning the bitumen was as hard as rock and the head fit perfectly tight. The hunter smiled. This stuff was good.

The human use of bitumen, the Neanderthal hunter's mastic, is one of the earliest markers of our civilization. Humans have used this black stuff for at least 70,000 years, and it had great value to our Neanderthal ancestors. They adopted it readily, because using bitumen-glued spearheads and flint knives on the long shafts of their weapons gave them more hunting power to kill wooly mammoths and bison, and defend their families against saber-toothed tigers.

However, this new-found power also led to the extinction of the big animals they hunted. The large lumbering beasts were no longer able to escape or defend themselves against circles of spear-wielding humans.[1]

. . .

As the Ice Age diminished and the Neanderthal hunters moved north to follow the dwindling herds of large animals, the less-hairy tribes of homo sapiens moved into the valleys of the Tigris and Euphrates rivers 10,000 years ago. They too started to harvest the abundant bitumen, first using it to attach flint chips to sickles to harvest their grain, then to waterproof and seal their reed baskets of grain and pottery jars of beer. Some scholars say that humans became civilized when they started brewing a weak beer that let them avoid the spread of water-borne illnesses.

We tend to think of the oil industry as a twentieth-century phenomenon, and certainly it is the largest single business in the world today, but it also was a major industry in the ancient Middle East, and bitumen was at the heart of the business, employing tens of thousands of people making many of the products we still use today—for building, waterproofing, preserving, paving, and decorating.[2]

As early as 5000 BC, the world's first oil industry was centered around the present-day city of Hīt in Iraq. Workers harvested the globs of bitumen as it seeped out of the ground or into pools of water, where it stayed soft. They scooped it out, covered it with sand, and wrapped it in reeds or bags to keep it moist. Then

[1] *ScienceNews* (12 December 2008); ref. Boeda, E., et al., "Middle Paleolithic bitumen use at Umm el Tlel around 70,000 BP," December 2008, Antiquity, vol. 82, no. 4, p. 853–861.
[2] Shell's "250 Uses For Bitumen"; Web Support Site, *Black Bonanza* Footnotes—Chapter 2. < * >

they traded it upriver as far north as Armenia, south down to the Persian Gulf, west to Egypt, and as far east as India. At faraway Moenodaro in the Indus Valley a well-preserved water tank from 2000 BC is coated with Mesopotamian bitumen—without it their civilization would have failed.

In the Ur period of 2000 BC, the price of bitumen was much more than it is today—three to five shekels a ton, a shekel being 8.5 gm of silver.[3] The town of Ursu had to pay a tribute (tax) of 280 tons of bitumen to the king of Ur. It was delivered either poured into loaves or in baskets that were kept wet until it was used. Clay tablets indicate three main grades of bitumen from the workings at Hit. One text talks about mining rock asphalt from the hills, which was melted down into purer bitumen.

Civilization in the Middle East grew to depend on bitumen, particularly as the climate got warmer and drier. The Mesopotamians continued to rely on it as glue and for waterproofing. An old Babylonian saga tells how a priestess, the mother of the great King Sargon, saved him when he was a baby by placing him in a bitumen-caulked casket of rushes. Even today, large reed boats and their round river coracles called guffas are dipped into hot molten bitumen, which forms a completely waterproof shell.*[4]

Bitumen was also used as medicine, insecticide, and as a magic potion to ward off a Babylonian female demon named Labartu. She had a hairy body, the head of a lioness, donkey's teeth and ears, long fingers and fingernails, and the feet of a bird with sharp talons. Labartu menaced women during childbirth and, if possible, kidnapped children while they were breastfeeding.

Bitumen was also used to deal out justice—evildoers in Babylon were punished by having hot bitumen poured over their heads.

• • •

[3] R.J. Forbes, *Studies in Ancient Technology*, vol. 1. (Leiden: E.J. Brill, 1964) p. 17.
[4] Image of a modern guffa; Web Support Site, *Black Bonanza* Gallery—Chapter 2. < * >

The *Old Testament* is full of references to bitumen and other forms of petroleum.

During the diaspora in Babylon, the writers of the Jewish holy books borrowed many of their myths and stories from timeless Mesopotamian legends. The story of Noah tells how he used pitch to caulk and waterproof his Ark, and *The Bible* specifies the work had to be done both inside and out, much the same as we caulk the cement foundations of our houses with tar. Adopting the Sargon legend, *The Bible* says pitch was daubed on the reed cradle that hid baby Moses in the bulrushes of the Nile.

As they built Babylon and other cities, the Mesopotamians used bitumen increasingly on an industrial scale. They mortared their brick houses, roofs, walls, water tanks, and drainage pipes with the tarry stuff, mixed with 65 percent sand and fiber. Farther to the west, Jericho, the world's oldest city, had walls of stone and sun-dried brick, mortared with this bitumen mix. The great temple towers and ziggurat of Nebuchadnezzar, made for the royal astronomers, were made of even stronger burnt brick, enameled in brilliant blue, and cemented with a mortar containing about 35 percent bitumen. The old Jewish *Book of Jubilees* describes the building of one great tower:

> And they began to build, and in the fourth week they made brick with fire, and the bricks served them for stone, and the clay with which they cemented them together was asphalt which comes out of the water, and out of the fountains in the land of Shinar.

This was the Tower of Babel in the book of Genesis.

• • •

Nebuchadnezzar II, the most important king of the Second Babylonian or Neo-Babylonian Empire, is one of the "bad guys" of *The*

Bible. He destroyed Jerusalem, exiled the leading Hebrew families, and took many captives back to Babylon. But he was also known for restoring old religious monuments, improving canals, and building the fabulous Hanging Gardens of Babylon, one of the Seven Wonders of the Ancient World. The Hanging Gardens were made with bitumen-waterproofed terraces, supported by brick arches, and watered by bitumen-lined cisterns. Nebuchadnezzar's building projects included surrounding his capital city with a ten-mile-long double wall (sixteen km) with an elaborate entry called the Ishtar Gate, decorated with blue-enameled animal tiles attached with bitumen mortar.[5] He also built a 370-foot (113 m) bridge across the Euphrates River on wooden piers which were sealed with bitumen to prevent rotting.

Nebuchadnezzar writes that his father, Nabopolassar, in about 615 BC, made a processional road in Babylon for the great god Marduk using three or more layers of burnt brick: "glistening with asphalt and burnt brick ... Placed above the bitumen was a mighty superstructure of shining limestone."

● ● ●

Today, there are moral critics who condemn rampant commercial activity and what they view as a mania for building. They argue that human materialism, aided by petroleum, is an affront against nature. Similarly, the Jewish priests in Babylon were not at all pleased with the zeal of their captors for building up glorious structures toward Heaven. Jewish historian, Flavius Josephus, in his *Antiquities of the Jews* (c 94 AD), mentions seeing Nebuchadnezzar's tower, and warns that the building was a work of pride and a rebellion against God, who punished humanity for building the Tower of Babel by cursing them with languages.

---

[5] Ishtar Gate reconstruction in the Berlin museum; Web Support Site, *Black Bonanza* Gallery—Chapter 2. < * >

But the Israelites also relied on bitumen. They were supplied from the Dead Sea, a salt lake that the Romans called the Lake of Asphaltes, after the lumps of bitumen that sometimes float to the surface even today. Nearby was the Valley of Sodom and Gomorrah, which *the Bible* says was destroyed in a hail of fire and brimstone. The geologist, Frederick Clapp, has speculated that pressure from an earthquake may have caused the subterranean deposits of bitumen, which contain a high percentage of sulfur, to gush out through a fault line and catch fire, raining destruction on the cities.

● ● ●

Bitumen was also used by the people of the Middle East and Egypt to wrap, embalm, and mummify the dead; in fact, the Egyptian word "mummy" comes from the ancient Persian *mumiai*, meaning bitumen.

In the early Middle Ages, 600–700 AD, Arab and Persian chemists made Greek fire, a deadly napalm-like weapon, by mixing petroleum's lighter elements with bitumen and quicklime. Greek fire was used against cities, castles, and ships. In 670 AD, Byzantine Emperor Constantine IV won a great naval victory by catapulting flaming Greek fire against enemy ships.

Akkadian clay tablets refer to crude oil as naptu—from which derives the root of the Arabic naft, as well as the Greek naphtha. In about 850 AD, during the Abbasid Caliphate—the early Muslim Oil Age, Baghdad distillers made the first refined lamp oil or kerosene, from heating crude oil and cooling the vapors. They called it *naft abyad* (white naphtha), and refined it using clay or ammonium chloride (sal ammoniac) as an absorbent. The distillers repeated the process until they could remove all of the explosive volatile hydrocarbon fractions.

Arab chemists also made a form of kerosene during the same period from oil shale and bitumen by heating the rock to extract the oil, which was then distilled. The *Al-Qamus Dictionary* says it was used as a liniment and laxative: "The best grade of naphtha is the water-white. It is a good solvent, a diluent and an expectorant. Taken internally, it relieves cramps and aches of the belly, and, when applied topically, it can sooth skin rashes and infections."

• • •

Like the Neanderthals and the Mesopotamians, the Dene people of the Athabasca, in what is today northern Alberta, used and traded the same liquid bitumen that flowed into tarry pools along the eroded banks of the river.

The next part of our story shows how European explorers and fur traders first discovered this treasure of the Athabasca Valley, and how early geologists took its measure and slowly came to realize what an enormous bonanza lay hidden beneath the boreal forests of Alberta and Saskatchewan, an area larger than England.

• • •

One bitterly cold November in 1714, a Chipewyan (Dene) woman named Thanadelthur, a native of the Athabasca Valley, arrived at the fur trade post of York Factory on the shore of Hudson Bay (the Bay). She had been captured and adopted by the Crees during a raid in the spring of 1713. Hudson's Bay Company (HBC) chief trader, James Knight, was very interested in Thanadelthur because she was not a Cree, but rather one of their sworn enemies.[6]

---

[6] The Cree and Dene both moved into Athabasca country following the retreat of the glaciers at the end of the last Ice Age. They sometimes warred over territory, but each regarded the other tribe as cousins. The Crees are an Algonkian people, whose legends say they originated along the Atlantic coast as far south as Virginia. The Dene or Chipewyan speak the same language as the American Apache.

Trader Knight was a shipwright by trade. When he joined the HBC as a younger man, the company put his carpentry skills to good use repairing boats and making its fur forts as snug as well-built ships. Now age seventy, Knight's HBC masters in London asked him to start trading inland, and look for any "mines, minerals, and medicines" that were there. In 1713, Knight sent out two young traders, William Stewart and Henry Kelsey, to attempt to convince the Crees to make peace with their enemies and come down to the Bay to trade. It was Stewart who brought Thanadelthur back to the fort.

Knight could speak the Cree language like a native, which enabled him to convince the local people to help him make maps by chalking out an outline of their country. The Crees told Knight that there were seventeen rivers beyond the Bay—the fourteenth had "yellow metal," probably copper from the White River or Coppermine River. Farther west, after thirty-nine days' travel, were a people who lived beside the mountains that rose to the sky—this is the first European description of the Canadian Rockies and beyond them, tribes who had an abundance of white and yellow metals.

Thanadelthur filled in more of the blanks for Knight and give him some exciting news. She told him about a "large river or strait where the tide ebbs and flows at a great rate and it hardly freezes some winters."[7] Knight reckoned this must be the Arctic Ocean or possibly the Pacific. She also talked of metals, and about going to the land of the Crow Indians and personally taking the yellow metal out of the river—possibly she had seen the Klondike riverbed gold deposits. She said that from the hills in that country you could see large vessels on the western sea. Knight thought this was the Pacific Ocean and the ships must be Tartars or Japanese.

The following spring, Knight ordered Stewart to take Thanadelthur and travel west with a large party of 150 Crees (Home Indians) and try to make peace with the Dene. The following account

---

[7] James Knight, *Hudson's Bay Company Journals* 1714–17; Web Support Site, *Black Bonanza* Footnotes—Chapter 2. < * >

from his post journal of September 10, 1715, is the first description we have of bitumen seeping into a river 500 miles (805 km) west of Hudson Bay, and the first report by a European of the Sands of the Athabasca, laden with the same tarry substance used by the Mesopotamians:

> Before they went I talked to them about the great river that runs into the sea on the back of this [far] country. They tell me there is a certain gum or pitch that runs down the river in such abundance that they cannot land except at certain places. The river is very broad and flows as much water as here. They describe of many different colors and full of Minerals. The weather is very warm in those parts compared to what it is here . . .

Stewart, Thanadelthur and their party left that June and were able to negotiate peace with the "Northern Indians," but many of them starved on the rough trip across the Barrens and never made it as far as the Athabasca River. Most died when they ran out of food, and only Stewart, Thanadelthur, and a small group made it back to York Factory. A weakened Thanadelthur died of the flu a few months later, on February 5, 1717.[8]

Excited by the stories of yellow and white metal, Knight left his post at York Factory and sailed to England in 1718 to organize a treasure expedition. The company owners gave him two vessels, the Albany and the Discovery, and in 1719 he set off in search of the North West Passage and gold. But Knight's northern Eldorado was not to be, and his dreams of riches lured him to his death. A violent Arctic storm wrecked the ships on Marble Island in Hudson Bay, and James Knight and his crew never survived. They likely ended up as winter rations for itinerant polar bears, since searchers have found only one human vertebra and three teeth on the island.[9]

---

[8] Ibid.
[9] Ibid.

Knight's assistant, Henry Kelsey, took over as governor of York Factory. As a young man, Kelsey had traveled inland as far as the Canadian prairies in what is now Manitoba or Saskatchewan. He was the first European to see the grizzly bear and the immense herds of bison on the plains. He never reached the riches of the Athabasca country, but on June 12, 1719, in the year Knight disappeared, Kelsey was looking over his books when a Cree trader, Wa-Pa-Sun (The Swan), arrived with a load of beaver, marten furs, and castors—dried beaver oil glands that were used as a headache remedy. Wa-Pa-Sun also brought out of his deerskin pouch a moss-wrapped piece of black pitch he said flowed out of the banks of a river. He said it was useful for dressing wounds, waterproofing clothes, and patching birchbark canoes.

When Kelsey sniffed the substance it smelled just like oakum—the pitch-soaked rope fiber that shipbuilders used to caulk the seams in ship planking. He thought it might interest his Hudson's Bay Company masters, and he traded it for some tobacco. But the merchants were not interested in such a cheap substance, already available in London at a decent price. That was the last mention of Athabasca bitumen in the Hudson's Bay Company records for another half century.

● ● ●

In spite of making several trips inland, the HBC men preferred to huddle inside their trading posts on the shore of Hudson Bay and let the Cree come to them. But French traders from Montreal were now invading their territory, and after the fall of New France in 1760, a new breed of Scottish and American traders from Montreal and Detroit began to tap into the rich fur bonanza of the northwest.

The first into the Athabasca country was a hard-nosed venturer named Peter Pond, who had served in the British Army and was present at the French surrender of Montreal. Pond was originally from Connecticut, and began fur trading with his father down the Mississippi from Detroit. After the American Revolution, he sided with the British, left the United States, and soon partnered with the North West Company (NWC) merchants from Montreal, rivals of the Hudson's Bay Company in the far northwest. He respected and worked closely with the native people, and learned from them about the waterways and portages to the Arctic and Pacific Oceans, and to the Russian posts in Alaska.

In 1778, the 38-year-old Pond was the first person of European background to see the dark oil-laden sands along the river the Cree called the *Assenpiskew* (the Athabasca). North of the site of Fort McMurray, where Syncrude and Suncor now strip-mine the richest surface deposits, Pond noted simply that along the banks of the Athabasca were "springs of bitumen that flow along the ground."

The bitumen held little interest for Pond. It was the rich bonanza of top quality fur that drove him into the Athabasca region, where the colder weather made the animals grow thicker pelts. He built a fur trading post called Fort Pond further downstream to the north, and began trading with the Mikisew Cree (Woodland Cree) and the Denesolene (Athabasca Chipewyan First Nation). News of the Athabasca fur bonanza spread, and rival traders arrived ready to do battle with Pond. He moved his main post farther downstream to the south shore of Lake Athabasca, followed closely by the competition.

Pond had a talent for mapmaking, and during the winter of 1784–85, he drew the first chart showing the rivers and lakes from the Great Lakes and Hudson Bay westward to the Rocky Mountains and northward to the Arctic. He indicated a large river flowing from Lake Athabasca to Slave (Great Slave) Lake, and thence to the Arctic Ocean, noting the "extraordinary banks of salt" west of the Athabasca.[10]

---

[10] Pond's Map; Web Support Site, *Black Bonanza* Maps & Charts—Historical. < * > .

34

Pond had a dark side that cut his fur trade career short. He had killed another man in a duel as a young man and had a reputation as a hothead. Frustrated by growing competition, he likely counseled or agreed to the shooting of two rival traders in 1782 and 1787.

In 1787, NWC partner, Alexander Mackenzie, arrived at the Athabasca post on his way to the Arctic Ocean. When he heard of the second shooting, he likely censured Pond or even relieved him of his duties, sending him to Montreal to explain his actions before a tribunal. Pond sold his NWC share and left the fur trade in 1790.

●　●　●

In the spring of 1789 Mackenzie had a closer look at the oozing bitumen springs along the banks of the river, to see if there was any profit in mining them. He wrote in his journal:

> At about 24 miles from the fork [of the Athabasca and Clearwater Rivers] are some bituminous fountains into which a pole of 20 feet long may be inserted without the least resistance. The bitumen is in a fluid state and when mixed with gum, the resinous substance collected from the spruce fir, it serves to gum the Indians' canoes. In its heated state it emits a smell like that of sea coal. The banks of the river, which are there very elevated, discover veins of the same bitumenous quality.[11]

But the Sands were just a curiosity for Mackenzie; his passion was to explore the remaining blank spaces on the maps of North America and, of course, to make a good profit from the fur trade. Farther downstream, he founded Alberta's first permanent

---

[11] Alexander Mackenzie, *Voyages from Montreal*, 1801–29; Web Support Site, *Black Bonanza* Footnotes—Chapter 2. < * >

European settlement at Fort Chipewyan. On June 3, 1789, he and his party of French-Canadian voyageurs set out down the Slave River. The Yellowknife Indians had told him of a giant wilderness river flowing northwest from Great Slave Lake, and he wanted to find out whether it flowed into the Arctic or Pacific ocean, and complete the route from Great Slave Lake down the river system that Peter Pond had partially mapped. He and his voyageurs made it all the way to the Arctic Ocean down what is now known as the Mackenzie River, and a few years later hacked and portaged their way to the Pacific, becoming the first people to cross North America.

The early 1800s saw Mackenzie move to England, where he wrote up his travels, was knighted by the King, and retired in glory. But back in the Athabasca, the fur war had heated up. In 1805, HBC traders moved into the valley. The two companies started using ruthless tactics against each other, including scuttling canoes, sabotaging the hunt, and destroying produce, even attempting to burn down their rival's forts. By 1820, the two companies were exhausted by the fur fight and the shareholders of the two companies joined up in London, England, preferring monopoly to war. All the while, the black gold of the Athabasca still lay oozing out of the banks of the river, waiting for its time, 200 years in the future.

● ● ●

As the Northwest slowly opened up, other travelers began taking note of the Sands. On March 15, 1820, Royal Navy Captain John Franklin, on his way from Montreal to explore the Arctic coast east of the Mackenzie delta, descended the Clearwater River and found "pure sulfur deposited by springs and smelling very strongly." On March 17, his party reached Fort McMurray, where he noted the "sulfurous springs" and "bituminous salt" in the region. One of his mates, Dr. John Richardson MD, an amateur geologist, took the first detailed notes on the Sands, describing the bitumen beds, the clay outcrops, and the underlying limestone of the place.[12]

After a disastrous expedition along the Arctic coast, where his party starved and barely escaped with their life, Franklin returned to England, mounted another expedition, this time to the Northwest Passage, and some time after 1845 he and the pride of the Royal Navy disappeared without a trace.

While the last starving survivors of Sir John Franklin's doomed Arctic expedition were resorting to cannibalism, or being eaten by polar bears, Lady Franklin grew desperate for news. At her urging, the Hudson's Bay Company sponsored a search expedition led by Dr. John Richardson, who had been with Franklin on the earlier ordeal.

In 1848, Richardson again passed through the Athabasca territory on his way north to search for his old friend. Still intrigued by what he thought could be a resource of great value, he stopped to make the first proper assessment of Athabasca bitumen with scientific instruments. He noted that the oil sands were similar to the Devonian shales of the Marcellus Formation of New York. He did acid tests on the oil, looked at the sand under his microscope, identifying it as simple quartz, and modestly concluded, "I do not possess evidence of the facts to satisfy a geologist."[13]

• • •

The seasons passed and the valley of the Athabasca slept, while to the west, south, and east the United States expanded into

---

[12] Pierre au Calumet (pipe stone), near Bitumount, was a Hudson's Bay Company fort built in 1788 and seized by the North West Company in 1817; John Franklin, "Narrative of a Journey to the Shores of the Polar Sea in the Years 1819, 20, 21 and 22." See the original notes by Richardson and other travelers on the *Black Bonanza* Web Support Site.
[13] Berens House, the fur emporium of a free trader; John Richardson, "Arctic Searching Expedition: A Journal of a Boat Voyage Through Rupert's Land and the Arctic Sea, in Search of the Discovery Ships under Command of Sir John Franklin," (London, 1851) pp. 123–24.

Indian territory and suffered through a bloody Civil War. A new country called Canada came into being and soon bought the territories of the Hudson's Bay Company, and started to build a transcontinental railway. The entire continent began to open up, and with settlers pouring into the prairies, towns and cities sprang up almost overnight. Optimism was the ruling passion, and all those who experienced pioneer life could sense that a new future was being carved out of the empty plains and wilderness of North America.

• • •

One rainy evening in September 1875, a Canadian government survey party led by geologist John Macoun set up camp on the banks of the Athabasca River and ate their evening meal. Later, when the campfire died down, Macoun went into his tent, lit a candle, and wrote down these words in his diary:

> On account of the rain, our camp was formed in the woods, and was both wild and picturesque. Three rousing fires were built (one for each boat) and around these in the darkness flitted dusky figures, some cooking, others smoking, and all talking or laughing, without thought of rain or any other matter than present enjoyment.
>
> Long after the noises ceased I lay and thought of the not-far distant future, when other noises than those would wake up the silent forest; when the white man would be busy, with his ready instrument, steam, raising the untold wealth which lies buried beneath the surface, and converting the present desolation into a bustling mart of trade.

Today, close to where Macoun set up his camp, is indeed a bustling mart of trade, the modern city of Fort McMurray, the metropolis of the Sands. And billowing over the mines and pumped underground is the ready instrument used to raise the untold wealth of the Sands—steam.

• • •

In 1867, the newborn country called Canada wasted no time identifying its geological riches by forming the Geological and Natural History Survey of Canada, led by Dr. Robert Bell.

Three years later, in 1870, Canada acquired what was known as Rupert's Land from the Hudson's Bay Company—a vast tract of land draining into Hudson Bay, that extended from Ontario to the Rockies and north to the Arctic. In that same year, the Hudson's Bay Company trader, Walter Moberley, founded Fort McMurray as an HBC fur post and store, at the confluence of the Clearwater and Athabasca Rvers. It was named after William McMurray, chief factor of the Hudson's Bay Company for the Athabasca region.

While the fur trade started to decline, other natural products stepped in to fill the vacuum. The first recorded oil sale in the Canadian West was made by HBC factor, W. L. Hardisty, at Fort Simpson, who ordered five kegs of tar from Fort Good Hope, which were delivered to him by a canoe party of Dene people.

The Hudson's Bay Company closed its Fort McMurray store in 1898, but reopened it in 1912 to meet the demand for a warehouse on the Athabasca River to serve river traffic north to Lake Athabasca, then on to the Mackenzie River and the Arctic Ocean.

• • •

In August 1874, Geological and Natural History Survey of Canada scientist, George Mercer Dawson, in the employ of the Boundary Commission, noted petroleum seeps in the Waterton area of present-day Alberta. The following year in August and September 1875, geologist John Macoun also found "oil springs" (seeps) on the

Peace River, and then carried out the first government-sponsored study of the Athabasca Valley Sands, poling up the river for almost 125 miles (200 km) with his crew. Macoun was increasingly amazed at the huge size of the deposit. At one spot where they landed to track the boats upstream, the ooze from the Sands had completely covered a hundred yards of beach with a coat of smooth tar that was as hard as rock. But by noon, the surface had softened, like spots of tar on an asphalt road, and the men pulling the boats sunk into the tar up to their ankles.

At some point, Macoun's party found the small creek where the Hudson's Bay Company got their supply of tar for the boats:

> I noticed a little stream of water flowing into the pool, which was coated with an oil scum and under the stream was an abundance of tar. Along the beach it was oozing out in many places, and by gathering and washing the sand saturated with it, we obtained just as pure tar as we brought from the spring on the hillside.
>
> Instead of getting the tar on the beach, as I had expected, I took it from this pool, which was about forty feet down the stream. I filled one jar at the stream and another jar on the beach by taking the tar and washing it in the water. That there must be enormous quantities, I am quite satisfied, on account of having seen that tar along the bank for over one hundred miles.[14]

• • •

In 1882, the year Karl Benz invented the automobile, Dr. Robert Bell, new director of the Geological Survey of Canada, arrived in the Athabasca to gauge the commercial potential of the Sands. He

---

[14] John Macoun, "Report of Progress," Geological Survey of Canada (1875); Web Support Site, *Black Bonanza* Footnotes—Chapter 2. < * >

identified the "asphaltic sands" as Lower Cretaceous in age, and proposed that the bitumen was sourced in the Devonian strata.[15]

Bell shipped some barrels of the Sands back to Ottawa, and for two years he and his survey chemist, Christian Hoffman, analyzed samples of the "sandy pitch." Hoffman concluded that it was going to be a very valuable resource one day. He thought the sands were "admirably adapted for asphalting purposes" without the need to separate the sand and bitumen. The sands were suitable for roofing and waterproofing basements, and for "construction of roads, footpaths, courtyards, and for asphalting the floors of granaries." He felt it would be a simple matter to separate out pure bitumen. It could, he wrote, "be effected by simply boiling or macerating the material with hot water, when the bituminous matter entering into fusion will rise as scum to the surface and may be removed by skimmers, whilst the sand falls to the bottom of the vessel."[16]

In 1883, Bell asked Hoffman to experiment using hot water to separate the bitumen from the sand, and Hoffman reported back that it separated readily. Hoffman even took a stab at estimating the amount of bitumen in place in the Sands by assuming 1,000 square miles (2,590 sq. km), 28.5 cubic miles (119 cubic km) of sand, and 22.9 percent content of bitumen to equal 26 billion barrels in place.[17] As we shall see, he was way off the mark.

Bell was one of the first to suggest that the huge deposit might be merely dried-out crude oil that had seeped into the Sands from distant Devonian rocks, and that liquid petroleum lurked in the deeper formations. "The enormous quantity of asphalt, or

---

[15] See Robert Bell (center) and his Survey Party in the Athabasca, 1883; Web Support Site, *Black Bonanza* Gallery—Chapter 2. < * >

[16] G. Christian Hoffman, "Chemical Contributions to the Geology of Canada," Geological Survey of Canada, Ottawa; Web Support Site, *Black Bonanza* Footnotes—Chapter 2. < * >

[17] According to Earle Gray, "Hoffmann's macerating didn't remove quite all of the most minute particles of sand. The bitumen he extracted by this method still contained 50.1 percent very fine sand. It would take a little more than "simply boiling" to completely remove it. Hoffmann added that, given greater quantities than his few samples, the bitumen might be distilled and "advantageously employed as a crude material for the manufacture of illuminating and lubricating oils and paraffin." This was still the age of coal oil lamps.

thickened petroleum, in such a depth and extent of sand indicates an abundant origin. It is hardly likely that the source from whence it came is exhausted. The whole of the liquid petroleum may have escaped in some parts of the area below the sandstone, while in others it is probably still imprisoned in great quantities and may be found by boring."[18]

Bell was partially right, but wrong in the location and the hydrocarbon. In the same year he was exploring the Athabasca, Canadian Pacific Railway (CPR) drillers, looking for water for the CPR's steam locomotives, made Western Canada's first natural gas strike at CPR Siding No. 8 at Langevin, near Medicine Hat, east of Calgary. The gas flow caught fire and quickly consumed the drilling rig. The people of Medicine Hat were soon using the gas for lighting, heating, and cooking, prompting visiting British author Rudyard Kipling, viewing a gas flare up close, to comment that they had "all hell for a basement."

Canada's Parliamentarians suddenly wanted to know far more about the riches of the Northwest, and in 1888 a Senate committee was struck to find out how much oil and gas the territory contained. In his testimony to the Senate, Bell prophetically called the Athabasca and Mackenzie Valleys "the most extensive petroleum field in America, if not in the world ... it is probable this great petroleum field will assume an enormous value in the near future and will rank among Canada's chief assets."[19] He also proposed that a pipeline could be constructed from the eastern end of Lake Athabasca 500 miles (805 km) east to Hudson Bay, to ship the extracted oil to foreign markets.

● ● ●

----

[18] Robert Bell, "Report on Part of the Basin of the Athabasca River-NWT," Geological Survey of Canada, *Annual Reports* (1881, 1883, and 1884); Web Support Site, *Black Bonanza* Footnotes—Chapter 2. < * >

[19] Canada, Senate. "Report of the Select Committee Appointed to Enquire Into the Resources of the Great Mackenzie Basins," Session 1888; Web Support Site, *Black Bonanza* Footnotes—Chapter 2. < * >

Bell's colleague, R.G. McConnell, was next to survey the Sands, and he reported with a little more confidence that:

> The Tar Sands evidence an upswelling of petroleum to the surface unequalled elsewhere in the world, but the more volatile and valuable constituents of the oil have long since disappeared, and the rocks from which it issued are probably exhausted as the flow has ceased. In the extension of the Tar Sands under cover the conditions are different, and it is here that oils of economic value should be sought.[20]

McConnell gave the Senate committee a geological description of the oil sands and linked them with the Cretaceous Dakota sandstone in the Western Interior Basin of the United States. He reckoned that the reserves of bitumen in the Athabasca oil sands were at least 4.2 million "long tons" and suggested that there might be light oil underneath. He proposed an immediate program for drilling, and the Senators agreed.

In 1893, the Parliament passed a bill authorizing the Geological and Natural Survey of Canada to investigate the petroleum resources of the Northwest Territory and the Athabasca Oil Sands; Parliament gave McConnell a $7,000 grant to hire a contractor and move a drilling rig up to the Athabasca River. McConnell hired Ontario driller, A.W. Fraser, who brought a rig up to the Athabasca where he spudded his first well on August 15, 1894.

On June 16, 1894, the *Edmonton Bulletin* suggested that the government was preparing to boost a commercial oil industry. Stock speculators, suspecting a bonanza of oil wealth, grew frenzied by all this activity. There was a mini boom on the Calgary Stock Exchange, with hundreds of paper companies floated to tempt excited investors.

---

[20] R.G. McConnell, "Economic Geology," *Report of Progress*, Geological Survey of Canada (1890–91), p. 66D; Web Support Site, *Black Bonanza* Footnotes—Chapter 2. < * >

McConnell expected to encounter crude oil at between 1,197 to 1493 feet (365 to 455 m), but Fraser's drillers "ran out of hole," using smaller and smaller diameters of casing until further progress was impossible. McConnell and Fraser abandoned their first well in 1895. Two years later, Fraser got new pipe from Ontario, moved the rig, and started drilling a second well on the Athabasca at Pelican Rapids. After much difficulty, he reached a depth of 1,600 feet (250 m), at which time "a roar of gas at a pressure of 500 psi could be heard three miles (5 km) away." The Pelican Rapids well blew wild, and in one of the great resource losses in Canadian history, burned off 20 million cubic feet (566,337 cubic m) per day for twenty-one years, until it was killed in 1918 by a crew led by A.W. Dingman and Stan Slipper. Geological survey chief, George Mercer Dawson, who visited the Sands himself in 1895, was greatly disappointed at finding "maltha or tarry oil instead of liquid oil at Pelican Portage."

McConnell and Fraser abandoned the site and drilled another well downstream from the town of Redwater along the banks of the North Saskatchewan River. But after they had spent over $30,000, it was clear there was no "basement oil" under the Sands, and the government axed the program. All interest in exploiting the Athabasca died out in 1897 when news came of a colossal gold strike at Bonanza Creek in the Yukon.

• • •

Some of the promoters reportedly salted their wells by dumping volumes of crude oil downhole to be pumped up later for the edification of credulous investors.
—Earle Gray

In 1898, the town of Edmonton was a major jumping-off point for gold prospectors eager to reach the fabulous mines of the Klondike. On Bonanza Creek, it was said miners could peel the gold off the rock in thick slabs like a cheese sandwich.

One young treasure seeker who went west was twenty-four-year-old Alfred von Hammerstein, scion of an aristocratic German family; he would later capitalize the "von" to make it less aristocratic. The young Von Hammerstein began his career in the Prussian army, but was soon stricken by wanderlust. He found himself in New York just as news broke of a fabulous gold strike in Canada's Yukon.

At that time, there were two ways to get to the Klondike—via Skagway on the Pacific coast or cross-country from Edmonton. Von Hammerstein chose the latter, but on his way down the Athabasca River, he first encountered the Athabasca Tar Sands, and as he liked to tell it, he determined then to stay and develop the bonanza of the Tar Sands instead.

The first of the oilsands pioneers, Von Hammerstein was an ambitious serial entrepreneur who promoted a variety of businesses over his lifetime. Between 1898 and 1907 he ran German-language newspapers in Winnipeg and Edmonton. Inspired by news that the Geological Survey of Canada was predicting that crude oil underlay the Sands, Von Hammerstein raised capital, acquired Canadian government leases, and in 1907 he and his friend, "Peace River Jim" Campbell, took a drilling crew to Fort McMurray, hauling the rigs overland from Edmonton to Athabasca Landing, and then by barge downriver to the bitumen deposits. They spent the next five summers drilling twenty-four wells into the Devonian limestone under the Athabasca Sands, and although they fed speculation by talk of "promising results," they failed to strike the "free oil" predicted by Bell and McConnell.

In 1907, Von Hammerstein traveled to Ottawa and assured the Senate committee that the Sands would be of great value to the nation, once there was a reliable way to get it to market. "I have all my money put into it, and there is other peoples' money in it, and I have to be loyal. As to whether you can get petroleum in merchantable quantities ... I have been taking in machinery for about three years. Last year I placed about $50,000 worth of machinery in there. I have not brought it in for ornamental purposes, although it does look nice and home-like." He described the experiments he had carried out, even to using the tarry residue to produce tarpaper.

Von Hammerstein founded the Athabasca Oil and Asphalt Company in Winnipeg in 1909, and raised hundreds of thousands of dollars in capital for his drilling program. He did find salt at the confluence of the Horse and Athabasca Rivers, and it became the major industry in the Fort McMurray area for the following fifty years. But Von Hammerstein's dreams of a black bonanza in the Athabasca Tar Sands were shattered by reality, and rumors that he too had taken to "salting"—pouring oil into the wells to make it appear as if he had really struck pay dirt.

What finally skewered Von Hammerstein was the rising anti-German sentiment many Canadians felt as World War I approached. In the 1909 elections, he was a candidate for Athabasca, but withdrew his name two days before the elections. As the war approached, he tried to return to Germany, but was captured and interned for a time. He protested these measures imposed on the "enemy aliens" who happened to be from Germany or the Austro-Hungarian Empire. After the war, Von Hammerstein founded the Canada First Movement to promote friendship between different cultures. He intended to run for Parliament in 1915, on the Canada First platform, but received little financial support.

Exhausted by his failures to strike oil in the Athabasca, Von Hammerstein finally retired in Winnipeg, but he visited Alberta several times in the 1920s to keep his leases and his fading dreams alive. He offered the properties to Imperial Oil and Royal Dutch Shell for $250,000—later reduced to $110,000 during the Depression of the 1930s. Neither company took up the offer because there was clearly no free oil to be found.[21]

What happened to Von Hammerstein's leases? First of all, they were "freehold" leases for the production of asphalt (bitumen)

---

[21] "Overview of the immigration history of Alberta's German-speaking communities," University of Alberta, Institute of Germanic Languages, Literatures, and Linguistics (www.ualberta.ca/~german/PAA/German-speakingcommunitiesinAlberta.htm).

only. He owned six titles, one mile (1.6 km) apart, fronting along the Athabasca River. They were Dominion or Crown lands and extended back about three miles (5 km). In the 1930s, when the leases were virtually worthless, Calgary lawyer Eric Harvie gathered up as many as he could, and later sold all of his interests to Chevron. Eventually, the six Von Hammerstein leases made their way into the hands of Great Canadian Oil Sands (GCOS) and are now part of the Suncor Energy properties.

Von Hammerstein's dream eventually did come true, but not at all in the way he had imagined. What the Sands needed was a market for all its buried energy, and far-sighted investors who were prepared to wager hundreds of millions of dollars on developing an entirely new way of producing petroleum. That market started to emerge in the early years of the twentieth century with the dawning of the Oil Age.

* * *

On March 27, 1855, Halifax inventor, Abraham Gesner, was awarded U.S. patents for his kerosene distillation process, essentially duplicating what the Mesopotamians had discovered 1,200 years earlier. He and a group of investors set up the highly successful North American Kerosene Gas Light Company, to market the new lamp fuel that was to completely replace whale oil. Forty years later, after discoveries of crude oil in Ontario and Pennsylvania, John D. Rockefeller's Standard Oil Company ended up controlling most of the lamp oil industry.

As the new century dawned, western civilization was still built upon the coal-fired steam engine and the horse. In 1900, annual world coal output was 700 million tons, up from 15 million tons in 1800. Horse power was still the major energy source for traction and shipping in Europe and North America. The horse population in Britain was 3.5 million. In the U.S., a quarter of agricultural land (90 million acres or 365,217 sq. km) was used to grow food for horses, and the cities reeked with steaming piles of manure.

The first stirrings of change was felt in the 1890s, with an increased demand for fuel oil to power oil boilers in trains and ships, and refined gasoline to drive internal combustion engines in automobiles. But the price of oil was still high, and the electric car was beginning to make major inroads.

Everything changed on January 10, 1901, at Beaumont, Texas, as the Spindletop gusher blew wild, ushering in the automotive age. Oil priced at less than twenty-five cents a barrel led to abundant gasoline supplies, just in time to supply the $600 cars being built by Henry Ford and Ransom Olds.

One of the major Beaumont operators was a Pennsylvania refiner by the name of Joseph Newton Pew. Pew quickly assembled some producing wells and built a pipeline to the nearby Neches River, to ship Texas crude to his huge new refinery at Marcus Hook, Pennsylvania. Pew then founded the Sun Oil Company to consolidate his holdings in Ohio, Illinois, West Virginia, and Texas, and was able to break the Rockefeller monopoly with low-priced gasoline. His son, J. Howard Pew, also had oil in his blood, and developed a way to make lubricants out of asphaltic Texas crude. Under Howard's presidency, Sun Oil was the first (in 1937) to use Eugene Houdry's catalytic-cracking process, instead of thermal cracking, to make its gasoline. Thirty years later, Howard Pew would also be the first to pioneer a large-scale Athabasca Oil Sands plant, as the major investor in what is now Suncor Energy.

●　●　●

As the twentieth century began, the area south of the Athabasca was gradually opening for settlement, and drillers were finding gas and the first whiffs of petroleum. As the new Canadian Prime Minister, Wilfrid Laurier, predicted, the twentieth century would belong to Canada.

To get the golden goose to lay, the Laurier government brought in the Petroleum Bounty Act of 1904, paying one and a half cents for every gallon of oil produced in Canada, including petroleum produced from oil shales and sands. This subsidy ended in 1925.

In 1905, the federal government created the new provinces of Alberta and Saskatchewan out of the Northwest Territories. A more northerly transcontinental railway was soon built, linking Winnipeg with Saskatoon and Edmonton, and all the way to the Pacific coast at Prince Rupert. In 1910, the Alberta government committed to building railway connections to the Athabasca near Fort McMurray. The railway reached Waterways, east of the town, in 1921.

While granting provincial status, the Canadian government held back giving title to the mineral rights and natural resources to the new provinces, not giving them the same Crown lands as the older provinces; these rights would not revert to Alberta and Saskatchewan until 1930. Part of the reason for retaining these rights was strategic, related to Canada's role as part of the British Empire. The Canadian Pacific Railway and steamships were still a part of Britain's imperial "All Red Route" to the Far East, and the Royal Navy Pacific Fleet had a secure supply of coal at Nanaimo, British Columbia.

As the twentieth century dawned, the British were faced with German imperial expansion. Winston Churchill,[22] First Lord of the Admiralty, quickly moved to maintain Britain's mastery of the seas by converting Royal Navy battleships from coal-fired engines to diesel, because of faster fueling and greater efficiency. The bulk of the British fleet was converted by 1910, and the days of the Pacific fleet coaling station at Nanaimo ended abruptly; however, the British imperialists were confident that they would be able to replace coal with Canadian oil. The Athabasca Sands were one of the most promising resources.

Churchill ignored offers of fuel from Shell Oil's Marcus Samuel, and promoted British oil rather than Dutch—Shell was headquartered in the Netherlands. Instead, he persuaded Lord Strathcona,

---

[22] Winston Churchill's Canadian roots were deep. His ancestor, the Duke of Marlborough, was a Governor of the Hudson's Bay Company.

Canada's High Commissioner in London and chief shareholder of the Canadian Pacific Railway, to finance the Anglo-Persian Oil Company (today's BP plc). Canadian drillers were soon at work in the Middle East, and they struck oil at Masjid-e-Soleiman, Persia, on May 26, 1908.

While the Age of Oil was beginning worldwide, in western Canada, all that could be found was natural gas. In 1908, an Ontario driller named Eugene Coste spudded the "Old Glory" gas well at Bow Island, Alberta. Four years later, in 1912, his Canadian Western Natural Gas Company built Alberta's first gas pipeline, 170 miles (275 km) from Bow Island to Calgary, and 12,000 Calgarians gathered to watch Mrs. Coste light the inaugural flare with a roman candle.

However, most observers and investors felt it was only a matter of time before drillers made the first oil strike in Western Canada, somewhere beneath the prairies or foothills or even hidden under the Sands of the Athabasca.

3

Gearing Up

The Years of Frustration

For the first half of the twentieth century, the Athabasca Sands were a kind of slow motion Klondike. During the 1898 Yukon gold rush, a stampede of prospectors from all over the world battled mountainous terrain, cold, and starvation to get to the gold fields. They staked their claims and started panning the river sands for dust and sluicing for yellow metal. A few got rich, some sent home a few bags of nuggets, but the rest lost their shirts. Three years after it began, the gold rush collapsed as big dredgers replaced the small sluice operators who washed the river gravel until the gold played out.

In the case of the Sands, there was no stampede or panic to get at the treasure. No more than fifty prospectors and teams came to the remote Athabasca frontier over a forty-year period before World War II. All of these starry-eyed dreamers lost money. But they believed they had the chance to strike it very rich by finding a large pool of crude oil, or at least make a modest buck by producing barrels of tar or from mining the Sands to pave the muddy roads of the Canadian Prairies with Athabasca asphalt. They did make some progress in understanding the riddle of the Sands. The

Athabasca River was not Bonanza Creek, and bitumen-soaked sand was not gold dust—at least not yet.

As with many projects in Canada, what kept the dream of the country's bitumen bonanza alive into the 1950s was the government's involvement in research and development, and the need to develop a synthetic crude oil resource during the two great wars of the century.

In 1913 as World War I neared, the Canadian government agreed to meet the potential demand for Canadian oil for Royal Navy warships. Ottawa placed all oilsands activity under a reserve, halting speculation and development in the Athabasca and Turner Valley southwest of Calgary, a potential site for oil and gas. The Geological Survey of Canada (GSC) also sent a young mining engineer named Sidney Ells to undertake a full inventory of the Sands, and to search for other potential sites that could be drilled for oil, since none had been found by Von Hammerstein and the other private operators.

Sidney Ells was the son of Robert Ells, a veteran of the GSC. In 1902, Ells senior had studied the New Brunswick oil shales with Sidney as his assistant. They also visited Trinidad together to view its famous tar lake. Ells junior graduated from McGill University with a science degree in 1908, then worked for a time in private industry helping to develop a coal mine as well as toiling as a railroad surveyor and roadbed engineer. He joined the Mines Branch of the GSC in 1912 as secretary to director Eugene Haanel, working there until retiring in 1946.

Sidney Ells grew obsessed with the potential of the Athabasca Sands, and said he was "so enthralled with the possibilities of the oil sands that I preferred resigning my position rather than being deprived of making an investigation."[1] His boss, Haanel, caved in to him and came up with a budget to survey and pinpoint the

---

[1] Alberta Energy and Utilities Board, *Historical Overview of the Fort McMurray Area and Oil Sands Industry in Northeast Alberta*, Earth Sciences Report 2000; Web Support Site, *Black Bonanza* Footnotes—Chapter 3. < * >.

richest deposits in the valley. For the next thirty-two years, the Sands became Sidney Ells' passion.

In the spring of 1913, Ells pulled together his gear and set out on his first trip to the Sands. At Athabasca Landing, a transfer point eighty miles (128 km) north of Edmonton, he was greeted by a "crew of three white men and an alleged native pilot." The party boarded a thirty-foot scow pulling a twenty-two-foot (7.2 m) freight canoe, and for the next nine days they poled through fourteen sets of rapids and floated down the 240 mile (400 km) stretch of river to Fort McMurray.

For the next three months, the twenty-eight-year-old Ells energetically surveyed 185 miles (298 km) of wilderness frontage along the Athabasca and its tributaries, photographing and charting 247 tarry outcrops, while meticulously measuring and recording the thickness of the deposits along the riverbanks that today are being chewed up by oilsands miners. The 1913 crew took more than 200 core samples down to depths of five to seventeen feet (1.5 to 5.2 m) using hand augers, then carefully wrapped them in burlap and placed them in wooden barrels.

Early in September, a new twenty-man crew of Métis and Dene rivermen arrived to pack and load the ten tons of core samples onto the scow and barges. Then they started the backbreaking work of hauling the precious cargo all the way back upstream, using tracking lines along the banks and shallows and through the rapids of the Athabasca. Ells wrote that, in some places, they had to fight their way "grimly along the shores, often through tangled overhanging brush, knee-deep in mud and waist-deep water. The ceaseless torture of myriads of flies from daylight till dark, the harassing and heavy work which only the strongest men could long endure made tracking one of the most brutal forms of labor." It took them twenty-three days of twenty-hour effort to drag the scow and barges upstream to Athabasca Landing. By that time, only twelve men were left. Three had been injured and five simply deserted, disappearing into the endless forest that lined the banks of the river.

Today, the same deep forest along the Athabasca is still largely intact, but you can drive the same stretch of territory in only six hours over a paved blacktop road.[2]

• • •

Back in Ottawa with his samples, Ells wrote up a meticulous ninety-two page Preliminary Report on the Bituminous Sands of Northern Alberta.[3] He reported that, "certain areas should lend themselves to large-scale commercial development." At that time, he felt the most promising use was as a road-making material—the automobile was making its appearance all over Western Canada, and roads that were dusty, muddy, or frozen could be made passable with a bitumen coating.

Ells was realistic about other possible uses of the Athabasca Sands, noting that, "discovery of petroleum fields in Western Canada will have a direct bearing on the development of Alberta's bituminous sands." After William Herron found oil along the banks of the Sheep Creek in Turner Valley, and after the Dingman Discovery Well southwest of Calgary blew in on May 14, 1914, it was clear to everyone that the Sands would not be a source of petroleum for many, many years.

In August 1914, the war in Europe changed the prospects for Ells and his work on the Sands. He attempted to enlist, but his superiors told him to continue his work on Athabasca bitumen, which might contain substances useful for the manufacture of wartime explosives or fuel.

Ells needed more bitumen for his road surfacing experiments, but was not inclined to repeat the barging of Sands upriver, so he arranged for a Fort McMurray contractor to pack up sixty more tons

---

[2] See Google Maps; Web Support Site, *Black Bonanza* Footnotes—Chapter 3. < * >
[3] See "Preliminary Report on the Bitumenous Sands of Northern Alberta"; Web Support Site, *Black Bonanza* Footnotes—Chapter 3. < * >

from the Horse River and bring them upriver to Athabasca Landing and south to Edmonton in January of 1915 by horse-drawn sleigh, "in temperatures ranging from 20 to 50 below zero and without tents for men or horses."

Ells ran into some territorial trouble in Edmonton, when he failed to defer to city engineers before going ahead with his paving project. He laid three road surfaces on sections of 82nd Street using three mixtures of Athabasca asphalt. His boss at the Mines Branch had to smooth ruffled feathers, but continued to back Ells. Ten years later, a city road engineer stated that the surfacing Ells had done in Edmonton was still in excellent condition.

But Ells was convinced that with proper study and research, the Sands would eventually be able to deliver up their petroleum riches. Later that year, he went on a fact-finding tour to Kentucky and California to examine other bitumen plants. He also shipped some Athabasca oil sand samples to the Mellon Institute of Industrial Research,[4] a brand new and richly endowed engineering research center in Pittsburgh, Pennsylvania. The Mellon Institute was a scientists' dream, set up to do contract research in the heart of the U.S. coal and oil fields, and its main focus was petroleum. The Mellon scientists were fascinated by the Athabasca bitumen and the challenge it presented of separating the bitumen from the sand and turning it into lighter petroleum.

Ells was invited to visit Pittsburgh, where he spent several happy months in the luxurious surroundings of the Mellon Institute, and chemist William Hamer educated him on the true nature of what were then called "tar sands." Tar, Hamer said, was a by-product of coal. The Athabasca samples were in fact "bituminous sands," that is, silicates impregnated with asphaltic bitumen, or oil that was simply low in hydrogen but high in carbon.

Using all of the lab tools in their kit, Hamer and his researchers first tried thinning the raw sands with petroleum solvents to get the

---

[4] Merged with the Carnegie Institute of Technology in 1967 to form Carnegie Mellon University.

bitumen to release its sand. They heated it to a high temperature to vaporize the bitumen and then distill the gases that were given off. They tried using centrifuges and flotation cells to skim off the oily froth. But they got their most promising results, an extraordinary 99.7 percent pure bitumen[5], using hot water combined with acidic or alkaline reagents to strip the bitumen off the finer particles and then put it through a "filter press." This is much the same process that is used today.

Later, in 1915, with the Great War raging, Ells enlisted with the Royal Canadian Field Artillery. But because of his skills and the potential use of bitumen for fuel, Ells was allowed to continue his research and his work at the Mellon Institute until April 1917. This time, he was able to bring the bitumen out of Athabasca by train. In 1916, the Northern Alberta Railway was completed to Waterways, seventeen miles (27 km) from Fort McMurray.

Before leaving for the European Front, and in case he died on the battlefield, Ells quickly wrote up most of the Mellon research and paving experiments in a rambling two-volume, unpaginated report, with twenty-three appendices. In it, he talked about his paving experiments, noted other attempts to extract bitumen in California by means of chemical or petroleum solvents, and confidently concluded that the Mellon Institute's hot water process with chemical reagents had the best chance of success.

Ells concluded his report with a plea for further research to be conducted on the deposits, suggesting that premature development would do harm and that he supported the 1913 decision to close the Sands as a reserve. He doubted if private business would agree to invest research funds while the Sands were under government control. He suggested the best route was government sponsorship leading to commercial development.

• • •

---

[5] Barry Ferguson, *Athabasca Oil Sands: Northern Resource Exploration 1875–1951* (Canadian Plains Research Center, 1985), Appendix, p. 55.

By late 1916, the Canadian war cabinet's "Honorary Advisory Council for Scientific and Industrial Research" had taken over wartime projects. They tried to arrange for Ells to move to Edmonton so he could do joint work with the University of Alberta, but the university's president, Henry Marshall Tory, decided to look over the subject himself before making a decision.[6]

In 1917, the year the United States entered the war against Germany, the Canadian Army asked Tory to set up an educational section of the force, which later became known as "Khaki University" to train soldiers. In the spring of the same year, Ells was finally posted to Europe, and he would not return until Christmas 1919—after peace was declared—because Tory had posted him to teach engineering to demobilizing troops.

While Ells was away in Europe, Mines Branch Director, Eugene Haanel, hired two young graduates, Karl Clark and Joseph Keele, to evaluate Ells' work.

Clark, a geeky looking chemical engineer in glasses who had been rejected for military service because of his eyesight, was hired to evaluate road-making materials. He was already conducting his own experiments on extracting oil from Ells' Athabasca samples using chemical solvents instead of the hot water process Ells had recommended after his work at the Mellon Institute. After going through the loose, un-indexed papers that Ells had left behind, and seemingly ignoring the quality of the 1914 report, and the fact that it was a rush job, the ambitious young chemist belittled Ells' work, declaring it a "hopeless mess," intimating to Haanel that he could do better.

Clearly Ells never intended his pre-war notes to be published, and knew that more work and editing was needed, but Clark and Keele tore into the absent Ells, slamming his "Notes" as illogical

---

[6] Tory was a McGill-trained mathematician and physicist, and a hard-nosed manager. He was the major driving force in the founding of the University of British Columbia, and in 1907, when the first Alberta government wanted to set up a university, they selected Dr. Tory as the first president.

and incoherent, and claiming that their review was a way to make sense of Ells' report. In a self-serving manner, they admitted Ells raised some important questions and gave a good summary of current research, but they argued he hadn't proven his case—there were too many gaps in the data and too much incoherence to allow publication.

Already annoyed by Ells' behavior during the street paving trial in Edmonton, Haanel wrote his superior, R.W. McConnell, that Ells was incapable of the quality of work that Clark and Keele demanded—he lacked the ability to write a sound scientific study.

While Ells was still away, Haanel removed Ells from the project and put another Mines Branch engineer to work on the road-making issue. The new man came to the same conclusions as Ells—more trials were needed.

• • •

Some commentators are convinced that the ambitious young Clark was jealous of Ells and essentially stole his work. According to Montreal writer William Marsden, Clark purloined Ells' work and used it to launch his own career. He committed "a simple act of academic pilfering... Clark and two other researchers then took Ells' ideas and used them as the basis for their own 5,000-word research paper."[7]

When president Tory returned to the University of Alberta and looked through all the published material from the Department of Mines, he asked Haanel for more information on Ells' research. Haanel sent a package containing Clark and Keele's 1917 critique of Ells' unpublished notes plus the Clark research paper.

At the time, Tory was actively recruiting a teaching team for the university, and Karl Clark, who had recently been awarded his PhD, seemed credible. Tory offered him a job.

---

[7] William Marsden, *Stupid to the Last Drop* (Knopf Canada, 207), p. 30.

When Ells returned from the Front, he was at first baffled by what had happened, and then grew suspicious and angry. Before leaving, he had happily shared information with University of Alberta chemist, Adolph Lehman. When he got back, everything had changed. Says Marsden, "When Ells returned to his desk in Ottawa in 1919, however, he found that his work had been usurped and the perpetrator had disappeared west to Alberta."

Ells then took the unusual step of writing directly to Alberta Premier, Herbert Greenfield, arguing that Haanel had tried to discredit him, because he blamed Ells for accusing him of having pro-German sympathies during World War I. In this highly charged time, many other German Canadians had felt the sting of prejudice. We have already seen how it affected Von Hammerstein. University of Alberta chemist, Adolph Lehman, was German by ancestry. Even Clark was named Karl Adolph by his father, a professor of German at McMaster University. Perhaps after the war they wanted to put all of that behind them, and Ells, a veteran of the war, was a reminder of the prejudice.

Whatever the reason for these actions, when the Alberta oilsands research started up in 1920, the Edmonton scientists all went out of their way to shun Ells. The project was now theirs to exploit, and the word went out—have nothing to do with Sidney Ells.

Other factors helped persuade Henry Marshall Tory to ignore Ells and pick Clark. It's clear he felt that Ells was more of a field entrepreneur than a team player, more practical than suited for the ivory tower. Ells would have chafed under academic discipline. And, of course, he didn't have a PhD. But first, and foremost, the Honorary Advisory Committee back in Ottawa wanted to control Ells' work at the University of Alberta. Tory argued that the war was over, and that any work on campus must be under his control. In addition, he had already battled with the wartime research establishment in Ottawa and Montreal, and they had ignored or sabotaged his suggestions for a national research council. So he set one up himself—the Alberta Council of Scientific and Industrial Research—installing himself as its first chairman.[8]

For Ells' part, it is clear he regarded the actions of Tory and Clark as a form of theft and betrayal. But he knew how the game was played, and kept his mouth shut in public. For the next thirty years, in any of his work, it is hard to find any reference, kind or otherwise, to Karl Clark.

Marsden may well be right about pilferage, although "borrowing" may be a better term. Ells was advised by the Mellon Institute scientists to patent his results, but declined to do so, believing them to be for the public good. The evidence shows that Karl Clark was heavily influenced by the work of Sidney Ells, particularly at the Mellon Institute, and for most of his career, Clark did not shy away from following up and duplicating the research that was written up in Ells' pre-war notes, and later published by him in 1926. In fact, Clark would eventually move to patent the results of his own "process" in 1929.

When I examined all of Sidney Ells' published work for the Mines Branch and later the Fuels Branch, I found it to be uniformly thorough and, at times, even brilliant. Ells never claimed to be a chemist, but he had taken a course in laboratory practice in New York. His work with the Mellon Institute scientists, which he documented in detail in his 1926 work, *Bituminous Sands of Northern Alberta*,[9] was well thought-out and even imaginative. His sometimes heroic fieldwork was precise, and his maps were superb.[10] His business instincts and economic analyses were always clear-headed. Clearly, Ells got sandbagged, but perhaps the culprit was more Henry Marshall Tory than Karl Clark, a naive young man

---

[8] Ironically, when the Canadian government finally set up the National Research Council in 1923 and appointed Tory to the board, he quickly took over operations because no one else had his vision and talent. He became its first full-time president in 1927, at age 64.

[9] Sidney Ells, *Bituminous Sands of Northern Alberta: Occurrence and Economic Possibilities, Mines Branch Report 632*. Ottawa: Department of Mines, 1926.

[10] See Ells' major chart of findings; Web Support Site, *Black Bonanza* Gallery—Chapter 3.

< * >

who let himself be caught up in the hardball academic politics of the day.[11]

Whatever the outcome, the ambitions of all the players involved poisoned the well, and Ells had no further dealings with Clark until the 1950s, when they started writing to each other and likely met at conferences. The rivalry that festered between these two men in some ways mirrored the rivalry between the two governments of Alberta and Canada, as the young province struggled to find its way through a half century of boom and bust before the Athabasca Sands finally delivered its black bonanza.

This political rivalry and rancor between Edmonton and Ottawa would persist over the years, and as we shall see, will come to a boil in the 1970s and 1980s. Just as oilsands production finally came onstream, the world was shaken by skyrocketing energy prices while the two governments scrapped incessantly, even as oil royalties streamed into their eager hands.

●　●　●

The years during and after World War I saw many of the companies that are now major oil sands producers start up business in Canada or take their first timid forays into the Sands. One reason for this was the fear, expressed by the U.S. Bureau of Mines, that petroleum would run out in ten years.

In 1915, Shell had proposed it take control over the northern half of Alberta to secure petroleum for Royal Navy warships. Winston Churchill turned them down flat, because Shell was not a British-based company and had German connections. He turned the job over to the Anglo-Persian Oil Company and Burmah Oil, forerunners of BP plc, which today is a major oil sands player.

---

[11] One librarian at Natural Resources Canada confirmed the bitter infighting and politics of the Mines Branch and G.S.C. in the early years of the twentieth century.

Imperial Oil, another major investor in the Sands, was founded in 1880 by a group of Ontario refiners, but was swallowed up by John D. Rockefeller in 1898. From 1917 to 1919, the Northwest Company Ltd., an Imperial Oil subsidiary, drilled for oil in Township 85 in the Athabasca region.[12]

As the Roaring Twenties began, there were almost 10 million automobiles on North American roads and gas stations opening up everywhere. Roads needed asphalt and there were high hopes that the Athabasca Sands could supply that growing market.

As for the gasoline supply, Imperial Oil and its Royalite Ltd. subsidiary signed a profit-sharing agreement with the Canadian Pacific Railway (CPR) in 1921 to develop the CPR's mineral rights. They struck gas near the original Dingman well in Turner Valley and built a pipeline to Calgary. They also discovered oil beneath the Turner Valley field's gas wells with the Royalite No. 4 well, and Imperial built Alberta's first oil refinery in Calgary in 1923. In the early 1920s, with a new crude oil frontier to be tapped, exploiting the Athabasca Sands was the farthest thing from any company's mind.

* * *

On the other hand, Sands research was steaming ahead steadily at the University of Alberta. In June 1920, Karl Clark came up with his

---

[12] Imperial was now part of Jersey Standard or Esso (Standard Oil Company of New Jersey), created in 1911 when the U.S. Supreme Court declared the Standard Oil group to be an "unreasonable" monopoly under the Sherman Antitrust Act. It ordered Standard to break up into thirty-four independent companies with different boards of directors. Apart from Jersey Standard which eventually became Exxon, the companies included Socony (Standard Oil Company of New York), which eventually merged with Vacuum and was renamed Mobil, now part of ExxonMobil; Standard Oil of California (Socal) was renamed Chevron, became ChevronTexaco, but returned to Chevron; Standard Oil of Indiana (Stanolind) was renamed Amoco (American Oil Co.) and is now part of BP; Standard's Atlantic and the independent company Richfield merged to form Atlantic Richfield or ARCO, now part of BP. Atlantic operations were spun off and bought by Sunoco; Standard Oil of Kentucky (Kyso) was acquired by Standard Oil of California, currently Chevron; Continental Oil Company (Conoco) is now part of ConocoPhillips; Standard Oil of Ohio (Sohio) is now part of BP; The Ohio Oil Company, more commonly referred to as "The Ohio," is now known as Marathon Oil Company.

own version of a hot-water flotation process for separating bitumen from Athabasca Sand. Perfecting his process would be the focus of his career and his passion for the next fifteen years until 1935, when his project was suspended during the Great Depression.

There had been interest in the Sands at the University of Alberta since 1913, when engineering professor W. M. Edwards encouraged Tory to let faculty members study samples from the Mines Branch. Professor Adolph Lehman had already studied the chemistry of the Sands and essentially agreed with Ells that it could, some day, be refined into pure gasoline. This was the holy grail they were all working toward—this would be the eventual bonanza of the Sands.

In 1921, the Alberta government set up the Alberta Research Council (ARC) at the University of Alberta, with a mandate to doc-ument Alberta's mineral and natural resources.[13] Two years later, the ARC gave Clark and his associate, Sid Blair, the task of study-ing ways to exploit the oil sands.

Working away from their offices in a cramped basement lab under the University of Alberta power plant, Clark and Blair built the first scale model of a hot water flotation-separation plant. What came to be called the Clark Hot Water Separation Method was essentially a variation of the Mellon process, where mined oil sand was mixed with hot water and a sodium hydroxide (caustic soda) base; then the resulting slurry was rotated in a horizontal drum at eighty degrees centigrade to aerate it. The rich floating bitumen froth was skimmed off the top, while the clean layer of sand would settle to the bottom of the tank.

At least that was the theory. The real problem was purity, and research became an inch-by-inch battle to squeeze out 100 percent of the water, clay, and other impurities from the bitumen in larger and larger scale operations. The two researchers found that freshly

---

[13] Today, the ARC is a wholly-owned subsidiary of the Alberta Science and Research Authority (ASRA) within Alberta's Ministry of Innovation and Science.

dug and ground sand was best, because it was wet and moisture stopped bitumen from sticking to sand. For the next few years, Clark and Blair went through eighty-five tons of oil sands, with Sid Blair shoveling the raw oil sand in through the basement window and then shoveling the clean sand out again.

During the 1920s, Clark and Blair moved from their lab-bench operation to a larger one-man plant in the Dunvegan railway yards in North Edmonton, and then to a field-scale separation plant at Clearwater near Fort McMurray.

• • •

While the ARC moved forward with coal and tar sands research, the Canadian government continued to control the Crown Lands and natural resources of Alberta, Saskatchewan, and Manitoba, and would do so until 1930. Ottawa argued that since Canada had acquired the territory from the HBC and invested millions in railway development and settlement, the time had not yet come to transfer control.

This attitude angered Henry Marshall Tory, and when a federal official quoted two McGill scientists who suggested, in error, that Athabasca bitumen was only good for asphalt and not for making petroleum, a furious Tory shut down all cooperative research projects with Ottawa.

The University of Alberta president had spent much of his career battling what he called the "stuffed shirts" in Ottawa, but this was too much. Yet Tory knew that Canada desperately needed any and all potential sources of petroleum, and the Athabasca deposits were a huge resource waiting to be explored and exploited. In 1920, with demand for oil skyrocketing, there was talk of very real shortages in the near future—much like the peak oil discussions of today. At that time, Canada was almost completely dependent on oil imports from the U.S. and Venezuela, with only limited production from Ontario. Turner Valley would not add much to the pot, and by the mid-1920s, Canada was producing only about 4 percent of its own oil.[14]

At the same time, global panic was easing somewhat with new oil strikes in Oklahoma and California and the beginning of large-scale exports from Saudi Arabia and other countries in the Middle East. Lacking the futures markets we have today, the large oil companies put in place their own supply management and cartel schemes to stabilize prices. By the late 1920s the world was glutted with oil—the price was collapsing and the supply emergency had passed.

The Athabasca Sands were not on anyone's radar as a petroleum source, yet Ottawa still backed Sidney Ells and Alberta funded Karl Clark as they forged ahead with their research and development during this roller coaster of a decade. Backed by president Tory, Clark increasingly had the upper hand. Having fully digested (and presumably copied) Sidney Ell's notes about the Mellon research, Clark knew what direction to take to duplicate that research and try to surpass it, even though his research budget was miniscule compared to the research funds available today.

It was only a matter of time before Ottawa would be forced to hand over control of the Athabasca Sands to Alberta, and Clark had to work toward that goal. Step one, in his mind, was to set up a demonstration of the hot water process and to publicize his work.

• • •

In August of 1921, Clark reported to Tory that his bench lab was set up and that, "something definite has been accomplished and a very considerable glimmer of daylight let through the problem. Most of the inventive work has now been done," he wrote bravely. "There remains to be accomplished the practical application of the new method to the production of bitumen from the tar sands."

---

[14] Today, with the Sands in full production, Canada is a net exporter of oil, although it is still cheaper to ship crude into eastern Canada by tanker and export it from the West by pipeline.

Clark claimed to Tory that he had discovered a "new method," a distinct way to crack the Sands by a hot water separation process, distinct from the two known methods of "retorting" bitumen by heat or using solvents to distill the oil. In his mind, all that was needed now was a scaling up to commercial development.

Apart from appropriating and claiming as his own processes those that had been used in mining since the 1890s and the pioneering work that had been done at Mellon, the young chemist was getting ahead of himself. Way ahead. He still had to match the 99.7 percent pure bitumen standard that Ells described at Mellon and then take it to 100 percent. He had to solve problems such as preventing the dense bitumen from sinking back into the water and sand. He had to perfect the process with different grades of bitumen, and he had to ramp-up the scale of production into an industrial process, producing pure bitumen for road materials, as well as refined petroleum. This was a tall order for a project whose first-year research budget was $300.

By 1922, Clark's youthful arrogance had changed into resignation—it was going to be harder than he had thought. He hesitated to publish "his" process for obvious reasons, and he was clearly not confident about getting it patented without further unique discoveries and better results.[15] Yet he told Tory that he was near to solving the extraction problem for road material at least. The university president wrote to Alberta Liberal MP, Charles Stewart, then Federal Minister of the Interior, that, "We have solved the problem of the separation of bitumen, in so far as its relation to the problem of roads is concerned. Clark has succeeded in getting out by a very simple process nine-tenths of the sand in one operation."

In his reports to the Research Council, Clark was less confident, writing that the bitumen he was producing would probably

---

[15] An English chemist named Ernest Fyleman had recently patented a method similar to Clark's.

not be able to be refined into gasoline. In 1923, he had a bout of optimism, suggesting that his development of a hot water and silicate of soda process was the key to separating bitumen from sand. The problems that remained were finding the best mix of sand and silicate-water solution, and the most efficient pulping and separation technology.

In 1924, Clark and his research assistant, Sid Blair, built a larger scale plant on a siding of the Dunvegan railway yards in north Edmonton. The site had the advantage of a direct connection with the Northern Alberta Railway (NOR), the Alberta government railway that would finally reach the steamboat docks at Waterways near Fort McMurray in 1925.

Unlike their basement bench "washing machine," Clark and Blair's Dunvegan plant could simultaneously wash one hundred tons of sand *and* skim off the bitumen. But they soon found that due to design flaws, the bitumen had a 30 percent average mineral content, compared to 9 percent for their lab product. Part of the problem was using "weathered sand," which had dried out and dropped much of the thin water layer that kept the oil from sticking directly to the sand. In 1925, they rebuilt the plant, got a better mixing machine, and found that "fresh" wet sand yielded much better results, with only 7 percent mineral content.

In the meantime, they had sent forty-five liters of filtered crude oil to the Universal Oil Products Company in Chicago for analysis. Universal confirmed it was clean enough for refining into gasoline, fuel oils, and kerosene. They were also so impressed with Sid Blair they offered him a job, and he went off to work for Universal in 1926.

By 1927, the Research Council printed its *Report No. 18* on "The Bituminous Sands of Alberta." Volume One, on the "Occurrence" of the Sands, summarized a survey made by Clark and Blair on the geology of the Sands, together with maps and tables on the analysis of the Sands and their chemistry. Clark and Blair noted that the bitumen content of the Sands ranged from 10.5–13.5 percent of total volume, combined with extensive silt and clay, and a 4–6 percent sulfur content. Volume Two, entitled "Separation," talked about the "Clark Hot Water Separation Method."

"When bituminous sand which had been kept in contact for some time with a hot dilute solution of silicate of soda was introduced with agitation into a comparatively large body of hot water, a complete dispersion of the bituminous sand took place." Agitating the emulsion with a flood of hot water resulted in an inversion from water-in-oil to oil-in-water, and "minute globules of bitumen form and rise to the surface of the water," whence they can be skimmed off as relatively pure bitumen.

Clark and Blair further explained that the process was crucial for creating a product that could be taken to market. In concluding, they did mention it could deliver an "outstanding" base for road material, but downplayed the costs of freight and capital. They also mentioned its potential for "cracking" into petroleum.

In the third volume, written by Clark alone, he argued for development of the Sands for road material and motor fuel, but said that far more work needed to be done before that could happen. Clark knew that Universal Oil Products and Canadian Oils Limited in Sarnia, Ontario, were already working on uses for heavy oil and bitumen. So that summer, taking some bitumen samples with him, he started a two-month tour of the U.S. and Canada, visiting Blair in Chicago and getting opinions on the bitumen from U.S. and Canadian petroleum refiners. Earl Smith of Canadian Oils said the bitumen was like a heavy Texas crude, maybe good for lubricants, but not so useful for refining into gasoline.

Clark was hugely disappointed when he found that in a market now glutted with crude, there was really no interest in Athabasca bitumen. The only message he got from the refiners was "some day."

• • •

While Clark was working away in Edmonton, over thirty other operators tried their luck working the Sands.

In 1920, Daniel Diver was the first leaseholder to try and produce oil from the bitumen by an *in situ* (underground) method. He tried to distill oil directly from the oil sands by lowering a heating unit to the bottom of a well near Fort McMurray. That technique didn't work very well. In the mid-1920s, a Montana oilman named Jacob Absher tried injecting steam into shallow thirty-foot wells. When that method didn't have any real effect, he tried kerosene instead. That experiment also failed when Absher's pipes melted in the extreme heat.

Starting in 1920, Thomas Draper, an oil equipment manufacturer from Petrolia, Ontario, had slightly better luck. He originally started working with heat to try and draw bitumen directly from sand. Draper acquired a lease near Fort McMurray and got permission to start mining the Sands for paving roads and streets.

Draper spent the next sixteen years in the paving business with his McMurray Asphaltum and Oil Company. From 1922 to 1926, he mined more than 1,500 tons of oil sands for Karl Clark's experiments. As a sideline, Draper was also fascinated by the hot water flotation method and spent $35,000 building the first plant near Fort McMurray, but in 1924 it was destroyed by fire.

On Karl Clark's recommendation, Draper got contracts to pave a portion of Parliament Hill and a short stretch of Wellington Street in Ottawa, as well as roads and streets in Medicine Hat, Vegreville, and Camrose, Alberta. But his business suffered when the City of Edmonton told Clark that Draper's costs were higher than outside suppliers. Clark concluded from this that paving with raw Athabasca Sand was not a paying proposition.

Clark was still convinced that bitumen tar taken from the Sands could be used for road paving, and in 1927, he conducted his own experiment on a half-mile (1 km) stretch of the Edmonton–St. Albert Trail. But his emulsion of bitumen and gravel did not bond well with the gravel, and the surface broke down quickly.

Sidney Ells was also involved in the asphalt game and managed a successful three-mile (5 km) paving program in Jasper National Park and at Jasper Park Lodge. Ells used raw Athabasca tar sand, heated and then mixed it with gravel. It wasn't a permanent surface and needed re-rolling, but Ells claimed it was better than a plain dirt road and cheaper than conventional asphalt at ninety-three cents per square yard versus $1.25. Karl Clark was not impressed.

In 1927, Clark also suggested to the Research Council that they fund a full-scale bitumen plant right on the Sands at Fort McMurray. "A process has been worked out and has been demonstrated by fairly large-scale applications to be practical. All data so far obtained indicate further that the process is economical. The basic general problem of bituminous sand separation has been solved." Henry Marshall Tory and the Council were impressed, and Clark was able to hire a young PhD in organic chemistry from McGill University, David Pasternack, to help with the problem of completely dehydrating the wet oil produced by the plant, which still contained 30 percent water. The only stumbling block was cost, and Tory realized that if the project was to move ahead, there had to be some cooperation with Ottawa.

A major breakthrough happened in 1928, when Tory was appointed to take over the new National Research Council of Canada in Ottawa. Also in 1928, the new government of Alberta, led by Premier John Brownlee, passed a Natural Resources Act to fund northern research.

On May 7th that same year, Karl Clark pulled together the eight years of notes and diagrams that he and Sid Blair had been working on, and worked out a patent application for the "Process and apparatus for separating and treating bituminous sands." It was awarded in February 1931.

In May of 1929, in a major push to crack the nut of the Sands, the Research Council of Alberta and the Mines Department of Canada signed a two-year cooperative agreement to study coal, gas, and bituminous sands resources, including what to do with the incredible waste of natural gas being flared off from the Turner Valley field—an incredible 60 million cubic feet a day. The agreement also set up the Bituminous Sands Advisory Committee with a mandate to finance Karl Clark's full-scale separation plant on the Athabasca. The board consisted of Robert Wallace, new president of the University of Alberta, as well as Charles Camsell, Deputy Minister of Mines, and Henry Marshall Tory.

The raw sand would come from the federal government's reserve, and one of the goals was to move research toward extraction of petroleum from the bitumen.

As for Sidney Ells, who had spent much of the decade mapping and coring the Sands, he was given funding to proceed with his asphalt and road material experiments, which were having better results than Clark's.

●　●　●

Clark and Pasternack soon got to work redesigning the Dunvegan separation plant, then dismantling it, shipping it, and rebuilding it at the Waterways railhead of the Northern Alberta Railway, on the Clearwater River just east of Fort McMurray.

It was not a good omen that Clark's plant started operations on Black Tuesday October 19, 1929, the very day the Wall Street crash ushered in the Great Depression. In the three days of trial run operations it produced only eleven barrels of bitumen, with less than 10 percent mineral content but still over 30 percent water. That winter Clark and Pasternack worked on perfecting ways to diminish the mineral content to less than 2 percent and get out more water using clay emulsifiers.

They arrived back at the Clearwater plant the following May, and after some tinkering with the equipment, started up operations. Right away they ran into some devilish technical problems—the feed hopper failed to operate smoothly and they were only able to put through 20 tons of sand in a day, which was a great waste of steam. However, on June 24, Clark wrote that they were getting a product "rich in bitumen, soft and nice. The tar rolled out of the plant in great style." But not for long. The wheel that skimmed off the froth stopped turning and the dehydrator only worked sporadically.

Clark and Pasternack eventually figured out the problem—the sand had to be feed in uniformly, and so they had to add another step to the process by adding what was called a "pug mill" at the front end. This grinder served to ensure a continuous and consistent feed and screened out walnut-sized iron sulphide (Macasite) nodules in the sand that were so hard they jammed the feeder.

In spite of these start-up problems, the pair were able to process a total of 800 tons of sands by late August. To their delight, the yield was very good—75 tons of bitumen or about 15,000 gallons. Best of all, the mineral content was only 5 percent and the water only 1 percent. They later discovered that by mixing the bitumen with mineral salts in a steam-jacketed mixing and kneading machine, with the temperature precisely controlled, they were able to cut down the total water and mineral content to less than 2 percent, more or less what Ells claimed the Mellon Institute results were fifteen years earlier.

Clark and Pasternak had at last succeeded in proving that a hot water flotation system could work on a large scale, and in spite of their frustrations, it appeared they had cracked the riddle of the Sands. Clark was immensely relieved. He wrote in the 1930 Research Council report that they had successfully operated a bitumen separation plant on the Athabasca, and "this has had psychological as well as technical values."

As for financial values, well, that was another matter.

• • •

While Clark and Pasternack were perfecting their process at Clearwater, Sidney Ells, with funding from the Bituminous Sands

Advisory Committee, built a large portable mixing plant at Edmonton, housed on a railway flatcar, which could prepare 700 tons of paving material per day. But the experiment only lasted two months. With the Great Depression beginning to grip North America, demand for asphalt and road materials from towns and cities dried up completely. While Ells' back was turned, his equipment was sold for scrap.

Ells knew that transporting and marketing raw tar sands for road making could be cost-efficient on a larger scale, but the deepening Depression made progress impossible. Funding stopped with the arrival of the dust bowl on the prairies. By 1933, the government of Alberta was nearly bankrupt and, indeed, went into technical bankruptcy three years later when it stopped honoring the provincial bonds held by private investors. Premier William Aberhart, battling Ottawa and the eastern banks, declined to join the Canada Loan Council created to help the provinces stave off the Great Depression. So Alberta had to suspend the work of the Research Council and sell off the Waterways plant. Karl Clark was forced to retreat from oilsands glory and do simple soil analysis and part-time teaching. But even in those dark days there were still private entrepreneurs who believed in the potential black bonanza of the Sands. One of them was a real estate promoter named Robert Fitzsimmons. The other was a brilliant American oil entrepreneur named Max Ball.

• • •

Max Ball was a rotund, jolly looking man with black horn-rimmed glasses. A graduate of the Colorado School of Mines and George Washington University Law School, Ball had worked for the U.S. Geological Survey (U.S.G.S.), and then as a consultant for both Shell and Standard Oil, where he honed his ability to appraise and analyze potential oil deposits. In 1928, he struck off on his own as a consulting geologist and in 1929, eager to make a buck as a developer, he partnered with Denver mining engineer, James McClave, president of the Western Research Corporation. McClave was a specialist in hydrometallurgy, the science of using water to extract valuable minerals. McClave had visited the Athabasca Sands in 1921, took out samples, and started tinkering. In 1923, he patented a hot water-steam process that involved using additives of 1.5 to 2.5 percent sodium bentonite or driller's clay to take away silt and help separate bitumen from oil sand.

In 1929, Max Ball invited a government man from Ottawa named Sidney Ells to come down to Denver to talk about the oil sands deposits on the Athabasca River. Ball found Ells' enthusiasm infectious, and traveled to Ottawa where Ells introduced him to the Minister of Mines and the Director of National Parks, who managed the oil sands leases. Ells recommended to Ball that he secure a lease on the Horse River Reserve.

All of this activity happened before the 1930 Natural Resources Transfer Agreement, which gave all provinces, including Alberta, control of their own lands, but the federal government retained ownership of the national parks and several leases around Fort McMurray and on the Horse River, claiming it had put development money into the Sands and also needed the site to produce bitumen to pave the western national parks. Some in Alberta were not pleased by Ottawa's actions, but the crashing economy meant it was unlikely the province would have put up any roadblocks in the way of Max Ball's project. In fact, they embraced it, as did Karl Clark, who had also warmed to Ball when he had visited Edmonton in 1929. Clark was impressed by Ball's intelligence and charm, and the fact that he had clearly done his homework. But Ball also grilled Clark without mercy on his progress with the Clearwater plant, and was very interested in both Ells' and Clark's opinion that the McClave process was not particularly workable.

At that time, Max Ball had a lot more on his plate than just the oil business, and later events showed that like a few other knowledgeable Americans, he was fully aware of the long-term strategic potential of the Athabasca Sands to serve as an emergency reserve for what could be "Fortress North America." With the rise of Communism and Fascism in Europe, and with an oil-hungry Japan threatening conflagration in the Far East, oil tanker traffic from California and along the East Coast could be subject to attack by enemy forces and the valuable Middle East reserves were at risk and in play.

It is also clear that Max Ball's influence, even at that time, went up to the very highest levels of the U.S.G.S. and even the White House. Within a few years of starting work on exploiting the Athabasca Sands, he was appointed chairman of the Oil Board of the U.S.G. S.. In 1940, he wrote a lively bestseller called *This Fascinating Oil Business*, in which he precisely and shrewdly analyzed the huge and crucial role oil would play in the conduct of World War II. When the U.S. joined the war after Pearl Harbor, Ball became Special Assistant to the Deputy Petroleum Administrator for War, and had the ear of Presidents Roosevelt and Truman, who relied on his sage advice.[16]

In early 1930, even with the global economy sliding into a deep depression, Max Ball decided to take the plunge and build an oilsands extraction plant on the Athabasca River.

That August, Ball formally notified both governments of his intentions. After both Ells and Clark assured their superiors that Ball had the resources to mount the project, Ottawa agreed to give him the lease of the Horse River Reserve, located quite close to the railhead at Waterways, plus an option to select another 1,555-hectare, six-section parcel in any area of the Sands "under binding conditions with respect to development."[17] In return, Ball promised to open a plant by September 1, 1936 and mine 45,000 tons of sands in 1937 and 90,000 tons each year after 1938. His company

---

[16] Max Ball, *This Fascinating Oil Business* (Vintage, 1940).
[17] Barry Ferguson, *Athabasca Oil Sands: Northern Resource Exploration 1875–1951* (Canadian Plains Research Center, 1985) Appendix, p. 16.

would pay a rental of $2.47 per hectare per year, and a royalty of $0.063 per cubic meter on production for the first five years, and $0.31 per cubic meter thereafter.

Ball then asked Sidney Ells to advise his company on the choice of further lands, since Ells had done a great deal of core drilling five years earlier. But Ottawa refused, not wanting to get involved in commercial decisions. Ells was puzzled, but understood the reasons behind the decision. But Ball would not give up lobbying Ottawa and it paid off. Two years later, in the spring of 1932, the hoot of the HBC's paddle-wheeler woke Ells from a deep sleep in his cabin on the Athabasca. He ran down to the shore as one of the steamboat crew threw a large weighted package from the vessel, which landed with a splat in the river mud at his feet. It was an urgent message from the Minister of Mines, requiring him to make haste to Ottawa to advise on Ball's allocation. Ells suggested a rich lease in the Mildred and Ruth Lakes area twenty-five miles (40 km) north of Fort McMurray, which is now the current site of the huge Syncrude plant.

• • •

In September 1930, Ball incorporated the Canadian Northern Oil Company to work the lease. In late August 1930, the Bituminous Sands Advisory Committee mandate expired and Ball paid them the sum of $9,200 for Karl Clark's newly abandoned Clearwater plant and the records about his work in progress, which Ball started studying in Edmonton.[18] James McClave agreed to serve as the consulting engineer. When McClave arrived from Denver, he immediately started planning a 500-ton per day separation and refining plant modeled partly on Clearwater, along the Horse River near present day Abasand Heights, a subdivision west of

---

[18] Joseph Fitzgerald suggests the sale later fell through, or was waived because of Depression era realities. At least Ball and McClave had access to the Clearwater operating records.

Fort McMurray. But forest fires delayed progress, and a number of equipment suppliers had gone broke during the Depression. By June 1931, Ball had spent $22,900 on planning, and confessed to Clark that he was in a "desperate struggle" to keep the project going.[19]

After the Wall Street crash, Ball lost some major investors, but he was able to tap the Toronto Stock Exchange, the world's top mining exchange, for capital through the firm of Nesbitt Thomson.[20] At Nesbitt Thomson's request, he set up a new company based in Toronto, changed the company's name to Abasand Oils Limited, and built a lab to analyze a trainload of samples sent down from the Athabasca. In 1934, McClave's lab was also moved to Toronto from Denver for the investors' due diligence. At that point, Ball hired Kansas City engineers A.I. Smith to evaluate the Abasand project and come up with detailed production records to show that the process was workable.

Finally, in December 1935, with Ottawa waiving royalties for three years and with working capital from Nesbitt Thomson, the planning stage ended. McClave's Abasand engineers got the pilot plant up and running in the following summer. After a year of operations and analysis, they had worked most of the kinks out of the process and started to build an improved 400-ton unit, with a pipeline to the railhead at Waterways, which was finally completed in the fall of 1940.

After burning through $1 million in research and development costs, the Abasand plant started its first stage of operation. But McClave ran into trouble with the quarrying and strip mining equipment, and keeping a wartime workforce in place. He was only able to ramp up to full production on May 19, 1941. By the

---

[19] Barry Ferguson, *Athabasca Oil Sands: Northern Resource Exploration 1875–1951* (Canadian Plains Research Center, 1985). p. 88.
[20] This firm of stockbrokers, founded in Montreal in 1912, was acquired by the Bank of Montreal in 1987, and is now operating as BMO Nesbitt Burns, a wholly-owned subsidiary of the Bank of Montreal Financial Group.

end of September, the company had mined 18,475 tons of oil sand and produced 2,690 cubic meters of synthetic oil, which was reprocessed into 137,550 gallons of fuel oil, 70,700 gallons of diesel fuel, 42,265 gallons of gasoline, 375,235 gallons of "residuum," and 319 tons of coke.

The entire production from Abasand was purchased by Consolidated Mining and Smelting (CM&S), operators of the Trail, BC smelter, after a glowing report on Abasand from Karl Clark. CM&S, a giant subsidiary of the Canadian Pacific Railway, wanted to lock in a secure fuel supply for their mining operations and were prepared to invest in, and even consider owning, an oilsands plant.

McClave's Abasand process added one more step to the process developed by Clark—a diluent mixer. As Ball described it:

> Mild abrasion in warm water breaks the films and gives a pulp of water and sand through which are disseminated particles of oil. In a properly designed flotation cell, the oil particles will be picked up by air to form bubbles that float to the surface.[21]

If you then added a solvent such as kerosene or naptha to dilute the oil, then the sand, clay, and dirty water would settle out, "leaving a clean oil that can be pumped through a pipeline." The diluent could then be removed in the refinery and returned for reuse.

This complex process, which added solvent reaction to the mix, went the last mile and delivered a refinable diluted bitumen— basically what is produced today.

Unfortunately, just as Max Ball had achieved his dream, a wartime rivalry swiftly overtook the Abasand project. In April 1942, urged on by the U.S. Army, engineers Bechtel-Price-Callahan and the 388th Engineer Battalion started the brutal job of building the strategic Canol Pipeline to secure oil supplies in case of a Japanese invasion of Alaska and to supply trucks and planes using the Alaska

---

[21] Barry Ferguson, *Athabasca Oil Sands: Northern Resource Exploration 1875–1951* (Canadian Plains Research Center, 1985). p. 90.

Highway corridor to Fairbanks and the Pacific port of Skagway. In fact, Japan invaded the Aleutian Islands on June 3, 1942.

The four-inch (10 cm), 621 mile-(1,000 km)-long Canol Pipeline ran from Imperial Oil's Norman Wells discovery near the Arctic Circle in the Northwest Territories, 1,100 miles (1,770 km) downriverfrom Fort McMurray, to a 3,000-barrel-a-day refinery in Whitehorse, Yukon. The job was so tough and the conditions so extreme that the cost soared seriously over budget, from $20 million to over $125 million, leading to a U.S. Senate committee investigation chaired by soon-to-be President Harry Truman.

It was increasingly clear to Ball and his fellow players that the Abasand plant would not be called on to meet wartime needs, and could only be a backup. Whether due to sabotage or not, the plant burned down in November 1941. Max Ball, now exhausted and bleeding red ink through his pores, turned to the Canadian government for help.

* * *

In 1942, Canadian Oil Controller, George Cottrelle, decided that Canada had to support a workable oilsands plant to supplement Canada's dwindling reserves and aid in Canada's energy security. Cottrelle told Canada's wartime "Minister of Everything," C.D. Howe, who was an American-born engineer, that "if anyone is likely to solve the problems attendant on this deposit, and which at one time seemed insurmountable, Mr. Max Ball and his associates will do it."

Abasand was rebuilt on a larger scale during 1942 and 1943, when the Canadian Wartime Oil Administration took over operations as a test site for a cold water extraction process. But C.D. Howe, the Minister responsible for the operation of the plant, was finding it hard to justify the costs of Abasand with its high expenses and limited results. The government essentially mothballed the plant, putting most northern resources into supplying the engineers building Canol and the Alaska Highway. Abasand was again destroyed by fire in June of 1945, the same year that the Canol Pipeline was abandoned. This time, it wasn't rebuilt.[22]

So while Abasand lost its battle to play a starring role in the conflict, it had to be supported during the conflict as a backup or even emergency resource. Peacetime killed the Abasand project outright, and most of the participants moved on. As for shrewd and feisty Max Ball, he found himself back in Washington where he served with the U.S. Board of Economic Warfare, and from 1947–1948, as Director, Oil and Gas Division, in the U.S. Department of the Interior, before he got the itch again, and went back into the consulting business.

During his fifteen years developing a workable Sands project, Max Ball and his partners had funneled at least $700,000 into their oilsands lease, with the remainder —about $2 million—financed by Ottawa during the wartime emergency. To console themselves for their losses, Ball and his investors did retain a 25 percent interest in certain Athabasca properties, including a 4,000-acre lease beside Tar Island where Great Canadian Oil Sands would develop its first oilsands plant.

● ● ●

Max Ball's Abasand was not the only oilsands plant operating in the 1930s. The other was Bitumount, a small potatoes operation run by a starry-eyed promoter from Prince Edward Island named Bob Fitzsimmons.

---

[22] Earle Gray notes: "The Abasand plant was rebuilt and one of those involved in this wartime effort was Harold Rea, first chairman of GCOS. Rea had been manager of sales with Canadian Oil Companies, Limited—best known for its White Rose gasoline—when he was loaned to the federal government's Wartime Oil Administration. "During the dark days of World War Two, Canada was hard-pressed to meet even essential petroleum needs," Rea later recalled. "Submarine warfare had already closed down a large East Coast refinery. The Canadian Wartime Oil Administration was forced to initiate development of every known Canadian source of petroleum, including the Athabasca tar sands." After the war, Rea returned to Canadian Oil Companies where he became president until 1963 when the company was acquired by Shell."

As a young man, Fitzsimmons had moved west to farm in Manitoba and Nelson, BC, then invested in real estate in Washington State. In about 1919, he heard stories about the fabulous oil wealth waiting to be found under the Athabasca Sands, and filed this news in the back of his mind. After a legal dispute with his real estate partners in 1921, he cashed out and turned up in Vermilion, Alberta, to find his black bonanza. In 1923, Fitzsimmons snapped up an important lease on the east bank of the Athabasca fifty miles (80 km) downriver from Fort McMurray. The property had been operated by the newly bankrupt Alcan Oil Company, founded by a group of New York City policemen who had fallen in love with the Sands after World War I. They quickly lost their shirts, although one of them decided he preferred the peace of the Athabasca to the bustle of New York. He built a log cabin along the river, trapped muskrat for a living, and became a well-known hermit who came into town only once a year to get his hair cut.

Bob Fitzsimmons' dream was to find those elusive pools of oil that Sidney Ells said didn't exist, but after three years and eight dry holes, he was persuaded that Ells was right. Undeterred, Fitzsimmons switched focus and built a rinky-dink backyard hot water flotation unit, using less than $50 worth of materials. It was, in fact, the first field plant to extract oil from the Athabasca oil sands. On August 12, 1927, he reorganized Alcan as the International Bitumen Company (IBC). Ever the promoter, he was able to persuade the Canadian post office to give the IBC its own address—Bitumount.

In 1930, with fresh capital, Fitzsimmons developed a larger hot water flotation plant based on Karl Clark's Clearwater operation. That summer, fifty miles (80 km) north of Fort McMurray, his seven-man crew produced about 300 barrels of Athabasca bitumen, which he shipped to buyers in Edmonton. But the following year, the Depression hit him hard and he had to suspend operations between 1932 and 1937. Starting back up again in January 1938, Fitzsimmons hired a young engineer, Elmer Adkins, to rebuild his old extraction plant. IBC started to produce bitumen again and

Adkins even tried his luck with distilling, producing a small quantity of passable diesel oil.

Even though Fitzsimmons was lucky to sit on a very rich and deep deposit, his nickel-and-dime operation had only mixed success. His bitumen was never completely free of sand or clay particles, making it unsuitable for refining, but he was eventually able to market a good product for waterproofing roofs through a western Canadian chain of hardware stores.

The advent of the Second World War cut into his business, however, and by 1941, the Sands had claimed another dreamer as a victim. Fitzsimmons was flat broke, claiming to have had invested and lost over $300,000 in the Sands.

• • •

In 1942, Montreal mining promoter, Lloyd Champion, snapped up International Bitumen and renamed it Oil Sands Limited. He retained Fitzsimmons to work the leases while he tried to raise capital to turn the operation into a refinery to produce diesel fuel for the war effort.

One of the people Champion talked to in 1944 was Jack Pew, Sun Oil's exploration and production vice-president, and a nephew of the founder. The Sun board decided that the time for oil sands was not quite ripe, but Sun Oil was already ramping up a modest oil drilling program in southern Alberta.

An undeterred Champion then visited Edmonton to propose a private-public partnership to the Alberta government. Karl Clark gave the project a thumbs-up when he was asked to evaluate the proposal. In December 1944, Premier Ernest Manning announced $250,000 in funding for a proper pilot plant at Bitumount to be known as Oil Sands Limited.

Constructed for $725,000 over three years, the plant was ready to start production when Champion ran out of capital and called it quits. In November of 1948, he transferred his share of the Bitumount plant complex to the ARC. The government-owned plant finally started up in the summer of 1949, processing 450 tons of oil sand a day. At the official opening, all the members of the Alberta legislature were ferried up to attend the festivities.

Unfortunately for oilsands development, Imperial Oil's Leduc discovery in 1947 ensured that the development of the Athabasca Sands was no longer on the energy radar. Leduc, just south of Edmonton, was a huge conventional light crude oil reservoir, and other large discoveries followed close behind. The oil industry quickly lobbied Alberta to get out of direct investment in the oilsands business, and in 1955, the ARC unloaded the whole Bitumount operation for $180,000 to an entrepreneur named Stan Paulson. Paulson's CanAmera Oil Sands Development Ltd. confidently installed new Coulson separators based on spin-dry washers. Unfortunately, the abrasive quartz of the sands chewed up the separators in no time flat. Paulson unloaded the operation to the Imperial's Royalite Oil Company for $180,000 plus royalties. Royalite, in turn, was taken over by Gulf Oil and eventually became the property of Suncor Energy.[23]

Karl Clark was keenly disappointed with the result, but his spirits lifted when the government of Ernest Manning commissioned the vice president of Bechtel Canada, his old research assistant, Sid Blair, to write a full evaluation of the Athabasca Sands. Back in 1926, Blair had gone off to work for Universal Oil Products Company's laboratories in Chicago to help research heavy oil refining, and during the war he managed a secret British Air Ministry project in Trinidad to turn bitumen from the island's tar lake into high-octane aviation fuel. Now he was back in Toronto, and eager to get going.

•   •   •

---

[23] In 1974, Bitumount was declared a Provincial Historic Site, and the government of Alberta is working to preserve it properly before allowing public visits; Web Support Site, *Black Bonanza* Gallery—Chapter 3. < * >

In spite of the apparent failure of Abasand and Bitumount, these projects went a long way to putting together the final pieces in the puzzle of Athabasca oilsands production and moving it closer to being a paying proposition. The question of choosing a site for wartime supply became crucial. In 1942, when Abasand was finally producing at capacity, Canada's oil controller, George Cottrelle, warned the War Cabinet that the plant would only pay its way if it could boost output to 10,000 barrels a day. Ball, McClave, and Smith had found that the Horse River site was a real problem; its bitumen was too thin and laden with rock. They suggested that a move to the Mildred Lake lease was necessary to reach that goal, but a plant of that size would cost at least $4.5 million to build, not including a $300,000 pipeline to Edmonton and a $3 million refinery to handle the output. Ball told the government that the $8 million bill matched what oil companies were spending in Turner Valley, with marginal results. George Cotrelle agreed.

The question remained, who had that kind of money to spend and was the risk worth it?

Thanks to promoters like Max Ball and researchers like Karl Clark, most of the hard chemistry of the Sands had been done, and recovery rates for bitumen from it were approaching 100 percent purity. The wilderness of Athabasca's topography had been mapped and the frontier was no longer unknown. Sidney Ells and several private companies had drilled hundreds of core samples to determine the thickness and quality of the Sands. Pilot plants had been erected and had worked, with some exceptions. Rough rail and road were in place. South of the Sands, pipelines and refineries were being built to exploit Leduc and other conventional resources that could one day enable Athabasca synthetic crude to get to market. Alberta and Ottawa were at peace. Even Karl Clark and Sidney Ells were on the same page. The world price of oil, if not quite high enough, was at least firming up at about $2.50 a barrel, keeping the Middle East potentates happy. It was time to kick-start development. Or was it? Were the Sands ready for prime time?

Enter Sidney Blair.

• • •

Sid Blair was born in Parry Sound, Ontario in 1897. His family moved to Dewberry, Alberta, to farm when he was four-years old. In order to attend high school in Edmonton, Blair lived with an uncle while attending Strathcona Collegiate Institute and while studying mining engineering at the University of Alberta. From 1917 to 1919 he was a flying instructor with the Royal Air Force, and like Sidney Ells, taught at Khaki University. Blair received his BSc in Mining in 1922 at the University of Birmingham, then went to the University of Alberta to do graduate work on the oil sands under Karl Clark. His Master of Science thesis, "An Investigation of the Bitumen Constituent of the Bituminous Sands of Northern Alberta," was accepted in 1924, after which he toiled beside Clark as a research engineer with the Scientific and Industrial Research Council of Alberta. After working with Universal Oil Products in Chicago and with a refinery project in Trinidad, he returned to Canada as vice president of Canadian Bechtel, with its head office in Toronto.[24]

In September 1949, Sid Blair brought Ed Nelson, vice president of Universal Oil Products to Edmonton. They spent some time with Karl Clark, who gave them a guided tour of the Bitumount plant and showed them the latest ARC data. It was clear that Bitumount had served its purpose, and that it was time for larger scale commercial

---

[24] Blair was later involved in planning and building oil refineries and chemical plants, pipeline systems (including Trans Mountain and Trans Canada). He helped build the Great Canadian Oil Sands plant at Fort McMurray and the hydroelectric power projects at Churchill Falls and James Bay. He officially retired as president of Canadian Bechtel Limited in January 1974. His son, Bob Blair, followed him into the oil industry.

development. Alberta had given the plant one more year of support, but in the Legislature, an embattled Minister of Industry, John
Robinson, declared that he didn't know whether the project was "a
lemon or a plum."

Shortly after their visit to Bitumount, Blair and Nelson went
back to Edmonton to meet with Alberta Premier Ernest Manning. At
that time, the recent Redwater discoveries northeast of Edmonton
had caused more oil glut in the province, and Manning was being
pressured by the Alberta oil industry to shut down any government
support of the Sands. Clearly, after millions of dollars had been
spent by a succession of Alberta governments and Ottawa, something had to be done about Athabasca. So the Premier asked Blair to
write a report for the Alberta government on the economic viability
of the Sands, estimating what it would cost to produce and deliver
a barrel of synthetic Athabasca crude.

● ● ●

Blair was fully aware of the politics behind Manning's request—
the Premier was engaged in creative delay to keep the oil companies off his back. But Blair gladly undertook, with Nelson,
a detailed examination of all the technical tasks involved in
producing synthetic crude. A year later, in 1950, he presented
his report to Manning. In it, he argued that development was
possible, rather than probable. In his view, economies of scale
mattered a lot. Only by processing large quantities of sand—
3,200 cubic meters per day or greater—and piping out large
volumes of oil could an investor expect to reap any return on
investment.

Blair suggested that a plant costing $43 million, with an output
of 20,000 barrels per day, would generate a 5–6 percent annual
return on investment, with conventional oil currently at $2.70 a
barrel on the market. A barrel of high-quality synthetic Athabasca
crude could be delivered to the head of Lake Superior by rail car

for $3.10. In comparison, Alberta Redwater crude delivered to the Lakehead sold for $3.00 a barrel.[25]

The "Blair Report" was the first analysis of the Sands by a respected engineer, and because of Blair's involvement with Bechtel—the planet's premier energy engineering firm—it created a huge stir in the industry worldwide. Even before Alberta could follow up on Blair's suggestion for hosting a symposium on the oil sands, scores of petroleum executives and engineers suddenly started flying into Alberta from around the world. Dr. D.A. Howes, the head of Anglo-Iranian's research and development division, was quoted in the *Edmonton Journal* as saying his company came "to see if the 'Blair Report' could be believed." As Howes and others later pointed out, it could not. Blair's estimates did not include capital costs, taxes, or royalties, or any formal allowance for technical problems. At a time when world and Alberta oil prices were falling, oilsands output was still below commercial viability.

But for the moment, Blair's report had the province euphoric, and Alberta offered to make available all technical data and research produced and compiled by Karl Clark and the ARC. On Sid Blair's advice, the province started to prepare for the very first Oil Sands Conference. In October 1951, hundreds of oil company executives, government officials, and scientists gathered at the University of Alberta to discuss oilsands geology, mining, recovery, transport, and refining.[26]

Sidney Ells attended the Edmonton symposium, but there is no record that he met or had any discussions with Karl Clark or Sidney Blair. However, Ells and Clark did start to correspond in the 1950s, perhaps through the intervention of Sid Blair, or through a desire by both Alberta and Canada to bury the hatchet.

---

[25] Sidney Blair, *Blair Report* (Province of Alberta, 1950), p. 75.
[26] Both Blair and Clark insisted on calling what were then known as the Athabasca tar sands "oil sands," since they were not properly tar (a product of coal), but rather naturally occurring bitumen.

On the final day of the conference, Nathan Tanner, Alberta's Minister of Mines and Minerals, argued for a North American perspective on the Sands, calling its development "in the interest of the people of the Province and of Canada as a whole, and, further, to the security of this continent."

To spark industry interest from around the world and especially the oil company majors, Tanner put forward a suite of leasing and royalty strategies for the development of the Sands. The province would offer leases of 50,000 acres (20,230 hectares) to interested companies. The catch was, the properties had to be explored over the following three years. If companies were interested in going further than core drilling, they had to build a commercial plant within one year of obtaining the lease. At first, few companies were willing to take the risk, so the province changed the rule—the leaseholder was only required to proceed with a commercial plant within one year if instructed to do so by the province.

Ten oil companies took up the Alberta challenge in 1952, beginning the next stage of Sands development. One of the leaseholders was J. Howard Pew of Philadelphia, who optimistically took out a double 100,000-acre lease for his Sun Oil Company.

• • •

After the Leduc discovery, Karl Clark grew more and more pessimistic about the future of oilsands development. Back in 1947, he had written to a friend in Ottawa, "I do not think there is any use trying to make out that the tar sands are other than a 'second line of defense' against dwindling oil supplies."

But wiser minds than Clark had other ideas. Canny old oilman, J. Howard Pew, knew far more about the world oil business than Karl Clark, and Pew realized the time had come to abandon pessimism and yield to a new optimism. The bonanza of the Athabasca was there for the taking.

4

Pay Dirt

The Oil Sands Today

No subversive forces can ever conquer a nation that has not first been conquered by 'subversive inactivity' on the part of the citizenry, who have failed in their civic duty and in service to their country.

—J. Howard Pew, 1953

J. Howard Pew, president of the Sun Company Inc. of Philadelphia, was one of those innovative Yankee mavericks that American business sometimes throws up. A competitive hands-on oilman, Pew was a true independent thinker. He wouldn't play the monopoly game and join "any price" management schemes or an oil cartel set up by the majors. It's hard to think of a modern equivalent to Pew. Perhaps Steve Jobs of Apple in his relations with IBM and Bill Gates of Microsoft.

As the 1940s drew to a close, Howard Pew was already well aware of the massive potential of the Athabasca Sands. He maintained an open file on the Sands, and in 1944, sent his nephew, John Edgar (Jack) Pew, Sun's vice president of exploration and production to meet with Montreal financier Lloyd Champion to find out more about the operations of Oil Sands Limited, the former International Bitumen Company (Bitumount). In the end, Pew and the Sun board decided to pass for the time being on investing in the company.

But Howard Pew also came at the Sands from a very unique perspective—he was a world expert in the science of asphalt.

• • •

As we saw in Chapter 2, Pew was the second son of Sun Oil founder, Joseph Newton Pew, a Pennsylvania oil and gas producer who made his fortune in the huge Spindletop discovery in Texas, buying productive leases and shipping the oil by tanker to his new refinery at Marcus Hook, Pennsylvania. Sun and other firms like Gulf and Texaco were able to put a large dent in John D. Rockefeller's near monopoly of the oil business, and they drove prices down so far that they kick-started the American auto industry.

Young Howard got his schooling at the Massachusetts Institute of Technology, where he studied engineering with course work in thermodynamics and structural design. After graduating, J. Howard Pew was given a challenge by his father—find a use for the thick black residue, much like bitumen, that was left over when heavy Texas crude was refined. The young man didn't disappoint his father and the Marcus Hook labs were able to turn the waste gunk into a superb lubricating oil with a very low cooling point. Marketed under the name Sun Red Stock, it became a global success.

The young Pew was so diligent, it was said he sometimes slept in the labs over night so he could get right back at the process he was developing. In 1904, all his hard work paid off when he came up with another use for the black stuff—it served as the base for North America's first commercially successful petroleum asphalt. Called Hydrolene, it was also Sun's first trademarked product.

J. Howard Pew was only thirty years old when he was picked to lead the Sun Company when his father died suddenly in 1912.

Ever an innovator and always an ardent American patriot, Pew was visiting Europe in 1915 when he learned of the German U-boat program. Knowing that transatlantic shipping routes would be in danger from the submarine menace, he decided that many more oil tankers would be needed to ensure a continued flow of oil across the Atlantic and along the eastern seaboard. Sure enough, after two years of war, the U-boats had destroyed 2 million tons of shipping, and Pew was finding it hard to get supplies from Texas to his refinery at Marcus Hook. The railways were operating at capacity and there were no major pipelines in place.

Pew quickly moved to build his own tanker fleet, setting up a company called Sun Shipbuilding. During World War I, the Sun shipyard in Chester, Pennsylvania, employed 16,000 men and women, building hundreds of tankers and minesweepers. In the 1920s, the yard pioneered welding instead of riveting hulls, and built oil tankers not only for Sun, but for other clients like Standard Oil. During World War II, Sun Shipbuilding was the largest shipyard in the world, employing 40,000 workers to build hundreds of freighters and 40 percent of the U.S. tanker fleet.[1]

Following World War I, Pew watched American society enter a period of explosive growth, as the auto age took flight. Sun opened its first service station in Ardmore, Pennsylvania in 1920; within a decade, the Pews owned or controlled 500 filling stations across the U.S. When General Motors and Jersey Standard formed the Ethyl Corporation to make higher octane gas with a lead additive, the Pew brothers declined to participate. Instead, they made

---

[1] Sun Shipbuilding constructed a number of unique vessels, including the Glomar Explorer, built for the CIA through a Howard Hughes company to retrieve the hull of sunken Soviet submarine K-129 in the Pacific, and the SS Manhattan, a reinforced oil tanker that navigated Canada's Northwest Passage from Greenland to Prudhoe Bay, Alaska, in 1969. Foreign competition finally killed Sun Shipbuilding in the 1980s.

one of their innovative gasolines, Blue Sunoco, without poisonous tetraethyl lead. J. N. Pew Jr. insisted on coloring the gas blue for romantic reasons. It matched the blue tiles seen by Pew and his wife on their honeymoon trip to China.

The Sun Company of Philadelphia also started doing business in Canada in 1915, supplying lubricating oils, kerosene, and spirits to war plants in the Montreal area. After the war, in 1919, Sun opened its first Canadian office in Montreal as the Sun Company of Canada. The company soon added new product lines, including fuel oil and gasoline brought in by rail from the U.S. In 1923, the company incorporated as the Sun Oil Company Limited. In 1927, Blue Sunoco gasoline replaced Sun's previous gasolines and was advertised as "the high-powered knockless fuel at no extra price." In 1930, the company opened its first Sunoco-branded service stations in Toronto, Montreal, and Quebec City, and built a lubricating oil and grease storage plant in Toronto. In 1934, the company moved its Canadian headquarters from Montreal to Toronto.

The Sun Company went public on the New York Stock Exchange in 1925. The following year, Sun provided its employees with one of America's first stock-sharing plans in order to enhance worker involvement in Sun's success. During the Great Depression of the 1930s, J. Howard Pew blamed the downturn on employers who paid inadequate wages, which dampened demand. Pew had to cut back days of work, but no Sun employee was laid off, and many could support their families on two days work a week. When President Franklin D. Roosevelt wanted to bring in the New Deal and the National Recovery Act, he asked the oil industry to come up with ways to help Americans cope with the Depression. Pew helped draft these guidelines, but as a supporter of free markets, he was shocked when Roosevelt rewrote them to fix the price of oil.

While Howard Pew's Sun companies provided the fuel and the ships that helped lead the Allies to victory in 1945, after the war,

Pew fought against continued wartime regulations and the pro-posed cartelization of the Anglo-American oil industry.

• • •

Now, three years after World War II ended, sixty-six-year-old J. Howard Pew was restless, and he started casting his eyes north-ward to the largest deposit of naturally occurring asphalt on the planet. He was fascinated by the Sands, and with his asphalt sci-ence background, it represented a special, personal challenge.

In addition, the Sun Company had always been a crude deficit company, with never enough producing wells to meet its needs. Sun was continually having to buy more and more outside crude to feed its refineries. Anticipating the arguments of experts such as Shell geologist, King Hubbert, Pew was also convinced that U.S. production was peaking and would one day start to decline. This would put even more of a squeeze on Sun.

Concern was growing in the Alberta industry as well. On Janu-ary 30, 1948, Calgary's *Nickle Oil Bulletin* reported to its readers:

> U.S. worried about its own oil supply, but ban on exports to Canada considered unlikely. The United States, by far the world's larg-est producer and consumer of petroleum products, is becoming increasingly worried about future supplies—to the extent that a ban on exports of oil is being suggested. The U.S. oil industry is pressing for a larger share of the nation's steel production to permit increased oil drilling, and the American Government is recom-mending to Congress a five to ten year, nine billion dollar program to develop a synthetic oil industry in the U.S.

J. Howard Pew was determined to do something about the problem. Sun's board had already taken a pass on investing in Lloyd Champion's Oil Sands Limited. In 1949, he went back to the board and told them he wanted to go ahead with developing an

Athabasca property. It was time to do it now, or drop it entirely. As the directors debated, Pew warned them: "I have been closely following progress at the Athabasca tar sands for twenty years. If Sun does not go ahead with this project, I will on my own." The board said yes.

After the meeting, Sun assigned a talented engineer named Ned Gilbert to head its Alberta operations. Just before Gilbert left, Pew called him into his office, pulled out a thick file marked "Athabasca Tar Sands" and went over the maps, reports, and notes with Gilbert. "I believe the Athabasca tar sands will, some day, be of great significance to the needs for petroleum in North America," Pew told the young man. "I want you to be sure that Sun Oil always has a significant position in the Athabasca tar sands area."[2]

When Gilbert arrived in Calgary, he camped out for a time in the Palliser Hotel and started shopping for prospects. The following year he began to identify site locations for a possible Sun Oil bitumen processing plant. In 1950, he started a three-year core drilling program. Results were so poor that some on the Sun board wanted to drop its Canadian leases. Gilbert argued for staying the course, and J. Howard Pew quietly backed him up in his purchase of two new Alberta leases. As Gilbert recalled, "It was a wonder I did not get fired on the spot for recommending things that my management were not approving." For a time, the company called one piece of its land holdings "Gilbert's Folly." Today, that land holding is known as Firebag, one of Suncor's more productive properties. In 1954, Gilbert redeemed himself by acquiring a 75 percent interest from Abasand Oils in a 4,000-acre lease number 86 at Athabasca. Lease 86 is the site of Suncor's major oilsands mining operations today.

Meanwhile the Sun Company Inc. set up a Canadian Production Division in Calgary and started to search for oil. In 1950, Sun

---

[2] Earle Gray, *History of the Oilsands*, p. 9; F.N. 18. John Dixon, "Sun and Suncor: Notes and Reflections," George Dunlap (ed.), *The Suncor Story* (nd). Glenbow Archives, Ned Gilbert Papers, M8057.

drilled its first Canadian-producing well in New Norway, Alberta. Also in that same year, oil replaced coal as Canada's first source of energy.

● ● ●

The year 1956 was a significant one in petroleum history. In September 1956, at a meeting of the American Petroleum Institute in San Antonio, Texas, Shell's head geologist M. King Hubbert made the precise and shocking prediction that U.S. conventional oil output was going to peak in the early 1970s and, thereafter, decline, making the U.S. increasingly dependent on foreign suppliers. This was such bad news for the industry that Shell's public relations department made a desperate attempt to stop the speech, and failed.

The founding father of the peak oil theory was the first to grasp the mechanics of oilfield depletion and the first to accurately assess recoverable oil reserves. Hubbert was right on the money about America, formerly the world's number one oil exporter. By 1970, production of petroleum (crude oil and natural gas plant liquids) in the lower forty-eight U.S. states would reach its highest level, peaking at 9.4 million barrels per day. North Slope discoveries in Alaska gave the U.S. a couple of years of grace, but output steadily declined ever afterward, and from that time forward, the U.S. grew more and more dependent on foreign oil.

But Hubbert was wrong in his other prediction, that global oil production would taper off after 2000, but only because he lacked clear statistics and did not factor in Canada's Athabasca Sands. He also did his reckoning without 3 billion new players—the Chinese and the Indians—that were not in the market until the year 2000.

Hubbert liked to use a 10,000-year graph to show that humanity's use of oil was simply a pimple, a "nonrepetitive blip" in history. He suggested that, "when the energy cost of recovering a barrel of oil becomes greater than the energy content of the oil," our fossil-fuel dependent society would come to a dead end.[3] Hubbert originally suggested nuclear energy as a passable option, but in 1976, as he came to realize its dangers, he retracted this opinion and quite correctly plumped for solar energy as our salvation and the way to ensure the future of our civilization.

Also in 1956, the year of Hubbert's speech, a Richfield Oil geologist named Manley Natland was also pondering nuclear power as he lounged on a sand dune in the Saudi Arabian desert watching the sun go down in a fiery ball. Natland's mind wandered off to the Athabasca Sands and, suddenly, as the sun sank under the horizon, he had a brainwave. Perhaps the fireball of an underground nuclear bomb could release stubborn Alberta bitumen from the sand and make it flow like warm molasses.

Richfield agreed to back the idea. In a period when the U.S. Department of Energy was championing "Atoms for Peace," and talking about hammering nuclear swords into peaceful atomic plowshares, Natland's vision got a ready reception. H-bomb physicist, Edward Teller, also championed it, giving Natland even more traction.

Suggesting a small nine-kiloton bomb, Natland wrote that, "The tremendous heat and shock energy released by an underground nuclear explosion would be distributed so as to raise the temperature of a large quantity of oil and reduce its viscosity sufficiently to permit its recovery by conventional oil field methods." A whole series of bomb blasts, he argued, would give the U.S. a secure supply of oil for decades to come.

By 1958, Project Cauldron was under way with Richfield Oil, the Alberta government, and the U.S. Atomic Energy Commission all onside. Richfield leased a site in the middle of the bush sixty-two miles (100 km) south of Fort McMurray, and the U.S. navy agreed to sell a bomb to Richfield for $350,000.

---

[3] See Hubbert's "pimple" and his peak oil estimates; Web Support Site, *Black Bonanza* Gallery—Chapter 4. < * >

The Canadian government was not onside with this scheme, however, and set up a technical committee to study the proposal and hopefully delay it to death. Alberta's health minister also expressed caution about the dangers of radioactive crude oil. So what was now dubbed "Project Oil Sands" was quietly shelved in 1960 during a debate in Canada over nuclear testing, and Richfield Oil diverted its attention to Alaska.

• • •

Lloyd Champion was a decent stock promoter, but not a good manager of an oil business. In 1948, he was unable to honor his part of the deal with Alberta and bowed out of the Bitumount project, while retaining a share of the leases for future promotion.

At this point, Karl Clark grew quite despondent that anything would come of his oilsands research. He shared his feelings with Sid Blair, and perhaps due to Blair's intervention, started to correspond with Sidney Ells.[4] The problem, he told Ells, was that engineers had still not been able to design a plant that worked for long periods without getting into mechanical difficulties. The whole oil sands process had to be continuous. So obviously, more funds had to be spent on engineering.

In 1952, Lloyd Champion re-emerged and incorporated Great Canadian Oil Sands Ltd. (GCOS) in Toronto. A year later, he pulled Abasand Oils and Canadian Oils Ltd., along with his own Oil Sands Ltd., into the GCOS pot. The three companies controlled some attractive leases, and with them, the company hoped to entice a major investor, ideally Sun Oil and the Pews who had talked to him ten years earlier.

Conditions were becoming more favorable. In 1954, U.S. President Dwight D. Eisenhower cancelled Harry Truman's synthetic fuels

---

[4] Paul Anthony Chastko, *Developing Alberta's oil sands: from Karl Clark to Kyoto* (University of Calgary Press, 2004), p. 74.

program, a holdover from wartime, which gave fresh impetus to plans for synthetic crude made from Athabasca sand. As Champion had hoped, the Pews bought into the GCOS consortium in 1954, acquiring a 75 percent interest from Abasand Oils in the 4,000-acre lease number 86 beside Tar Island. Sun moved quickly and in 1958, hired GCOS to mine and process the sands from lease number 86 (subject to royalty payments to Sun and Abasand), while Sun also contracted to purchase 75 percent of production from a plant proposed by GCOS which would produce 31,500 barrels per day of synthetic crude.

The project ran into a major roadblock in November 1960, when the Alberta Oil and Gas Conservation Board rejected the Great Canadian Oil Sands project on technical and economic grounds. As feared, conventional oilmen were mounting a ferocious lobby against bitumen extraction because of a continuing oil glut in Alberta, and they were afraid that prices would drop even further. For a time, the Alberta government stalled all oil-sands development for the same reason. To show the depth of rage felt by conventional oil people, Suncor veteran Joe Fitzgerald tells of being accosted in the Petroleum Club in Calgary where an angry and over-refreshed oil executive threatened to have him expelled because he was not a "real oilman."[5]

At that point, J. Howard Pew mounted a major charm offensive against Premier Ernest Manning. It was not difficult. The two were already fast friends, held similar opinions about nearly everything, and their wives got along very well, even sharing a cottage in Jasper Park.

Manning was motivated by real old-fashioned stewardship. He wanted to alleviate the boom-bust cycle of agriculture that had plagued the people of Alberta. He supported Sands research when conventional oil started to run out at Turner Valley, and backed Howard Pew in the 1960s even after new conventional finds were

---

[5] Fitzgerald got the opposite treatment a few years later at a mining convention, when he was lambasted for not being a "real miner."

making Alberta rich. He understood the cycle of oil prices and discoveries, and wanted some kind of certainty for the future of Alberta—a certainty that Howard Pew persuaded him was possible and his duty to provide.

By September 1962, Manning's government had worked out an oilsands policy he hoped would satisfy conventional oil people, and provide for the orderly development of the Sands. The Alberta Oil and Gas Conservation Board finally gave the green light to the GCOS project. The deal was, the proposed $122 million GCOS plant could produce up to 30,000 barrels per day, but it could not displace current market arrangements. GCOS oil could not exceed 5 percent of total volumes in markets already supplied by conventional Alberta crude. Sun Oil would, of course, be the major purchaser. The plant was also to produce 240 tons of sulfur and 900 tons of coke per day as by-products. One of the conditions of the approval was that the plant was to be in production by September 30, 1967.

By 1963, prior to the construction start-up, majority ownership of GCOS rested with the Sun Oil Company. But by 1964, the pioneering project was starting to ooze red ink due to equipment failure and problems supplying the remote location. With other investors dropping out, the Sun Oil Company had to take over the GCOS project entirely. With operating control, Pew was able to clean up the finances and negotiate an even larger project with the province. On April 13, 1964, *Nickle's Oil Digest* issued the following bulletin:

ALBERTA GOVERNMENT GIVES FORMAL APPROVAL TO GREAT CANADIAN OIL SANDS FOR $190 MILLION OIL SANDS PROJECT

April 13, 1964

The Hon, E. C. MANNING, Premier of the Province of Alberta on Friday of last week, April 10th, 1964, gave formal approval to the Application of GREAT CANADIAN OIL SANDS LIMITED for a $190,000,000 project to extract 45,000 barrels of oil daily from the famed ATHABASCA OIL SANDS. As soon as the Government's final approval was officially registered SUN OIL COMPANY, who will have the major common stock equity in GREAT CANADIAN OIL SANDS, revealed that its preliminary planning and actual work carried out at plant site in the past number of weeks will assure a construction start this summer.

A deadline of September 1st, 1964, for start of construction was one of the stipulations in the ALBERTA OIL & GAS CONSER-VATION BOARD's recommendations that the project be given the go ahead. Another, clause was proof of financing by a date yet to be set by the Government. This important phase is also virtually assured of success, as Sun Oil will provide $67,500,000 of the required financing in equity type capital and assist in arranging the remainder of the financing.

• • •

September 30, 1967 dawned grey and cold at the Fort McMurray airport. Sometime before noon, the first of 600 dignitaries began to arrive on a fleet of thirty charter aircraft. They had come to witness the official opening of Great Canadian Oil Sands (now Suncor). It was the world's first complex dedicated to mining oil sands and upgrading bitumen into synthetic crude oil. After being ferried up to the GCOS plant site in driving rain and buffeted by sharp winds, they were herded into a big inflatable shelter nicknamed "the bubble" to hear a glowing address by the Alberta Premier Ernest Manning.

"This is a red-letter day," said Ernest Manning, "not only for Canada but for all North America. No other event in Canada's centennial year is more important or significant. It is fitting," he said, taking the goals of the site to the higher plane of the lay preacher that he was, "that we are gathered here today to dedicate this plant not merely to the production of oil but to the continual progress and enrichment of mankind."

Then it was the turn of Philadelphia patriarch, J. Howard Pew, chairman of Sun Oil, to speak. Pew had been waiting eagerly for the delegates. The eighty-five-year-old Sun veteran and asphalt expert had spent several weeks on the site shepherding his project along. But now he had to hide his disappointment that an equipment glitch had shut down production, so his guests were not to be treated to the sight of bucket wheels tearing into the sand, big bitumen extraction vessels steaming, and upgrader systems humming.

GCOS was more than a project for Pew. It was nothing less than a challenge of Darwinian proportions. After cutting the ribbon, he declared to the hushed assembled throng:

> I am convinced this venture will succeed, and it will be the means of opening up reserves to meet the needs of the North American continent for generations to come... No nation can long be secure in this atomic age unless it be amply supplied with petroleum... It is the considered opinion of our group that if the North American continent is to produce the oil to meet its requirements in the years ahead, oil from the Athabasca area must of necessity play an important role.

Then, in words that would prove prophetic, Pew mused that, "at the outset I told our stockholders that unless projects of this character were conceived and started, our organization would become soft and eventually useless." Continuing on, "This is a great challenge to the imagination, skill and technological know-how of our scientists and engineers ..."

In fact, the early years of GCOS would harden and temper the skills of any oil engineer. The frontier operation was plagued by expensive challenges, mostly related to subarctic cold weather operations and the abrasive qualities of the sharp Athabasca sand, which chewed up rubber conveyor systems and other equipment meant for something as simple as soft coal mining. The company had adopted the same huge O&K bucket wheel excavators used by the German coal mining industry. Each weighed 1,600 tons and was higher than a ten-story building. It took several trainloads to bring these behemoths up to the Athabasca from dockside in Montreal.

Sun also had to develop entirely new technologies from scratch to crack the continuous mechanical process problems predicted by Karl Clark. Indeed, special surfactants in the separation process had to be developed from scratch by Sun chemist Earl W. Malmberg. Sun got a lot of help from the Alberta Research Council, who had opened their Clover Bar pilot plant to assist GCOS and other operations to get under way.

GCOS aimed to process bitumen into synthetic crude oil at a starting rate of 12,000 barrels per day. But after full start-up in May 1968, the plant ran into a string of expensive shutdowns, and much of the operation had to be re-engineered on the fly. During a seven-year regulatory and construction nightmare, costs mushroomed from the original $110-million 31,500 barrels-a-day proposal, to a 45,000 barrels-a-day operation costing $240 million. It was the largest single private investment in Canada up to that time.

Operating losses also mounted to a staggering total of $90 million over the first seven years of operation. But in spite of doom and gloom warnings in the press and gloating from his competitors, Pew hung in there, although the old maverick didn't live long enough to see his operation eke out its first operating profits in the mid-1970s. Even then, in 1971, the year of Pew's death, Calgary firm Touche, Vincent Investment Consultants said, "For GCOS common shares to have any value whatsoever it is obvious that the company must have much higher prices for its products."[6]

Operational problems would persist for the next twenty years, but most of them were solved in the early 1980s when the company

---

[6] Earle Gray, *History of the Oilsands;* Web Support Site, *Black Bonanza* Texts and Documents—Earle Gray's Works. < * >

replaced its creaky German bucket wheel excavators and mile-long chewed up rubber conveyor belts with the dinosaur-sized power shovels and monster trucks it still uses today.

Rising world prices certainly helped GCOS engineers smooth the way to profitability. After spending a billion dollars in capital and operating costs, what had become known as "Pew's Folly" finally morphed into the world's first commercially viable oilsands operation, a great Canadian bitumen machine known as Suncor Energy.

• • •

Sidney Ells was present at the GCOS opening ceremonies and by all accounts was delighted by the work. But his lifelong rival, Karl Clark, the man who had tirelessly promoted Sands research, was not there to witness the start of a whole new era. He had died of cancer in England nine months earlier, at the age of seventy-eight.

Hired by GCOS as a consultant in 1958, Clark had his last look at the site a year before the official opening, watching in horror as giant backhoes tore into the ground to drain the muskeg, while rampaging bulldozers pushed away the overburden, exposing the rich black sand below.

Clark had started his life's work in a tiny lab at the University of Alberta, then scaled it up to a plant in the Edmonton railway yards, then ramped it all the way up to Bitumount on the Athabasca. It was a toy operation compared to what he saw that day, but it was an operation that worked at last. Now he was appalled by the size of large-scale strip-mining that was necessary to turn a profit. Clark was, at heart, a wilderness camper who loved to get away to his cottage or go on long canoe trips. After the site tour, he confessed to his wife that he hated it and would never go back again.

Clark's daughter, Mary Clark Sheppard, remembers:

> Despite working so long for this day, it broke his heart to see the devastation done to his beloved landscape when the bulldozers

began to clear the site. In 1963, as a first step, a small test plant was built at Tar Island. Clark had a standing invitation to visit it to offer advice and he went frequently, always enjoying being in the north again. Eventually in May 1966, when the machinery testing was still going on, his illness began to manifest itself and he had to cancel the visit. However, by then the main plant construction was well on its way and he was beginning to feel there was no real need for him at Tar Island.

He told me he had no wish to return since he wanted to remember the country as he had known and loved it for so many years. In any case, a new, third generation of oilsands scientists was on the job and he was content to let go.

Sheppard is convinced that if Clark were alive today, he would be a committed environmentalist, "doing whatever he could to urge government and industry to work together on stimulating more effort in their laboratories to find a solution to the environmental challenges of the oil sands."[7]

• • •

Under the Canadian constitution, Ottawa holds responsibility for cross-border trade, whether it crosses provincial borders or involves the U.S. It also "owns" the Northwest Territories and Canada's offshore resources. Back in the mid-fifties, with a gas glut developing in Western Canada, people in the oil business started arguing for Ottawa to get cracking and promote cross-border energy trading and pipelines.

In 1957, newly elected Canadian Prime Minister John Diefenbaker, a westerner, set up a Royal Commission on Energy, led by Toronto

---

[7] Mary Clark Sheppard, "Rooted in Nature," *Alberta Oil*, May 1, 2009; Web Support Site, *Black Bonanza* Footnotes—Chapter 4. < * > The City of Fort McMurray dedicated a street and school in Sheppard's name, and the headquarters of the Research Council of Alberta in South Edmonton is on Karl Clark Road.

industrialist Henry Borden, to look at the issue. Borden concluded that it was time to build a pipeline from Alberta to Montreal to provide an outlet for 200,000 more barrels of Alberta crude oil. In November 1959, Diefenbaker set up the National Energy Board (NEB) and picked a respected Albertan, Ian McKinnon, chairman of Alberta's Oil and Gas Conservation Board, to head the new NEB.[8]

In that same year, a pioneering Oklahoma firm called Cities Service Oil Co., entered the Athabasca arena, founding a Cities Service Athabasca subsidiary. The company started its own research into the Sands and in 1959, president Bill Mooney, a Regina-born engineer, acquired the old Bitumount plant and leases downriver from Fort McMurray at Mildred Lake. Mooney put together a strip mining operation and a 3,000 barrel-per-day pilot plant. After extracting the bitumen, it was shipped out by tank car to be upgraded and refined.

Cities Service Athabasca was the first operator to use a bucket wheel excavator. The big 60-ton electrically powered machine scooped away chunks of ore, and mined 200 tons of oil sand an hour. The buckets had replaceable teeth because the sands were so sharp they wore away hardened steel. The driver could watch the discharge conveyor on a closed-circuit TV.

Once his pilot plant was up and running, Mooney went out looking for partners. By 1962 he had pulled together a working group, later called Syncrude, with Imperial Oil, Atlantic Richfield (ARCO), and Royalite Oil. Royalite, an independent operator which had recently been sold by Imperial, had also pioneered some work in the Sands. The partners' initial goal was to do feasibility studies into mining the Mildred Lake property and then, if the parties agreed, to make a proposal to the Alberta Energy Resources Conservation Board (ERCB). Their 1964 plan called for a 100,000 barrel-per-day plant costing $56 million, with a pipeline to Edmonton. Construction was to begin in 1965 with the plant opening in 1968.

---

[8] In 1991, the board relocated from Ottawa to Calgary, Alberta.

However, Sun's GCOS proposal beat out the Syncrude bid and another rival one from Shell, which was a hard blow for Bill Mooney. At the time, the ERCB was worried that synthetic oil from the Sands would compete for the same limited markets as conventional crude, so they decided not to bring too many oilsands plants on stream at once. However, Mooney got the parties back to the drafting table, reorganized them as Syncrude Canada, and patiently put together a new application.

In 1969, the ERCB finally approved Syncrude Canada's proposal for a much larger 125,000 barrel-a-day oilsands project—over two times bigger than the first GCOS proposal. But the election of a new Alberta government and the sudden onset of the energy crisis delayed the Syncrude start-up until December 1971. That's when the real trouble began.

* * *

By this point, Alberta was producing about 1 million barrels of conventional crude oil a day and the provincial treasury was becoming an overstuffed piggy bank. In 1971, Peter Lougheed's Progressive Conservative party swept into power, ending the Social Credit's thirty-six-year reign. The young Alberta Tory leader was not at all like shrewd old Ernest Manning, content to sit back and collect rent and royalty checks. Lougheed was a hurry-up interventionist, eager for a piece of the action—a piece that was growing larger and larger as the price of oil began to rise. One of his first acts was to get his senior bureaucrats to craft a new oilsands development policy that would keep more jobs and royalties in Alberta. Lougheed wanted no more "long-term costs arising from exported energy, technology, job opportunities, and environmental damages, in addition to the depletion of non-renewable resources."

To get Ottawa onside, Lougheed's draft policy was also nationalist, asking for development "shaped and influenced by Canadians for the benefit of Canadians," that would alter the trend of "ever-increasing foreign control of non-renewable resource development in Canada."

While Lougheed was crafting a stick to beat the oil companies, the outside world was getting its own beating. The culprit was not oil, but inflation.

After World War II, many countries signed the Bretton Woods Agreement, fixing their exchange rate to the U.S. dollar and pegging the price of gold at US$35 an ounce. While the Vietnam War was still raging, President Richard Nixon's advisors convinced him that the U.S. had to pay for the war by inflating the dollar rather than raising taxes. Countries holding U.S. dollar reserves were essentially being asked, or even forced, to subsidize the American military in its role as lead global cop. In 1971, French President Charles de Gaulle refused to go along with the Americans, and France pared down its dollar reserves by trading them for gold from the U.S. government. When this French disconnection threatened to turn into a run on Fort Knox, Nixon ordered the U.S. to go off the gold standard.

With the abrupt breakdown of Bretton Woods and the cheapening of the U.S. dollar, the oil exporting nations of the Middle East also started to grumble about being paid in greenbacks, which suddenly weren't buying as much as they did before. And so did the blue-eyed sheiks up in Canada, including the new Alberta government of Peter Lougheed, who was determined to get full value for his province's resources.

• • •

The Organization of Petroleum Exporting Countries (OPEC) was founded in 1960 by Iran, Iraq, Kuwait, Saudi Arabia, and Venezuela, and it has since grown to include eleven member countries. OPEC was modeled on the Texas Railroad Commission, a government-backed cartel whose job was to match oil production to demand and maintain price levels by regulating each well to a percentage of its capacity.

From 1949 until the end of 1970, Middle East crude oil prices had averaged about $1.90 per barrel. But on October 16th of that year, OPEC members meeting in Vienna suddenly decided to boost oil and gas prices by 70 percent, from $3.01 per barrel to $5.11. The following day, the Arab members—Saudi Arabia, Kuwait, Iraq, Libya, Abu Dhabi, Qatar, and Algeria—announced that they were going to cut their production below the September level by 5 percent for October and an additional 5 percent per month, "until Israeli withdrawal is completed from the whole Arab territories occupied in June 1967 and the legal rights of the Palestinian people are restored."

OPEC had the West over a barrel, and within a year, the majors had lost whatever control they had over pricing. Oil prices quadrupled, generating the world's first "oil shock," which rocked the global economy. The resulting energy crisis hit Europe and North America hard, with long lineups at filling stations and rapidly inflating prices.

The energy poker game that followed OPEC's announcement would change the world utterly and give fresh impetus to the development of the Sands.

In 1973, at the height of the energy crisis, Peter Lougheed moved aggressively to control development. Under Alberta's new Land Surface Conservation and Reclamation Commission (LCRC), all operators of coal mines, oilsands sites, and pipelines had to submit their plans for conservation and reclamation and obtain approval from the LCRC before they could develop a project. Alberta also moved to capture a higher percentage of the profits associated with rising oil prices. Soon, millions more petro-dollars were streaming into the Alberta Treasury.

While Alberta was moving ahead to boost royalties and lock in the value of its resources, the federal government of Pierre Trudeau also realized what was happening and determined that the treasury of Canada needed a piece of the action. In their budget of May 6, 1973, the Trudeau Liberals declared war on Alberta.

•   •   •

For years, many Albertans had chafed under real or imagined griev-ances against faraway Ottawa. Before 1905, the territory was a federal colony. The proud people of the Northwest had yearned to found one great province, but the Laurier government, not want-ing to give birth to a western powerhouse, created two instead—Alberta and Saskatchewan. Not only that, Ottawa waited for twenty-five years before handing over control of natural resources to the new provinces, at least until railway development had been paid for. Albertans griped over the power of Ottawa to award oil-sands leases and after 1930, chafed over the federal government's decision to hold back a small section of the Athabasca Sands for its own uses.

During the Great Depression, many Albertans backed Premier William Aberhart's proposal to print provincial currency (the so-called prosperity certificates), preferring this inflation-ary approach over Ottawa's tight money and stingy national welfare program. It hurt Albertans when the Supreme Court of Canada declared Alberta's "funny money" unconstitutional. It also hurt when the Royal Canadian Mounted Police had to take over policing from a bankrupt province. During World War II, Albertans grumbled even more when they had to go along with Ottawa's dictatorial powers over the wartime economy. After the war, when Ottawa bowed out of oilsands support, Alberta decided to go ahead with its own Bitumount project. Karl Clark quipped to a friend that the province's motive was entirely politi-cal, that Alberta "pleases to regard the Ottawa government as the lowest thing on earth, incapable of doing anything right, but capable of the lowest forms of political dirt such as deliberately sabotaging the chance of development of Alberta's great tar sand resource."[9]

And now, on budget night May 6, 1973, Ottawa was again dumping on Alberta, proposing to directly tax royalty payments

---

[9] William Marsden, *Stupid to the Last Drop* (Knopf Canada, 2007), p. 33.

to provincial governments. Peter Lougheed responded to the Trudeau budget by calling taxation of Alberta oil royalties "the biggest rip-off of any province that's ever occurred in Confederation's history."

Lougheed's blood continued to boil, and he and his Energy Minister, Don Getty, decided that the best way to hold off the Ottawa wolf was to get an ownership stake in Syncrude before allowing the development to proceed. In August of 1973, with Syncrude construction about to begin, Lougheed called the players to Edmonton for a meeting. Present were Lougheed and Getty, Syncrude president Frank Spraggins, Jack Armstrong of Imperial, Jerry McAfee of Gulf Canada, Gordon Sellars of Cities Service, Bob Anderson of Atlantic Richfield Canada (Arcan), and scores of industry managers and cabinet officials. Earle Gray tells the story:

> The first meeting, involving only the vice presidents and cabinet ministers led by Getty, was almost the last. When the Syncrude people said that the terms under which the consortium was prepared to continue were not negotiable, Getty and his group walked out of the meeting. The next day, when Lougheed outlined Alberta's terms, the oil companies were close to walking out. Lougheed wanted 50 percent of Syncrude's net profits for Alberta; a back-in option to acquire a 20 percent interest in Syncrude, after final costs and probable profits were determined following the startup of production; and for Alberta Energy Company (half owned by the government), half ownership of the oil sands-to-Edmonton crude oil pipeline plus 80 percent of the project's large power generating plant. The pipeline and the power plant were the only aspects of the project that were almost certain money makers.[10]

---

[10] Earle Gray, *History of the Oilsands;* Web Support Site, *Black Bonanza* Texts and Documents—Earle Gray's Works. < * >

Several more nail-biting days followed before the consortium caved in to Alberta's demands and the province put Syncrude back on track.

Two weeks later, on September 4, 1973, Ottawa responded to Lougheed's poker play with a so-called voluntary oil price freeze to be followed nine days later by a new export tax on crude oil of forty cents a barrel.

Alberta countered a month later by cancelling the Alberta Oil Revenue and Royalty Plan, eliminating all maximum royalty provisions in all leases and bringing in a new royalty system—price related rather than production related—to try and keep money out of Ottawa's hands.

• • •

In 1973, right on schedule, the U.S. reached Hubbert's Peak, cruised over the top and started on the downward slope, consuming more oil than it was producing.

During a lull in the middle of the Ottawa–Alberta energy war, U.S. futurist, Herman Kahn, founder of the Hudson Institute think tank and a confidant of both Henry Kissinger and Richard Nixon, decided to pay a visit to Canadian Prime Minister Pierre Trudeau in Ottawa. Like J. Howard Pew, Kahn saw the Sands as a kind of a salvation for an America being held to ransom by oil sheiks, while its own reserves went into decline.

With the OPEC embargo driving up oil prices to $11 from $3 per barrel, the U.S. Congress passed an Emergency Petroleum Allocation Act, imposing oil price controls and lowering highway speed limits in an ill-starred attempt to protect the consumer. But President Nixon wanted more—he was determined to break OPEC's hold on the American economy. He outlined his vision to the American public in what he called Project Independence, declaring, "Let this be our national goal: At the end of this decade, in the year 1980, the United States will not be dependent on any other country for the energy we need to provide our jobs, to heat our homes, and to keep our transportation moving."[11]

Well, not exactly. There was one other country that could be depended on, and that was America's northern neighbor Canada. Nixon's Project Independence also stated, almost as an aside, that "there is an advantage to moving early and rapidly to develop tar sands production," because it "would contribute to the availability of secure North American oil supplies."

Precisely. Pew's Sun Oil had shown that mining Canadian bitumen was certainly possible and would only get cheaper. Kahn felt that more projects of that kind would give the U.S. some breathing room while it looked for technology to exploit its own locked-in treasures such as the Colorado oil shales.

In the fall of 1973, Herman Kahn flew up to Ottawa with his associate, Montreal economist Marie-Josée Drouin.[12] In his opening gambit, to try and gauge Canadian reaction, the pair proposed a breathtaking crash program of "overnight go-ahead decision making" to solve the energy crisis. And it wouldn't cost Canada a penny!

With Trudeau and his Energy Minister Donald Macdonald listening raptly, Kahn framed the American case in one of his usual super hyperbolic scenarios. He called for the immediate building of twenty Syncrude-scale projects that would produce 3 million barrels of oil a day for export to the big oil-consuming counties.[13] The governments of Japan, the United States, and northern Europe would put up the $20 billion cost, and South Korea would provide up to 40,000 workers, who would pay dues temporarily to the local unions. Canadians would benefit through royalties, refineries, and a secure market.

---

[11] In 1970, Nixon also proclaimed that he was: "inaugurating a program to marshal both government and private research with the goal of producing an unconventionally powered virtually pollution free automobile within five years."

[12] Drouin, the wife of New York hedge fund manager, Henry Kravis, is a senior fellow at the Hudson Institute.

[13] Kahn's target is coming true, but in slow motion, since the Sands will shortly be producing that amount of oil.

When news of Kahn's scenario got out, Canadians were underwhelmed. One Canadian government biologist reckoned that Kahn's megaproject would foul the Athabasca River and wipe out the Mackenzie Valley ecosystem all the way to Tuktoyaktuk on the Arctic Ocean. Clair Balfour of the *Financial Post* wrote, "It would be as though the 10,000 square miles of oil sands were declared international territory, for the international benefit of virtually every nation but Canada."

The Trudeau government politely declined to participate in Kahn's crash program, even when the Nixon government said it was ready to sign an $8 billion check to kick-start the project. Ottawa argued that the plan risked overheating the economy, creating steel shortages, upsetting the labor market and wiping out Canada's other exports by driving up the value of the Canadian dollar. "I don't know, within the world community, why we should feel any obligations to rush into such large-scale production, rather than leave it in the ground for future generations," sniffed Energy Minister Donald Macdonald.[14]

Instead, on December 6, 1973, Trudeau announced a new "made in Canada" national oil policy, "designed to reach Canadian self-sufficiency in oil and oil products before the end of this decade."

Premier Lougheed was still not buying it and escalated the war even further, instead of bowing to the advice of advisors and friends in the oil industry. At a luncheon on March 4, 1974, he warned the Prime Minister that Alberta planned to bring in a 65 percent super royalty on oil effective April 1, 1974.

Trudeau simply stonewalled. While his Liberal budget of November 18th had made some concessions to Alberta, Canada still retained the right to tax provincial royalties.

● ● ●

---

[14] Larry Pratt, *The Tar Sands: Syncrude and the politics of oil* (Hurtig, 1975).

Faced with Ottawa's hardball tactics, Lougheed switched tactics and proposed to bring direct provincial investment into the
Syncrude support system, by creating a new provincially owned
company, the Alberta Energy Company (AEC), to hold a stake in
the proposed Syncrude pipeline and power plant.

Three months later on December 3, 1973, Pierre Trudeau
countered the creation of AEC with the news that his government
would create a national oil company, Petro-Canada, and take other
steps to promote Canada's energy security. This would include a
pipeline from Sarnia to Montreal to carry Alberta oil into Quebec
(then served by cheap Venezuelan crude), federal funding for oilsands research, and approval for the Mackenzie Valley pipeline
to bring natural gas south from the Northwest Territories, which
Ottawa controlled.

• • •

As if Syncrude didn't have enough worries, on December 7,
1974, ARCO announced that its Atlantic Richfield Canada
(Arcan) subsidiary was pulling out of Syncrude, and abandoning
its 30 percent interest in the project.[15] The company said it was
being squeezed by high interest rates and needed more capital
to develop its share of the Prudhoe Bay field in Alaska. A few
days later, the three remaining partners, Imperial, Gulf Canada,
and Cities Service Canada, informed the Alberta government that
project costs had more than doubled, to $2.3 billion, and the
maximum risk capital they were willing to spend on the project
was $1 billion.

Arcan's departure had left a gaping hole that the three remaining partners were not inclined to fill. With Syncrude on the brink
of collapse, Alberta Energy Minister Bill Dickie sent out letters to

---

[15] Atlantic Richfield Company (ARCO) and Exxon had jointly discovered the phenomenal
Alaskan oilfield, North America's largest, on March 12, 1968.

other potential investors, including Shell and the governments of Ontario and Quebec, proposing a meeting to discuss salvaging Syncrude. He pointedly did not invite Ottawa to the table. But people like Bill Mooney of Cities Service and Dave Mitchell of AEC soon persuaded Alberta to enter a temporary truce with Ottawa to try and save the megaproject.

After weeks of working the phones, Mooney finally pulled together a rescue meeting for February 3, 1975 in a Winnipeg hotel room. Present were Peter Lougheed and Don Getty, Ontario Premier Bill Davis, Canadian Energy Minister Donald MacDonald, and the three CEOs of Imperial, Gulf Canada, and Cities Service Canada, who wanted the governments to fill the 30 percent hole Arcan had left or come up with at least another billion dollars for the project.

To keep Syncrude on track, Lougheed knew Alberta would have to put up some equity, so after three days of hard bargaining, he pledged the province to a 10 percent share and committed AEC to fund the entire cost of the pipeline and power plant. Ottawa and Ontario staked the remaining 20 percent, Ottawa 15 percent and Ontario 5 percent. Alberta also agreed to lend $200 million to Gulf and Cities Services, with an option to convert the loan to a 20 percent interest in Syncrude. The oil company shares were as follows: Imperial, 31.25 percent, Cities Service, 22 percent, and Gulf, 16.75 percent. To celebrate, Lougheed's government cut the province's personal income tax by 28 percent, making Albertans the lowest-taxed Canadians.

So Syncrude was saved. However, the Trudeau government was not done yet. On April 30, 1975, they passed another zinger—the Petroleum Administration Act—allowing Ottawa to set the domestic price of oil and natural gas without the agreement of energy-producing provinces. Of course, inside the province, Alberta could charge whatever it wanted.

• • •

On July 30, 1975, Pierre Trudeau asked his friend Maurice Strong to return to Canada from his UN environment post to head the newly created national oil company Petro-Canada. Strong, who had started his career as a fur trader with the Hudson's Bay Company, was the ex-president of Montreal's Power Corporation and a strong supporter of the Liberal government.

Trudeau himself came from an oil company background. His father, Charles-Émile, had built his company, Champlain Oil Products, into a chain of gas stations and a home fuel delivery service in the Montreal area. In the early 1960s, the company was acquired by Imperial Oil, leaving the family multimillionaires.

The bill to create Petro-Canada had been tabled in Parliament by the New Democratic Party (NDP) in 1973. Trudeau's Liberals were then in a minority and depended upon the support of the NDP to stay in power.

The national oil company hit the ground running on January 1, 1976, with Maurice Strong setting up temporary shop in the International Hotel in Calgary. Strong and his executive vice president, Bill Hopper, had $1.5 billion in spending money, a 15 percent holding in Syncrude, and a 45 percent interest in Panarctic Oils. They soon started shopping around for assets to build a national oil major. Later that year, they acquired U.S.-owned Atlantic Richfield Canada (Arcan) for $342 million. Arcan, with its staff of 300, was morphed into Petro-Canada's main operating subsidiary, Petro-Canada Exploration, so the company gained operating expertise and a cash flow of $50 million a year from the production of 430,000 barrels of oil and liquids a day. Arcan also came with 90 million cubic feet of gas reserves in Western Canada, plus gas processing facilities, 11 million undeveloped exploration acres, and some oilsands leases on another 1.2 million acres.

Petro-Canada soon invested in several East Coast offshore programs using its funding to pick up the pace of exploration. In 1978, it bought a stake in the Hibernia oil discovery off Newfoundland and major gas finds off Nova Scotia, and in 1980, drilled its first offshore wells as operator of an exploration program off Labrador. The company's next major purchase, in 1979, was the Canadian assets of U.S.-controlled Pacific Petroleum. This included oil and gas properties and a small refinery and marketing network in Western Canada. In 1981, Petro-Canada bought Belgian-owned Petrofina Canada, giving it a larger refining and marketing presence in Eastern and Central Canada. Other Petro-Canada refineries and service stations were acquired from British Petroleum Canada in 1983. Finally, in 1985, Petro-Canada gobbled up the Canadian retail stations of Gulf Canada in its last major acquisition.[16]

All this frantic activity paid off. In 1982, Petro-Canada discovered oil at Valhalla, Alberta. It was the largest new oil field of the 1980s in Western Canada. Two years later, the company made its first big offshore discovery as operator in the Terra Nova oil field off Newfoundland.

Many Canadians were annoyed at having to pay a patriotic surcharge at all of the country's gas pumps, which Ottawa used to finance Petro-Canada buyouts of foreign-owned oil companies. But Albertans complained the most. According to Earle Gray, the arrival of Petro-Canada caused howls of bitter protest all over Alberta, bitching that was not always justified:

> In Calgary, Petro-Canada was at first about as welcomed as a hooker at a matronly tea party. Bumper stickers would later proclaim, "I'd rather push this car a mile than fill up at Petrocan." No one seemed to notice that it was Alberta that had the second biggest corporate interests in the oil business, in Alberta Energy, in its 20-percent stake in Syncrude, and in Nova, with its province-wide gas-gathering grid which, while not government-owned, was a tool of government policy.[17]

---

[16] Strong later became chairman of the Canada Development Investment Corporation, the holding company for some of Canada's main government-owned corporations.
[17] Earle Gray, *History of the Oilsands;* Web Support Site, *Black Bonanza* Texts and Documents— Earle Gray's Works. < * >

Albertans joked that Petro-Canada stood for "Pierre Elliott Trudeau Rips Off Canada." And when Petro-Canada had finished building their ruddy colored, marble-clad headquarters, which cast a long shadow over a neighboring Calgary plaza, the complex was snidely referred to as "Red Square."

But the opposition softened as Petro-Canada proved itself a model corporate Calgarian. In 1988, the company went a long way toward redeeming itself in the eyes of all Canadians when it mounted a public relations offensive that culminated in the brilliant eighty-eight-day Olympic Torch Relay, which Petro-Canada organized and sponsored. People from all walks of life carried the Olympic flame through every province and territory on the way to the Calgary Winter Olympic Games.

• • •

While Ottawa participated in the Athabasca Sands with its share of Syncrude, Peter Lougheed and Don Getty asked Alberta oil veteran, Dave Mitchell, CEO of Great Plains Development Company to head up the Alberta Energy Company (AEC), the vehicle that would hold the province's share in Syncrude. They had to track him down in Honolulu. His Hawaiian vacation ruined, Mitchell agreed to come back and serve on condition that there would be no direct government interference and wide 50 percent public ownership by Albertans.

Mitchell proposed an initial capitalization of $150 million split evenly between the province and the public. He recalls that, "the actual mechanics of the 1975 offering were complex and required careful negotiations with the brokers as they initially did not think that more than $40 million could be raised." Mitchell stuck to his six shooters and also insisted that no Albertan could hold more than 1 percent of the issue. He then proceeded to offer stakes in AEC to Albertans at a bargain $20 a share. Mitchell's popular capitalism worked like gangbusters, and the issue was oversubscribed even at the $75 million target price.

AEC started out as a four-person operation and grew into a successful and sophisticated player in the oil and gas industry, with a big share of both Syncrude and the operations in the federal government's Suffield and Primrose military reserves. In 1983 alone, AEC drilled over 500 gas wells on the Suffield range in southern Alberta. The company had holdings in coal, forestry, and petrochemicals at one stage or other, but eventually they were sold off bit by bit. Under vice president Gwyn Morgan, the company focused primarily on oil and gas exploration. Alberta eventually phased out its 50 percent equity interest, selling it to AEC in 1993. Says Mitchell, "the role of government, by then just an artifact from the interventionist days of the 1970s and early 1980s, was over." AEC merged with PanCanadian Energy Corporation in 2002 to become EnCana, led by Gwyn Morgan. EnCana would sell out its stake in Syncrude in 2003, and by 2006 grow into one of the top two or three companies in Canada, rivaling the Royal Bank of Canada and Research in Motion in share value on the TSX.[18]

●   ●   ●

As for Syncrude Canada, the 50,000 barrels-a-day plant was complete by 1978 after five years of construction, and crude oil was soon heading south to U.S. refineries by pipeline. That year, the Energy Resources Conservation Board of Alberta (ERCB) gave it the green light to build a larger $1 billion expansion that would produce up to 129,000 barrels per day.

When Syncrude started up, the company used draglines like GCOS. These big $100 million cranes and buckets weighed more

---

[18] In 1980, David Mitchell founded the Ernest Manning Awards Foundation, which annually awards $75,000 prizes to Canadian innovators.

than fifteen full 747s each. Within months, the murderous climate extremes and sharp silica in the oil-soaked sand started giving the operators migraines. The conveyors that moved the sands to the processing plant would crack and split, having to be replaced and causing expensive slowdowns.

But on July 30th, Syncrude piped out its first barrel of diluted bitumen to Edmonton to be made into the product, Syncrude Sweet Blend, and the plant officially opened for business on September 15th. Syncrude produced 5 million barrels of oil within the next twelve months, and since world oil prices leaped skyward in 1979 and remained high until the mid-1980s, the operation seemed to be a financial success from the start.

To celebrate the occasion, Alberta hosted the World Energy Conference that autumn at the Banff Springs Hotel. After the conference ended in early October, a curious Sheik Ahmed Zaki Yamani, the Saudi technocrat who was OPEC's public face, asked his hosts for a guided tour of Syncrude, to see what all the fuss was about.

Not long after Yamani returned home, the Iranian Revolution and hostage crisis erupted. With all the chaos in that country, Iran saw a drop of 3.9 million barrels per day of crude oil production from 1978 to 1981. At first, other OPEC countries made up the shortfall, but in 1980, the Iran–Iraq War began and many Persian Gulf countries had to cut output as well. By 1981, OPEC production was about one-fourth lower than it had been in 1978, and prices had doubled.

Responding to higher prices, U.S. President Jimmy Carter appeared on U.S. television in late 1978 wearing a sweater and urging Americans to turn down their thermostats. The following July, he proposed a sweeping $142 billion energy independence plan for the following ten years. "Beginning this moment, this nation will never use more foreign oil than we did in 1977—never," Carter declared bravely to the television audience.

Carter put in place an import quota of 8.5 million barrels of oil per day and created a $20 billion synfuels program, aimed at producing 2.5 million barrels of synthetic fuels per day by 1990. He also proposed, in words that sound eerily familiar, to fund the "creation of this nation's first solar bank, which will help us achieve the crucial goal of 20 percent of our energy coming from solar power by the year 2000." Carter took off Nixon's price controls, but at the same time he warned people who insisted on driving large, needlessly powerful cars that they had to expect to pay more for the privilege.

●　●　●

Canada's first energy war ended in a truce in 1975, after Ottawa retreated from gouging the industry and let prices rise closer to world levels. It also let the companies write off royalties paid prior to the price upheaval as a legitimate business expense (via a 25 percent resource allowance effective January 1, 1976). The industry roared back to life and for the next five years the good times rolled in Alberta.

In 1976, Premier Lougheed created the Heritage Savings Trust Fund, setting aside $1.5 billion as a first installment. For the next decade Alberta put 30 percent of its surpluses into this provincial piggy bank. When revenues dipped in the 1980s, Treasurer Lou Hyndman cut the annual allocation to 15 percent. In 1987, with prices slumping further, new Premier Don Getty stopped topping up the Heritage Fund altogether. Since then, the Heritage Fund has generated over $26 billion in income during its lifetime, and revenues are pushing $1 billion a year.

In federal politics, a young Albertan in his thirties named Joe Clark took on the Trudeau Liberals in 1979 and led the federal Progressive Conservatives to a minority victory. On November 12th, Clark unveiled his own national energy strategy in a white paper called "Energy Self-Sufficiency by 1990." He advocated relying more on the private sector and the market moving toward world prices, and building a Canadian Energy Bank for national petroleum projects. But Clark also proposed raising the federal take from 10 percent to 19 percent of overall oil and gas revenue, to keep windfall profits out of the hands of the oil companies—the world price of oil had recently jumped 160 percent. He also wanted to replace the energy surcharge for Petro-Canada with a simple 18 perent tax on gasoline as a deficit-fighting measure. This measure, one of the cornerstones of Finance Minister John Crosbie's December 11th budget, proved fatal: the House of Commons narrowly defeated the budget, sparking another election.

The following February 1980, Trudeau's reborn Liberals swept back into power, eager to start Energy War II. Energy Minister Marc Lalonde fired their opening salvo on budget night October 28, 1980, bringing in a new National Energy Program (NEP), and the battle was back on.

The main impact of Trudeau's NEP was to remove the world crude oil price from the first 45,000 barrels per day of oilsands production. And Petro-Canada was used to administer the program, making the company even more unpopular in the Alberta oil patch.

Trudeau's timing stank. The NEP came into play just as oil prices were plunging around the world. Both factors caused petroleum land prices to plunge 65 percent in the first half of 1981. More than 25 percent of geophysical activity came to an abrupt halt, and the industry had to shut down or move south 227 drilling and 107 service rigs valued at over $1 billion, 40 percent of the drilling rigs in Alberta. It was the largest capital outflow in Canadian history.

Alberta responded by cutting oil production to protest Ottawa's energy policy, and Calgary Mayor Ralph Klein made headlines (and bumper stickers) with his growl, "Let the Eastern bastards freeze in the dark." In Ottawa, Marc Lalonde countered the move by bringing in what was soon called "the Lougheed Levy" to subsidize imports to Eastern Canada. It was a classic Mexican standoff.

By August 1981, the two sides had nothing but blanks left to shoot, and the petulance of the two governments had left the oil patch on life support. So Lougheed and Trudeau sat down for a six-day bargaining marathon, and emerged on September 1st with a new two-tiered price system—one price for old oil, one for new.

No tears were shed when two years later, Brian Mulroney's newly elected Progressive Conservatives dismantled the National Energy Program.

● ● ●

In 1984, the new Mulroney government told Petro-Canada to change its mandate and conduct business in a solely commercial manner, focusing on profitability. The following year, Mulroney deregulated oil prices allowing producers to sell at market value. But his actions didn't make much difference in the short run. A decade of high prices had led to more exploration and innovation, and the resulting supply glut put world prices on a sharp downward trajectory.

In 1985, the Saudis and other OPEC nations opened their taps, starting a price war that swamped world oil markets and pounded down prices by 60 percent in the late months of that year and early 1986. In July 1986, world oil prices bottomed out at $7.20 per barrel.

It was happy times at the gas pumps and North Americans started a love affair with SUVs, but the actions of Ahmad Zaki Yamani and his OPEC allies dealt a devastating blow to the Suncor and Syncrude projects. Losing $5 to $10 on every barrel of synthetic crude they produced, the companies had to make savage staff cuts and beg to the Alberta government to re-jig their royalty rate to avoid a complete shutdown.

The only bright spot in all the carnage was that producers were forced to re-engineer their mining and extraction operations in order to survive. The next few years saw them triumph, slashing the base cost of producing a barrel of synthetic Athabasca crude from CAD$35 to only CAD$13 a barrel.

• • •

Since the 1860s, Canadians had been trying to get the U.S. to sign a free trade deal that would ensure them fair access to the huge U.S. market. But there were always thousands of nagging issues. Say, for example, the Nova Scotia lobster industry wanted to export to Massachusetts, but state lobstermen were having a bad year. You could be sure the state assembly would pass a law to specify the size of shipping boxes that would prevent them from being sold at any fish market in the state.

In 1965, the big three automakers pushed Prime Minister Lester Pearson and President Lyndon Johnson to sign a Canada-U.S. auto pact that became a good model for free cross-border trade. Twenty years later, Canadian Finance Minister Donald Macdonald's Royal Commission on the economy issued a report to the Trudeau government recommending free trade with the U.S. Macdonald was, of course, a former Minister of Energy and knew that their growing concern over energy security would very likely get the Americans to the table. The new Mulroney government took up the cause, and on October 4, 1988 signed the Canada–U.S. Free Trade Agreement (FTA) with the Reagan government. The deal removed, in stages, several trade restrictions over a ten-year period, resulting in a huge increase in cross-border trade.

What really cemented the FTA were the energy provisions, two in particular which leveled the playing field for both countries and gave the U.S. the petroleum price and supply security it needed.

In **Article 903: Export Taxes**, the parties agreed not to bring in any tax or duty that would favor one country over the other.

Article 904: Other Export Measures, lets either party bring in energy supply restrictions or price hikes as long as it maintains the same price or percentage of supply to the other party.[19]

The 1994 North American Free Trade Agreement (NAFTA) negotiated with the U.S. and Mexico further guaranteed U.S. access to Canadian energy by limiting export/import restrictions, keeping the proportion of energy exports relative to total supply, and avoiding dual pricing.

●   ●   ●

In February of 1990, the Mulroney government announced it was taking steps to privatize Petro-Canada and passed a bill to that effect in October. On July 3, 1991, the first shares were sold to the public in an initial public offering. Mulroney continued the dismantling of Trudeau's NEP in March of the following year, by cancelling Ottawa's 50 percent Canadian participation requirement.

Petro-Canada was by then big enough to take care of itself, and the discipline of going private helped it to modernize and slim down. In addition, the Persian Gulf War of 1991 that followed the invasion of Kuwait by Saddam Hussein, boosted petroleum prices handsomely.

In 1995, the Government of Canada further divested shares amounting to 50 percent of Petro-Canada's common stock, reducing its interest to just 20 percent. Now, with the oil patch in much better shape, it eagerly awaited the inevitable ride back up the roller coaster to higher prices.

●   ●   ●

---

[19] For the text see: Canada–U.S. Free Trade Agreement, Energy Clauses (1988); Web Support Site, *Black Bonanza* Footnotes—Chapter 4. < * >

Oil sands projects are not "slam dunks" and certainly not for the faint of heart. It takes courage, deep pockets, staying power and experience in the building and operation of mega-projects.

—Neil Camarta, former Senior Vice President,

Shell Oil Sands

Higher prices also induced the Shell Oil Company of Canada to start building its own oilsands mega mine. Back in 1973, Shell had tried to launch a $700 million Athabasca oilsands plant at Muskeg River near Fort McMurray, and did build a pilot bitumen production plant near Peace River. The company decided to bring in partners and in 1978, the new Alsands consortium of Shell Canada and ten other companies applied to the ERCB for a 100,000 barrels-per-day mining operation. But when prices plunged in the early 1980s and the cost of Alsands had ballooned to $13.5 billion, Dome Petroleum and Hudson's Bay Oil and Gas withdrew from the project and it collapsed in May of 1982.

The early 1990s were not the best of times to build a new Sands megaproject, and none of the new projects were actually economic. But as Wayne Gretzky of the Edmonton Oilers said, "you skate to where the puck is going to be, not where it has been," and "you always miss 100% of the shots you never take." After a half century of trying, it took a gentle nudge from the Alberta government, who threatened to cancel its lease, to get Shell and its head office to move ahead. Shell Canada finally found other committed investors in Chevron Canada and Western Oil Sands, who each took a 20 percent share of the new $5.7 billion Athabasca Oil Sands Project (AOSP). In 1999, the partners started building the Muskeg River Mine, as well as a two-way pipeline and an upgrader near Fort Saskatchewan.

Shell Oil Sands vice president, Neil Camarta, who field marshaled the project, said that building AOSP "took lots of energy and lots of guts," and was something like the Normandy landings on

D-Day. Contractors installed almost 1,000 miles (1,600 km) of pipe, enough steel cable and rebar to reach all the way to New York, and poured enough concrete to build thirty-four Calgary Towers.

AOSP finally opened its 155,000-barrel-a-day project in 2003. But nothing came easy to Shell. As the project started up, a fire caused $150 million in damages and set back production for months.

Today, more than 6,000 workers toil at Muskeg River, where the operators of the world's largest trucks can make more than $120,000 a year, moving $10,000 worth of bitumen a load. After the monster trucks dump the ore onto a crusher, the sand rolls to the plant along a V-shaped conveyor belt, the world's largest, at 1,600 yards long. The bitumen is steamed off, diluted with lighter petroleum liquids, then pipelined down to the Scotford upgrader northeast of Edmonton.

* * *

In the early 1990s, with three major mines in operation and more being planned, the Athabasca Sands were finally coming of age. No longer were they a frontier deposit, scorned by naysayers as a backup resource. Now they were taking their place on the world energy stage, making Canada one of the world's major petroleum superpowers. In this enterprise, they were aided by new Alberta Premier, Ralph Klein, who took most of the brakes off of oilsands development.

The 1990s and the new century also saw a stampede into underground bitumen production by steam assisted gravity drainage (SAGD). This made-in-Alberta technology let smaller operators enter the oilsands game and ensured the development of the 80 percent of oilsands deposits that were too deep to mine. SAGD technology, I argue, is one of the astounding inventions of the late twentieth century, and could add up to two trillion barrels of oil to the world's energy account.

5

King Ralph and the SAGD Revolution

To have a long-range plan would be an interventionist kind of policy which says you either allow them or you don't allow them to proceed. The last thing we want to be is an interventionist government.

—Ralph Klein

On December 4, 1992, Ralph Klein was sworn in as Premier of Alberta, taking over from Don Getty. A former reporter and Liberal mayor of Calgary, the jovial politician, fondly called "King Ralph," was known to keep his ear very close to the ground, even hanging around beer halls to see what the boys were thinking. Klein was no green groupie, and liked to joke that global warming was caused by dinosaur farts.

Under Klein's fourteen-year reign, the oilsands business boomed, some say out of control, and it was a rare project that was not approved. Former Premier Lougheed often warned that the province was barreling ahead too quickly to develop its resources, but Klein just smiled at such suggestions.

Klein's goal was breathtaking. He wanted nothing less than to replace the King of Saudi Arabia as America's favorite petroleum potentate. In 1993, his government hosted a meeting of thirty oil companies and agencies to discuss the benefits of Canadian self-sufficiency in oil and frame a debate about the downside of "increased reliance on Middle East oil and politics." The following year, the group morphed into the National Oil Sands Task Force, including all levels of government, developers, trade unions, and suppliers. They also pulled together the Canadian Oil Sands Network for Research and Development (CONRAD), and gave it a $105 million annual budget to find ways to boost production and trim costs.

In its 1995 paper, "The Oil Sands: A New Energy Vision,"[1] the Task Force outlined a twenty-five-year growth strategy for the Sands, calling them, "the largest potential private sector investment opportunity for the public good remaining in Western Canada, and a 'national treasure'." The paper proposed investing up to $25 billion to boost production in stages from 450,000 barrels a day to a million. The Task Force confidently predicted that all of this activity would create 10,000 direct new jobs.

To speed this vision along, the Task Force asked the governments to put the whole tar patch on a level playing field. They wanted consistent royalties and tax terms for all projects, instead of deciding on a project-by-project basis. Ottawa was invited to bring in more corporate tax incentives, and the Alberta government was asked to consider an across-the-board 1 percent gross royalty until companies could pay off their multibillion-dollar investments. The Task Force also asked for a reduction from 50 percent to 25 percent on profitable production after recovery of capital costs, plus predictable rates of return equal to those paid on long-term Canadian bonds.

King Ralph's treasury was quite favorably disposed to the suggestion to "defer tax and royalty revenues until project expansions were completed." His government's new generic royalty

---

[1] This was later rebranded "A Declaration of Opportunity."

regime, announced December 1995, cut provincial payments to a minimum 1 percent of revenue from synthetic crude oil sales before project payout and 25 percent of net revenue after payout.

Way back east in Ottawa, the new government of Jean Chrétien brought their own bottles of champagne to the party, granting a speedy accelerated capital cost allowance that let oilsands companies quickly write off capital investments. Announcing the good news was a local Liberal, Chrétien's Natural Resources Minister, Anne McLellan, Member of Parliament for Edmonton Centre.

• • •

These generous write-offs and the new tax and royalty certainty opened the floodgates, and investment money started pouring into Alberta. The amount of funding quintupled in the seven years following the regime change. In the seven years up to 1995, $5.5 billion was spent on Sands projects. From 1995 to 2002, the amount was a staggering $24.5 billion, one of the biggest industrial expansions in Canadian history.

Much of the new investment capital was for mine upgrading, which benefited Athabasca Oil Sands Project (AOSP), Suncor, and Syncrude—Suncor started to clear-cut almost 300,000 trees for its Steep Bank mine, and on April 16, 1998, Syncrude celebrated sending its billionth barrel of bitumen upgrade down the pipeline five years ahead of schedule. Fort McMurray housing went into the stratosphere, and even a two-bedroom trailer cost upwards of $350,000. The price of a quality bitumen lease skyrocketed from $6 an acre in 1978 to $120 in 1998.[2]

The mines also started expanding their footprint, although Alberta's Ministry of the Environment said the companies were impacting less than 1 percent of Alberta's boreal forest, an area about the size of the built-up part of Edmonton.

---

[2] It would spike far higher, reaching an amazing and unsustainable $486 per acre in 2006.

The three big companies ditched the old dragline system and moved entirely to more agile mining shovels, dump trucks, and crushers, saving a few bucks a barrel. Syncrude replaced some of its conveyor belts with hydro transport, mixing the crushed sand with hot water and piping the slurry to the separators. The companies also heavily computerized their operations, with control-room sensors checking out everything from tire pressure to steam leaks. Dispatchers now use GPS to automatically track the 797B Caterpillar heavy haulers as they load and unload their payloads, 400 tons at a time.

The big three miners also started to pay more attention to research and development (R&D), and attached themselves to government and university research labs. At the Imperial Oil-Alberta Ingenuity Centre for Oil Sands Innovation (COSI), chemical and materials engineer, Jacob Masliyah, picked up where Karl Clark left off, bringing into the picture what is called coalite science— what actually happens at the interfaces of oil, sand, and water. Masliyah and his team found out exactly what happens to the oil droplet or bubble of air during the extraction process, and were able to suggest money and energy saving ways to use lower water temperatures. Says COSI's Murray Gray, "One project is examining not using water at all, or very little. We're hoping that some of the techniques we're working on could provide an alternative, without actually having to draw on the Athabasca River."[3]

Syncrude also opened a research lab in Edmonton in 1994 and began investing $30 million a year to tweak the whole extraction process for more efficient ways to extract bitumen from sand, recycle hot water, and cut down or solidify tailings. Shell's big research facility at the University of Calgary, which houses 200 scientists and technologists, actively looks for ways to boost oilsands production, solve the tailings pond issues, and diminish the industry's environmental footprint.

---

[3] Geoff McMaster, "Past, Present, Future: The race to unlock the mystery of Alberta's oil sands." University of Alberta; Web Support Site, *Black Bonanza* Footnotes—Chapter 5. < * >

While the companies were modernizing their mining operations, a large and increasing part of the R&D money in the oil patch was heading into new underground steam assisted gravity drainage (SAGD) developments, many by smaller, leaner operators eager to make their mark, but unable to shoulder the monster capital costs of developing a mine.

• • •

Roger Butler's invention of steam assisted gravity drainage (SAGD) has had a staggering economic impact. It will eventually change the whole geopolitics of oil in the world.
—Tom Harding, Head of Chemical and Petroleum
Engineering, University of Calgary

Neil Camarta, former Senior Vice President, Shell Oil Sands doesn't have too much respect for bitumen bearing sands—he calls it "dirt." But Camarta's true love is gas, and he is going back to his roots. After building Shell's colossal oilsands mine, then coming out of retirement to work for Petro-Canada, he went back to his roots as vice president of gas for the new Suncor/Petro-Canada company. Natural gas is the primary fuel used in oilsands extraction.

When I talked to Camarta about the prospects for SAGD,he said it represents the future of the Sands and is already producing more bitumen than mining. Camarta mentioned that, in about 1985, he visited the first successful SAGD site, an actual underground mine tunneled right into the limestone under the Sands to try and perfect the process.

SAGD is all about directional oil well drilling, which to me, and most other people, is a form of rocket science. Today's technology was first developed by the famous French oil service company Schlumberger, and others to fracture (or "frac") underground shale seams to liberate gas. It gives operators the incredible ability to drill down vertically and then, using a gyroscope and GPS, steer the drill bit while watching above in real time, and then change direction and tunnel horizontally in any direction or angle they desire. At the same time, they can monitor on a computer screen the position and boundaries of the formation and make fine adjustments to stay inside the zone. This is a bit like a mechanical version of the giant sandworms in the movie *Dune* or *Tremors*. But directional drilling is also a godsend for SAGD, which requires precision placement of the wells.[4]

With the SAGD process, you drill two horizontal wells, one about sixteen feet (5 m) above the other, and lay down perforated pipe for distances of about 875 yards (800 m). You have to precisely align the positioning of these wells relative to each other and to the boundaries of the target formation. You then inject warm vapor into the upper well at constant pressure, but not high enough to fracture the growing steam chamber. The heat rises and spreads, melting the surrounding bitumen off the sand. Then gravity takes over, draining the warm oil and condensed water down through the sand, where it seeps into the perforations of the lower producer well. Submersible pumps designed to handle hot fluids then lift the bitumen and condensed water to the surface. Over several months the chamber grows both vertically and laterally as the cycle continues, until the chamber flattens out and clean sand remains in place.

You can recover between 25 percent and 75 percent of the bitumen in place using SAGD, and recycle about 90 percent of the water. After recovery, you inject water into the bitumen-drained area to maintain the stability of the deposit.

The mine that Camarta visited twenty years earlier was the Underground Test Facility (UTF) at Dover River, now operated by Northstar Energy Ltd. It was built in 1984 by the Alberta Oil Sands Technology and Research Authority (AOSTRA) a government of

---

[4] See for example, Schlumberger Directional Drilling; Web Support Site, *Black Bonanza* Footnotes—Chapter 5. < * >

Alberta body set up to promote R&D for oilsands and heavy oil production, and particularly to test the SAGD process developed by Dr. Roger Butler of the University of Calgary.

• • •

There are quite a few Canadian inventors who have changed the world. Abraham Gesner's invention of kerosene in 1854 killed the sperm whaling industry, lit up the world for fifty years, and eventually gave birth to the Rockefeller fortune. Canadian cable and tool drilling techniques helped open North America's first commercial crude oil well in 1854, a year before Pennsylvania, and Canadian drillers struck oil in Iran for the Anglo-Persian oil company (today's BP plc) in 1906.

In 1892, Canadian botanist, Charles Saunders, invented frost resistant Marquis wheat, perhaps one of the most valuable products in the world, which opened up millions of colder acres around the globe for wheat production. In 1902, Reginald Fessenden pioneered radio wave broadcasting. Starting in 1958, two Canadian crop scientists, Baldur Stefansson and Richard Downey, patiently developed the fabulous canola seed from rapeseed, carefully breeding out the grain's heart-clogging bad fats, while leaving the healthy ones. Canola (from "Canadian oil") is now a huge global crop. Canada's Mike Lazaridis gave the world the BlackBerry, and Calgary's James Gosling created the Java programming language.

But the Canadian invention that will prove more valuable than all the rest combined is SAGD, a method of getting deep deposits of heavy oil and bitumen out of the ground, perfected at Fort McMurray in 1987 by chemical engineer Roger Butler. His technique is usable anywhere in the world where heavy oil and bitumen are found.

Since the oil industry could access less than 10 percent of the Athabasca Sands using surface mining, early mining was confined to mining on either side of the Athabasca River Valley where the overburden was thin. The arrival of SAGD in the 1990s meant that companies could now take out the majority of the Athabasca bitumen at a very competitive cost. In the Athabasca Sands alone, the advent of SAGD makes at least 330 billion more barrels readily accessible, and will probably yield over a trillion barrels of synthetic crude.[5]

It's a colossal number to be sure. But if Roger Butler's invention can tap two-thirds of the Sands that are out of reach of mining, it can also help ramp-up heavy oil production in places like Venezuela and Russia. The SAGD method just about doubles proven petroleum reserves in the world, estimated at 1.292 trillion barrels. In addition, it may have instantly tripled our planet's known recoverable oil resources, making Butler one of the true benefactors of humanity.

• • •

A mild-faced chemical engineer, Roger Butler earned his PhD at London's Imperial College of Science and Technology in 1951. He taught at Queen's University in Kingston, Ontario, joining Imperial Oil in 1955. Butler first pondered the SAGD process and developed his theory in about 1969 when he was working at Imperial's Sarnia refinery, at the time the company had discovered a huge heavy oil deposit at Cold Lake, Alberta, near the Saskatchewan border.

Butler had already tinkered with a process for mining Saskatchewan potash fertilizer deposits by injecting water down a well to dissolve the potash and salt. Gravity does the work. As he explained it, "Heavy brine falls to the bottom and the light water rises to the top. You end up with a turnip-shaped cavity in which the heavy material keeps falling while the lighter water goes to the top." He calculated that, "if we made the well longer, we could draw as much as 1,000 barrels a day. We'd be in business."[6]

---

[5] Bitumen is not equivalent to oil: it takes 1.2 barrels of bitumen to make one barrel of synthetic crude.

[6] Tom Kayser, "Roger Butler: Father of SAGD." *Energy Processing Canada*, March 1, 2005.

"I was really very impressed with the mechanism of this," Butler recalled. One day he was having a beer with a friend when the thought struck him—maybe his potash process could be applied to heat the molasses-like heavy oil at Cold Lake and create the same kind of steam chamber. The heated oil would flow down to the bottom of the chamber where another well would collect it and pump it to the surface.[7]

Butler wrote a patent memo on his gravity drainage concept in 1969, but it wasn't until 1975 when Imperial Oil moved him to Calgary to lead their Heavy Oil Research Department that he was able to tackle the concept. During the late 1970s, Imperial was testing a thermal cyclic steam stimulation (CSS) process, aka "huff and puff" in the Clearwater formation at Cold Lake. In this three-step process, you inject steam downhole at high pressure for several weeks, followed by several weeks of soaking to reduce the oil's viscosity, then you pump the heavy oil up using the same well.

Butler's radical notion for producing heavy oil by using heat and gravity to drain oil into collector pipes was at first scoffed at by the old hands at Cold Lake, but Butler wasn't deterred a bit. He was after a more efficient system that used continuous heating and production, rather than the six- to eighteen-month cycles with CSS and a process that lost less heat.

"Perhaps the steam will rise and the warm oil will fall," he mused.

He first tried injecting steam through one vertical well, letting the reservoir heat up and drain, then pumping the recovered oil to the surface through another vertical well. The results weren't promising. He reckoned that the oil was trickling down through the sand in an ever-narrowing cone, and more sand was plugging up the well used to pump the oil to the surface. "When you're extracting oil from in situ oil sands, the chamber (created by

---

[7] Mark Lowey, "An Interview with Roger Butler," *Alberta Oil Magazine*, April 1, 2006; Web Support Site, *Black Bonanza* Footnotes—Chapter 5. < * >

steam injection) is full of sand," Butler said. "The oil has to move through the sand and gather on the bottom of the chamber . . . but gravity won't assist the flow on a vertical well." So Butler had his "Eureka!" moment—vertical well production rates were too low to make SAGD economically viable. But a perforated horizontal well might be just the ticket.

Butler then asked Imperial to drill a horizontal production well low in the reservoir, with numerous drainage points along its entire length to capture the oil. "I could get a 1,000 barrels a day out of one of these wells on my paper calculations."

In 1978, Butler had numbers to support his idea, but Imperial moved like molasses, prompting him to get up during a high-level meeting and exclaim: "What the hell's the point of doing all this research if you fellas won't do something in the field?"[8]

Butler finally persuaded Imperial to drill what was the world's first modern horizontal oil well paired with a vertical steam-injection well. The horizontal well was about 165 yards (150 m) long, and, "The oil came out at about the right rate—I felt pretty damn good!" But 1,000 barrels a day from 150 feet (46 m) was too marginal for Imperial. Oil prices were dropping, most Cold Lake engineers were wedded to CSS, and Imperial put Butler's project on the back burner.

Butler grew convinced that vertical wells were the problem, but with little further support from the company,[9] he took early retirement and went to work at the AOSTRA for about a year, where he convinced them to test and refine the SAGD process at the organization's UTF near Fort McMurray. In 1983, Butler was appointed to the University of Calgary's first Endowed Chair in Petroleum Engineering.

• • •

---

[8] Tom Keyser, "Visionary's life work reverberates in oilpatch," *Business Edge*, May 2, 2005; Web Support Site, *Black Bonanza* Footnotes—Chapter 5. < * >
[9] Imperial suspended the $12 billion Cold Lake project in 1981, and scaled it down for a time, but ramped it back up again when prices rebounded.

In their first SAGD experiment in 1987, UTF engineers drilled three of Butler's proposed twin horizontal wells from mine shafts 220 yards (200 m) down, just above a tunnel dug into the limestone underburden. The first tests immediately proved the feasibility of twin well SAGD, and there was some quiet excitement in the industry when the UTF crew found they could recover about 60 percent of the bitumen in place. The UTF even went into the black in 1992, achieving positive cash flow producing at a rate of about 2,000 barrels a day from three well pairs.

Several years of testing followed. The engineers injected steam at various pressures, and then went under the wells to measure the actual results of their work. They finally got the best results, over 60 percent extraction, when they injected steam at a gentle low pressure so it didn't force open or fracture any of the deposit. Using this method, it stayed contained within the steam chamber, which got bigger as the warm bitumen drained out, just like Butler's old Saskatchewan potash well. The engineers also found that the best results came when they made sure the injector well and the producer well were drilled precisely parallel, and kept about five and a half yards (5 m) apart. Refining the process further, they also came up with ways to stop sand getting into the perforated pipe and prevent steam from getting into the producing well bore. Beginning in 1996, the engineers moved from the UTF up to the surface, where they drilled several well pairs and found, to their delight, that they performed as well as those drilled from the tunnels.[10]

These AOSTRA tests gave far better results than expected, and the timing of the SAGD discovery was perfect as well. While Butler was testing his process, oil service companies like Schlumberger were coming up with very sophisticated directional drilling technology. Suddenly, you could drill horizontal wells accurately, cheaply, and efficiently. So, with this drilling revolution, lower

---

[10] For SAGD imagery, please visit the Web Support Site, *Black Bonanza* Maps & Charts—Oil Sands Development. < * > .

capital costs, and the very high recovery rates, that Butler's process was showing, the major companies, as well as many independent oil companies, started to move quickly in the direction of SAGD. You could get into the oilsands business for $30,000 per flowing barrel, compared to $126,000 per flowing barrel for an integrated mine and upgrader.[11]

At the same time, AOSTRA developed a computer simulation program that it provided to companies so they could optimize the design and operation of their own thermal projects.

In 1985, EnCana, already a fan of horizontal drilling for gas, was first off the mark, starting its own advanced SAGD projects at Foster Creek and Christina Lake with partner ConocoPhillips. Petro-Canada followed with its MacKay River project, ConocoPhillips had a SAGD operation at Surmount, Suncor had one at Firebag, and OPTI Canada/Nexen had one at Long Lake, not to mention over a dozen smaller operations. It was soon found that one of the keys to high-profit SAGD production was to have thick cap rock (usually shale, as in the Kirby Lease) to keep in the steam heat. Some companies were soon reporting high-end recovery rates of over 70 percent of the bitumen in place. The first SAGD bitumen made it to market in late 2001.

SAGD technology also offered the oil patch some major advantages over the "huff and puff" in situ process, including lower steam-oil ratios and lower pressure needs, which cuts operating costs. SAGD has also allowed thermal recovery to be extended far beyond the thicker and deeper pay zones such as those at Cold Lake and Peace River.

The SAGD experience, however, has not all been rosy. When Suncor's 90,000 barrels-a-day Firebag project opened, engineers miscalculated the amount of sulphur the bitumen would produce during upgrading, and an "odor problem" resulted. The Alberta

[11] Cambridge Energy Research Associates, "Growth in the Canadian Oil Sands," 2009, p.18; Web Support Site, *Black Bonanza* Footnotes—Chapter 5. < * >

Energy Resources Conservation Board ordered a 50 percent cut-back until the problem was fixed. Suncor is now building its huge $20.6-billion Voyageur project, which will cost $9 billion for SAGD wells and surface facilities at Firebag and $12 billion for an upgrader. Production should rise to 370,000 barrels a day when the project is complete in 2012, rivaling the volume produced at a strip mine.

Suncor is now the owner of the MacKay River SAGD site with its purchase of Petro-Canada. Phase one performed well, with output rising toward 30,000 barrels a day. But with rising costs and Alberta's decision to raise royalties, Phase two is in a holding pattern.

Husky Energy's Tucker project also had problems with positioning its first wells, leading to "massive thermal inefficiencies, with heat being lost to the water at the bottom of the reservoir rather than soaked up by the bitumen in the pay zone," according to engineers at Calgary-based Ross Smith. Husky has learned from its experiences, and is fixing the problem, expecting to recover about 352 million barrels of bitumen over the next thirty-five years.

EnCana has been getting good results by increasing in consecutive phases of 30,000 barrels a day, and is aiming for production of 435,000 barrels a day (gross) by 2016, including 180,000 barrels a day from Foster Creek and 220,000 barrels a day from Christina Lake, both owned fifty-fifty with ConocoPhillips, plus EnCana's wholly-owned Borealis project is coming on-stream in 2015, which will produce 35,000 barrels a day. EnCana also operates the Senlac project in Saskatchewan.

These outputs compare favorably with Syncrude's capacity of more than 350,000 a day.

Perhaps the worst SAGD experience happened at Total's Joslyn SAGD project in northeastern Alberta in May 2008, when pressurized steam burst up through the thin cap rock, blasting out a crater twenty-two yards (20 m) wide and five and a half yards (5 m) deep. No one was hurt in the blast, but Total engineers had to go back to the drawing board to prevent a recurrence of such an expensive accident.

* * *

The major downside of SAGD and CSS is that they are voracious consumers of natural gas, while mines like Syncrude are generating more and more of their own energy from fuel gas and coke produced during upgrading. As Syncrude's Jim Carter says, "We could get off the natural gas pipeline. By just gasifying more of the heavy end of the barrel, we'd likely take out asphaltinenes. We can gasify those. But it's big capital investment and it doesn't make sense as long as gas prices are in the range that we are seeing them in today."[12] Syncrude mainly imports natural gas to provide hydrogen for upgrading its heavy crude. But most SAGD companies have to import gas to make steam for melting oil off sand, to generate electricity for their operations, and to create the hydrogen needed if they upgrade the bitumen.

Producers need to be near a source of fresh or brackish water and build large water recycling facilities to generate the copious amounts of hot water and steam needed. However, SAGD is proving more environmentally friendly than mining, as facilities are built on removable gravel and it disturbs no more than 15 percent of surface land in the area. No additional surface or groundwater is needed, and there is no tailings pond problem. Suncor's Firebag also husbands energy by recycling water in a closed system to generate steam.

A mine such as Syncrude now reuses 88 percent of all the water required for extraction. It currently pulls 47 million cubic yards (36 million cubic m) from the river, but also uses its stored 335 million cubic yards (256 million cubic m) of water that it continuously cycles through the extraction process.

---

[12] William Marsden, *Stupid to the Last Drop*, Knopf, 2007. p. 162.

The price of gas is a major governor of the industry, and higher prices have the potential to seriously slow down Sands development. A gas cost of US$5.00 per barrel of SAGD bitumen is decent, but SAGD economics don't look very good at twice the price unless, of course, the price of oil goes up concurrently.

In 2007, oilsands producers sucked in 13 percent of Canada's natural gas, enough to heat 6 million average-sized homes. With the rise of SAGD, demand from the Sands has nearly tripled to 1.1 billion cubic feet (bcf) a day. Natural Resources Canada estimates that by 2030, the Sands could consume five times more, up to 60 percent of Canada's annual natural gas supply. This pinpoints the urgent need to engineer new upgrading and energy technologies.

Nuclear is being talked about for power, but most people in the oil patch prefer to invest in gasification. Most engineers I talked to don't trust the nuclear option, and think it's too expensive. However, Calgary's Canadian Energy Research Institute (CERI), says that twenty to twenty-five nuclear reactors could serve all of the industry's needs. French oil company, Total, says that to produce its planned 200,000 barrels a day, it will need at least 3,300 metric tons of steam per hour, or the output of a 2,600 megawatt power plant.

The fuel would be easy to get—the nearby Key Lake mine in Saskatchewan is the largest uranium milling operation in the world and can supply 16 percent of global production. Ontario's Bruce Power and French nuclear giant Areva are standing by, waiting for the call.

•   •   •

Since natural gas makes up nearly two-thirds of the entire operating expense of a SAGD facility, the threat of rising prices prompted a search for sustainable ways to generate and recycle heat. Several newer steamless in situ technologies have been tried out as well, and several of these have been patented. Roger Butler also developed the VAPEX process—vapor-assisted petroleum extraction—that injects cold solvents like ethane or propane instead of higher cost steam, to displace oil and reduce its viscosity in a vapor chamber. When the heavy oil surfaces, the solvents are stripped off and recycled. VAPEX requires no water, no processing, nor any recycling and is 25 percent lower in capital costs than the SAGD process. Operating costs seem to be 50 percent less than the SAGD process.

In situ combustion (ISC) is another way forward. One patented process, ET-DSP, uses electrical heating to get bitumen to flow into simple vertical wells. The process involves passing an electrical current through large vertical underground electrodes placed in a grid pattern. Supporters claim this technology can produce an equivalent volume of bitumen in a tenth of the time required by SAGD, while using substantially less energy and water.

Petrobank Energy is using a promising ISC approach, called THAI (for toe to heel air injection), which also relies on horizontal wells and uses no water for production. The operator injects compressed air to generate a slow fireflood underground that drives oil to the extractors. The THAI process may have higher recovery rates and lower costs than SAGD, due to the minimal use of natural gas and water. It also has lower greenhouse gas emissions. THAI technology can also operate in reservoirs that are lower in pressure or quality, or have more shale.

"Combustion has always been seen as the Holy Grail because it's more efficient," says Chris Bloomer, Petrobank vice president and director of heavy oil, "but it's hard to manage." The company found that vertical wells didn't work out well. "You have to keep injecting more and more air to keep up a steady flow." Cool air was lowering the heat of the combustion, which meant the fire did not completely consume all the oxygen, resulting in oily emulsions that were difficult to process.

In the early 1990s, Malcolm Greaves, professor of chemical engineering at the University of Bath, found that drilling a vertical injection well at the toe of a horizontal production well at the bottom of the reservoir, could control the combustion air and the pressure would also lift the oil. Says Bloomer, "You're always having fresh air, so you can sustain high temperatures and can manage the combustion front more efficiently." Petrobank has done two successful pilot projects so far, starting with electricity off the Alberta grid to power its air compressors. The THAI process partially upgrades hydrocarbons in the reservoir by burning through the lowest-grade fraction, especially the high carbon coke, which saves diluent costs during processing. It also releases gases that can be used to fuel the compressors. "In a larger, commercial project, we will be self-sustaining," says Boomer. "We'll produce upgraded oil and our own power."[13]

• • •

One of the most promising ways out of the natural gas dilemma is a closed-loop SAGD process, which Nexen is perfecting at Long Lake.[14]

The Long Lake SAGD and upgrading project, a fifty-fifty joint venture of Nexen Inc. and OPTI Canada Inc., was sanctioned in February 2004 with a projected cost of $3.4 billion. It uses patented technology to produce its own fuel from gasified bitumen.

Unfortunately, the project ran into serious delays and a huge cost overrun to over $6.1 billion, mostly due to the construction boom and the cost of labor and services. But the company also decided it had to add more steam generation capacity and a sulphur recovery unit at a cost of $400 million. When it started up in August of 2008, Long Lake was only producing half the bitumen needed by the upgrader and had to buy from other producers.

---

[13] Bridget Mintz Testa. "Tar on Tap, "Power & Energy," *Mechanical Engineering*, December, 2008; Web Support Site, *Black Bonanza* Footnotes—Chapter 5. < * >
[14] See the animation on the Web Support Site, *Black Bonanza* Maps & Charts—Oil Sands Development.

Long Lake's eighty-one well pairs have an intended capacity of 72,000 barrels of bitumen a day, which will be converted to 60,000 barrels a day of synthetic crude oil.

Unlike conventional SAGD operations, Long Lake uses feedstocks derived from its own bitumen to fuel the project, which will give Long Lake the SAGD industry's lowest operating costs, and perhaps point the way to a more self-sustaining industry.

Today, there are more than fifty SAGD operations in the Sands learning by doing, and moving up the learning curve. It's estimated they will be producing more than a million barrels of bitumen a day by 2012.

• • •

So what of the inventor, the father of SAGD? There are those in the engineering community who speak Roger Butler's name with hushed reverence, but Butler was always modest about his fantastic discovery. He was quite proud of what he had done, and often cracked that Imperial Oil had missed the bucket by not continuing his research. Butler always showed reporters and pilgrims who visited his home two bottles filled with sticky black liquid. One contained the first heavy oil from Cold Lake; the second, a bottle he calls "more precious than all the finest scotch on the planet." It held the very first heavy oil produced in the world using SAGD.[15]

Dr. Roger Butler, the inventor of the SAGD and related VAPEX processes, died in May of 2005.

• • •

One could almost say the oil sands are one big science project.
—Deborah Yedlin, *The Calgary Herald*

---

[15] Mark Lowey, "An Interview with Roger Butler," *Alberta Oil Magazine*, April 1, 2006; Web Support Site, *Black Bonanza* Footnotes—Chapter 5. < * >

Canadian Prime Minister Stephen Harper has called tapping the oil sands of the Athabasca a bigger project than building the Great Wall of China. A total of $90 billion has been spent since 2000, and an additional $130 billion in development is underway or planned.

A lot of this money is going into R&D and a number of fantastic projects that are not just cutting back the environmental footprint of the Sands, but giving operators a lot more bitumen for the buck. We have already looked at THAI, VAPEX, Nexen's Long Lake closed-loop solution, but there are several other very cool developments in the field that should warm the hearts of all green activists every-where, and that includes just about everybody today:

- Glenn Schmidt's Calgary start-up, Laricina Energy, has filed for a patent on its solvent-cyclic SAGD technology[16], that the company claims can lower the steam-to-oil ratio by 50 percent and can be tacked on to current projects. The tech-nique involves, among other things, circulating propane in advance, so you can soften bitumen before steam chamber growth. Schmidt says companies can now recover twice the oil for the same amount of steam, cutting gas and water use for much better project economics.[17]

- Canadian Natural engineers have come up with a way to capture nearly all the carbon in oilsands mining and at the same time compact the tailings pond quicker. Murray Edwards of Canadian Natural says, "basically, when you produce a barrel of oil sands you take the sand, you haul it in a truck and you put it through a process to remove the sand from the bitumen oil. And in that process you release carbon, because carbon is naturally contained in the sand. In our project, as part of that process the largest release of

---

[16] Laricina Energy, "Capturing Opportunity Through Innovation"; Web Support Site, *Black Bonanza* Footnotes—Chapter 5. < * >
[17] See the Laricina home page; Web Support Site, *Black Bonanza* Footnotes—Chapter 5. < * >

carbon takes place in a thing called our hydrocheater. The hydrocheater actually allows you to capture that carbon in fairly pure concentrations. So in our process we're capturing that carbon. We've developed a process now where you can re-inject that carbon back into the tailings pond, and a process takes place where the carbon dioxide actually binds with the tailings of sand, and the end result is that carbon gets sequestered back into the Earth."[18]

- Bruce McGee's company, E-T Energy Ltd., claims it can produce oil at a profit with prices at $26 a barrel. Like heating molasses in a microwave, E-T's process puts electrodes deep underground in the bitumen deposit. When the power is turned on, a current passes through the oil sand and bitumen starts flowing into the collector well. No ugly mine, no tailings ponds, no greenhouse gas-spewing steam boilers. Just a big electric stove element in the ground. "Once we get out there, we're going to have more barrels on our balance sheet than Saudi Arabia in a very short period of time," says McGee. "If the price of oil stays at $40 a barrel, it will replace mining," predicts vice president of operations Craig McDonald.[19]

Meanwhile, back at the university labs in Edmonton and Calgary, there is some leading edge work going on that will make bitumen busting cheaper and better for the environment:

- Pedro Pereira Almao left the Venezuela of Hugo Chavez in 2003 to become co-director of the Alberta Ingenuity Centre for In Situ Energy (AICISE). AICISE is an idea factory at the University of Calgary that is continuing the work of Roger

---

[18] Remarks at Canada West Foundation, "Western Canada's Energy Future" community dinner, May 28, 2009.
[19] Nathan Vanderklippe, "Can science save the oil sands?" *Globe and Mail*, April 24, 2009; Web Support Site, *Black Bonanza* Footnotes—Chapter 5. < * >

Butler. Pereira Almao's main work involves using tiny nano catalysts underground, in situ, to replace the monster, billion-dollar upgraders that presently turn sticky bitumen into sweet crude oil. Pereira Almao is co-inventor of a process called aquaconversion, where steam and a catalyst extract hydrogen from coke or carbon-laden asphaltenes. If all goes according to his vision, it will work like this:

- Operators inject steam into the underground reservoir to heat the bitumen to 200 Celsius to get it flowing.

- When the bitumen gets warm enough, they then inject a mix of oil and the nano-catalyst, which looks a bit like sifted pastry flour, into the well and let it percolate through the bitumen.

- When the well monitor says conditions are ripe, the operators inject oxygen to ignite a small amount of bitumen and create a 450 Celsius "hot zone," where the catalyst and steam combine to crack the hot bitumen into smaller molecules and take up hydrogen from the coke.

- When the conversion is complete, operators pump the upgraded oil to the surface, where it is cleaned and pipe-lined to the refinery.

- Down below, the process continues, as the heat moving out from the hot zone liquefies more bitumen, cutting the need to make more steam.

"We are creating a reactor," says Pereira Almao. We are creating a zone that we can control. We can even control the size of it." With this process, companies will actually create refinable oil underground, leaving waste products such as sulphur, heavy metals, and carbon dioxide behind in the depleted reservoirs, hundreds of yards below.

- AICISE co-director, Steve Larter, a geochemist born in Britain, is working on monitoring what goes on underground using chemical analysis. "These reservoirs aren't like homogeneous tanks of sand," he says. "They have shale, they've got faults and they're basically very complicated. Even within one well, bitumen can be up to thirty times more viscous at the bottom of a deposit than at the top." Larter is also looking at biotechnology, and is starting a field test near Lloydminster, Saskatchewan to harness naturally occurring microbes to the job of fermenting unrecovered heavy oil into methane. Calgary producer Nexen is hosting the Lloydminster experiments.

- Scientists at COSI in Edmonton are looking at ways to do low-impact mining in mid-level deposits which are too shallow for SAGD, as well as "non-aqueous extraction," that doesn't use any water to produce bitumen, but instead relies on mineral sieves, acid, grinding, and heat. Goodbye tailings ponds. COSI's Steven Kuznicki used to work in New Jersey's chemical industry, where he helped develop a breakthrough molecular sieve that removed lead from drinking water. A molecular sieve is a kind of nano catalyst that can screen out impurities and let through the good stuff. The oil patch is increasingly using low-cost catalysts like these to help crack crude and liquefy gas. Kuznicki's team is also looking at solvents, and a water-free way to upgrade bitumen in situ. It works by injecting the molecular sieve into the deposit and then applying heat. The molecular sieve absorbs most of the undesirable stuff, leaving a much lighter oil that is pumped up, diluted, and piped to the refinery. The molecular sieve is cheap enough to be left behind underground.[20]

• • •

---

[20] Bruce White, "Dawn of the Clean Oil Sands," *Alberta Venture*, August 1, 2008; Web Support Site, *Black Bonanza* Footnotes—Chapter 5. < * >

The first years of the twentieth century saw strong steady growth in the Sands as mining matured and a small armada of SAGD companies came on the scene. Here's why:

- Companies with integrated surface mining/upgrading projects saw a sharp reduction in operating costs as the engineers got to work computerizing operations, recycling water and recapturing heat, cutting back on tailings, making their own fuel gas from coke and adopting many new technologies.

- Butler's SAGD method for in situ bitumen recovery opened massive new areas deep underground.

- Advances in horizontal well technology and well monitoring improved SAGD returns, allowing recovery of over 75 percent of deposits in some cases.

- Ottawa and Alberta leveled the playing field and set up a generic fiscal regime that gave all developers stable and predictable royalty and tax treatment.

- Conventional oil production in North America continued declining while demand continued to be strong.

- World crude oil prices stayed firm, and with the entry of India and China as mega consumers, optimism reigned regarding future oil prices.

But as oil people all know, the party can't last forever, and it was hangover time. Good times usually generate what Alan Greenspan famously called "irrational exuberance," and déjà vu was happening all over again. In 2007 and 2008, demand started seriously to outstrip supply, and a global commodity boom erupted fueled by hedging, hoarding, and the demands of China, India, and the other emerging nations. Price wars lifted metallurgical coal from $100 to $300 a ton (a few years ago it was $45). Potash, most of it produced in Saskatchewan, rocketed from $176 to $576 per ton (from only $30 in 1999). More ominously, the price of rice rose from $60 per ton to $1,000 per ton in the same period.

The price of oil is one of the governors of the world's economies and, perhaps, *the* most important price of all. In 2008, the oil market went mad, whipped by speculators and out-of-control hedge fund trading, while panic drove the price of crude up to a stratospheric $148 a barrel at the peak. The crash, when it came, was severe and the price landed with a sickening thud at $38 in February 2009.

• • •

With the bust came a severe banking and capital crunch, but after only a few months of settling, lower costs actually led to an upsurge in oil sands activity.

While the producing companies hunkered down burning capital and waiting for the deep freeze to end, there was carnage in the oil patch as thousands of jobs were slashed and many service companies went out of business. But there was also delight, as the nightmarish cost increases abated, suppliers came begging on their hands and knees, and there were sweet bargains to be had everywhere for people with cash.

Husky Energy and BP, who had paused development of phase one of their Sunrise SAGD project when costs reached an outrageous $4.5 billion, were now finding they could probably make the "sun rise" on Sunrise for only $2.5 billion. Husky CEO, John Lau, happily stated at his 2009 annual meeting that the market for steel, equipment, and labor was "completely different" from a year earlier. Sunrise would produce 60,000 barrels a day at an operating cost below $30 a barrel, and the "dilbit" (diluted bitumen) would be upgraded at BP's refinery in Toledo, Ohio.

The two companies quite naturally slowed down development of Sunrise to capture the lower costs expected from the oil price downturn.[21]

• • •

By early 2010, it cost an integrated mining project such as Syncrude about $32 to produce one barrel of bitumen. This cost includes the removal of overburden, mining the oil sands, and extracting the bitumen from the sands.

Add to this the cost of about $15.50 a barrel to upgrade the heavy bitumen so a conventional refinery can turn it into diesel fuel or gasoline.

At the same time, the Suncor Firebag SAGD project averaged close to $20 a barrel to produce a barrel of bitumen.

These costs do not include royalties, income taxes, interest, and so on.[22]

At current rates, governments will reap $123-billion in revenue from the Sands between 2000 and 2020. Federal corporate and other taxes will take out $51 billion, while the Alberta government will get $44 billion. The rest will go to local municipal governments, largely in Alberta.[23]

• • •

The first time I visited the Sands was on a dull October day in the 1980s with a busload of bored financial analysts from Toronto. There were no tourists. The Fort McMurray Oil Sands Interpretive

---

[21] Claudio Cattaneo. "Sunrise costs almost halved: Husky CEO." *Financial Post*, April 21, 2009; Web Support Site, *Black Bonanza* Footnotes—Chapter 5. < * >

[22] CAPP estimates.

[23] Govinda R. Timilsina, et al., "Economic Impacts of Alberta's Oil Sands," Canadian Energy Research Institute, October 2005, p.98; Web Support Site, *Black Bonanza* Footnotes—Chapter 5. < * >

Centre, opened in 1985, was empty. The Syncrude operation was idling because of some conveyor glitch, so the engineers and drivers were happy to chat, welcoming the break.

Today, it is completely different. Shutdowns are few, and the whole computerized operation runs like "hell on wheels." Companies run popular plant tours complete with screaming kids and hands-on bitumen demos.[24] Families gaze at the amazing devastation from a distance, and ask other families to take their pictures next to monster truck tires or the rusting hulks of the discarded bucket wheelers, each bigger than a brontosaur. Then they are herded over to look at the buffalo grazing on the reclaimed tailings pond. Many visitors are clearly Newfoundlanders, probably cousins of the workers who have made Fort McMurray into what they call their own "Fort McNewfie." But there are also license plates in the parking lot from all over North America.[25] Maybe it's no surprise that "Mordor" on the Athabasca has become such a tourist attraction. There's been so much press about how disastrous it is, so now it has a persona, much like a super-sized monstrous, oily version of Amy Winehouse. Tabloid-loving people like to see the ugliness up close.

There's also a Jerry Springer-like scrap going on in the media and blogosphere between warmists or alarmists and skeptics or deniers about all the greenhouse gas (largely steam) you can see belching from the smokestacks. Even though the Sands only accounts for about .01 percent of the world's greenhouse gas emissions, these big plants make for great visual backdrops in the nightly news media clip business.

Yes, it may be dirty and reek of sulphur, but the world's ugliest mine and biggest industrial project is attracting world-class attention. Bill Gates and Warren Buffett, the richest guys in the world, jetted up to the Sands in the summer of 2008 to make sure the riches were

---

[24] Oil Sand Separation Demonstration; Web Support Site, *Black Bonanza* Video—Production. < * >
[25] For some YouTube home videos and a Stan Rogers song about the tar sands sponsored by the Carpenters Union, please visit the Web Support Site, *Black Bonanza* Video—Music. < * >

real and their Gates Foundation money was in safe hands. At the other end of the spectrum, you'll see backpack-toting boys and girls from East or West coast college towns, weaned on green, coming to witness "Mordor" in person.

Fort MacMurray's campgrounds and hotels are packed in the summer with all manner of humanity, and out at the airport, pilots make big bucks flying enviro-journalists and other gawkers up and over the shimmering river, following the billowing plumes of steam, the flaring gas candles, and the enormous black sandbox where tiny Tonkas roar around beside toxic tailing ponds.

I catch myself asking, "Where the hell is Michael Moore?"

At the end of the 1990s, a new type of tourist started arriving, as the richest and best-endowed green groups enlisted celebrities to visit the Sands and express their horror about the destruction of the boreal forest. Newly minted green groupies like Canadian star Neve Campbell, star of the movie *Scream*, visited the Sands and, well, screamed. You get the picture.

Globe-trotting climate activists eagerly topped up their carbon credits and made the pilgrimage. Journalists joined the caravan, just as they had been doing for the past quarter century, snapping shots of Brigitte Bardot and Paul McCartney on the ice floes of the Gulf of St. Lawrence, snuggling up to baby seals. But the whitecoat seal pups were no longer being killed. Now the editors back home wanted news and views of tar sands and polar bears. Meanwhile, Greenpeace eco-warriors, knowing full well that funds had to be raised and eyeballs assaulted, stormed the fence of a mine again in the summer of 2009, disguised as Shell employees. They chained themselves inside a heavy hauler, hung up their dirty oil banners, took pictures on their smart phones, and uploaded them wirelessly to Flickr.[26] Yes indeed, it was "Tar Wars" time again.

---

[26] Greenpeace Canada Photostream on Flickr; Web Support Site, *Black Bonanza* Footnotes—Chapter 5. < * >

6

Tar Wars

Oil versus the Environment?

*North amid their noisome pits lay the first of the great
heaps and hills of slag and broken rock and blasted earth,
the vomit of the maggot-folk of Mordor ...*
　　　　　　　　　　—J.R.R. Tolkien, *Lord of the Rings*

When British author Rudyard Kipling told Albertans in 1903 that
they had "all hell for a basement," he was offering them a sincere
compliment. But today, critics of oilsands development are taking Kipling literally and blackening the reputation of the Sands
by comparing it to Mordor, the fictional black province in J.R.R.
Tolkein's fantasy trilogy, *Lord of the Rings*.

To Tolkien, Mordor was a "great mire of reeking mud and foul
smelling pools," where "great engines crawl across the field" and
orcs slave away feverishly underground. Here, "nothing lived, not
even the leprous growths that feed on rottenness. The gasping
pools were choked with ash and crawling muds, sickly white and
grey, as if the mountains had vomited the filth of their entrails
upon the lands about. High mounds of crushed and powdered
rock, great cones of earth fire blasted and poison stained, stood

like an obscene graveyard in endless rows, slowly revealed in the reluctant light."

Today, referring to the Sands as Canada's Mordor makes for very good press and helps attract scores of young pilgrims to the movement, but of course Maude Barlow knows that. In February 2009, Ms. Barlow, chairwoman of the Council of Canadians, decided to take a helicopter trip over the Sands to see the problem firsthand. Later, back in Edmonton, she held a press conference and compared the mines to the bleak, desolate landscape of Mordor, ruled by the Dark Lord Sauron.[1]

"When you experience the tar sands," said Barlow, in her best money quote, "you understand that this is Mordor, the place where nature has to die."

Barlow, newly appointed as an unpaid "Senior Advisor" to the United Nations (UN) on global water, is a well-known activist in Canada. She's a close collaborator of Ottawa's Polaris Institute, which specializes in water and tar sands issues. In 2008, Tony Clarke of Polaris wrote a book called *Tar Sands Showdown: Canada and the New Politics of Oil In An Age Of Climate Change*. Polaris now has its own dedicated oilsands attack website, Tar Sands Watch at www.tarsandswatch.org . Other partners on the same band of the political spectrum include the Canadian Centre for Policy Alternatives and the self-declared "nonpartisan" Parkland Institute at the University of Alberta.[2]

When pressed by Edmonton's finest "maggot folk" journalists to explain her Mordor comment, Barlow elaborated, "I wasn't being cute." She said she saw "steam rising from the ground," and (even though it was hibernation time), she saw "no birds in the sky or animals on the ground.... We were devastated by what we saw and smelled and experienced."

---

[1] One journalist allegedly asked Barlow, "Is Sauron Dick Cheney?"
[2] In Alberta, you're either Progressive Conservative or Non-Partisan.

Barlow told them she was deeply shocked by her experience. "The air is foul, the water is being drained and poisoned and giant tailing ponds line the Athabasca River. What stunned me from the air is how close they are to the Athabasca River and what might happen if there was a spill." Barlow said she was going to take her concerns about protecting the water supplies of the Athabasca to the floor of the United Nations General Assembly.

In truth, Barlow's Council of Canadians is fairly middle-of-the-road for Canada, and lines up pretty well with the policy of the country's union-backed New Democratic Party. When pressed, critics like Barlow are offended by the sulfurous stink of the Sands, but do not want a full stop to current oil extraction—thousands of good trades and construction jobs are at stake, particularly for laid-off Ontario autoworkers. But they really would appreciate a pause to look at the environmental impact on downstream areas like Fort Chipewyan. And green jobs are, of course, cleaner.

Jerry Lamphier of the *Edmonton Journal* spoke for a lot of weary Albertans when he snorted:

It's not that I don't appreciate it when Council of Canadians chief Maude Barlow, actress Neve Campbell, or their eco-warrior soul mates take time out of their busy schedules to fly out here to the frontier for a few photo ops. Clearly, their recent visits took real commitment. Not to mention excellent speechwriting skills. I particularly enjoyed Barlow's slick put-down of the oil sands by likening it to the bleak kingdom of Mordor, in Lord of the Rings. How awfully clever of her. As for Campbell, the Scream Queen managed to look both fashionable and "horrified," as she put it, during her all-too-brief visit to the ol' tar pit, which was conveniently captured by a Vanity Fair photographer.

Sadly, the glamorous Hollywood star had to jet off to Paris shortly after her brief stopover in Oilberta. I look forward to her return. Maybe she'll deign to talk to us plebeians in the local media next time. Must be oh so demanding to be both a horror flick star and an environmental expert.[3]

Back home, Barlow helped organize a Tar Sands Film Festival with the Sierra Club Canada at the University of Ottawa, in advance of President Obama's visit to Ottawa on February 19, 2009. The theme was, "Canada is trying to sell dirty tar sands oil as a solution to U.S. energy needs—our message is 'Don't Buy It!'" Films included *Tar Sands: The Selling of Canada*, and *The Dark Side of the Boom: Canada's Mordor*.

• • •

Canada's oil sands are now the major whipping boy of European and American green groups fighting the "Great Climate War." Canada is an easy target. It's a breeze to beat up on America's little brother and the world's boy scout.

When I began this book I was curious to find out more about the roots of all this attention. Is it because the world is jealous of Canada? Because Canada has abundant fresh water lakes, hydro power, gold, potash, uranium, wheat, scenery, seals, polar bears, Pamela Anderson, red-coated mounties, and now a trillion barrels of dirty oil too?

Apparently so, because the Sands have become the Rodney Dangerfield of petroleum—they "don't get no respect."

In the past few years, the mass media, perhaps whipped by President Obama's call for the U.S. to end its reliance on foreign oil, has focused its spotlight increasingly on the Sands, smelling blood. Members of the new profession of "environmental journalism" have become climate change cheerleaders, going after the Sands using their very best schoolyard taunts.

---

[3] Gerry Lamphier, "Learning to Love the Oilsands." *The Ottawa Citizen*, November 17, 2008; Web Support Site, *Black Bonanza* Footnotes—Chapter 6. < * >

Holding their noses at the stink coming from Canada's majestically ugly strip mines, they happily dub them "the biggest environmental crime on the planet" and "the worst environmental disaster in history."

Even Canadians like Simon Dyer of Alberta's Pembina Institute hasn't been able to resist joining the fun, calling the Sands "the worst project in the world." Toronto's Environmental Defence has also chimed in, producing a report called "Canada's Toxic Tar Sands: The Most Destructive Project on Earth." "With the tar sands," says Environmental Defence, "Canada has become the world's dirty energy superpower."

Calgary journalist, Andrew Nikiforiuk, backed by the Suzuki Foundation and Greenpeace, bluntly called his book *Tar Sands: Dirty Oil and the Future of a Continent*, and Montreal writer, William Marsden, taunted Albertans, calling his book *Stupid to the Last Drop*.

So what's going on here? Why are these enviro journalists so obsessed by trashing the tar patch and calling it the "biggest environment crime" on the planet when there are so many more worthy offenders?

Several genuine environmental crimes come to mind, for example, Saddam Hussein's draining of the Iraqi marshes, or the Soviet Union's use of the Aral Sea to grow cotton, which turned the whole region into a desert. But the Sands pale before the new China, model for growth, which builds another coal-fired power station every three days. And let's not forget the U.S. electric power generating industry that pumps out forty-four times the carbon emitted by Athabasca oilsands plants. The single top emitter in the U.S., the Scherer plant in Juliet, Georgia, spews out 25.3 million tons a year of carbon dioxide (CO_2) (not counting noxious substances like sulfur dioxide), compared to total emissions from all the Athabasca Sands of 40 million tons of relatively clean CO_2, primarily from the burning of natural gas to make steam, electricity, and hydrogen.

Note these enviro scribblers carefully use the word "tar," and scornfully demonize it as "dirty oil," as if it were some kind of devil's brew and not that sweet golden syrup coming from the Middle East that we lovingly refine and pump into our Priuses.

Okay, granted, bitumen's a few hydrogen atoms short of sweet, but Canada's bituminous sands are not "tar sands"—tar is a substance made from coal—they are properly oil sands. They were defined that way by Dr. Karl Clark fifty years ago. But who cares? In the battle for ratings and journalistic standing, "tar" is a dirtier word and the Sands make better copy. Who cares about China? Blame Canada.

Yet Canada is a fairly benign culprit, emitting a mere 1.9 percent of total greenhouse gas emissions (2006 data), whereas the European Union, often touted as achieving its greenhouse gas (GHG) targets, emits 13.8 percent despite its 196 nuclear power plants which emit no CO_2. Meanwhile, China produces 21.5 percent and the U.S. 20.2 percent.

Canada comes in at number twelve in the 2008 Environmental Performance Index, ahead of countries like Denmark at twenty-six, Ireland at thirty-five, the U.S. at thirty-nine, and Australia at forty-six. Although Canada went from the number eight spot in 2006 to twelve in 2008, its actual score in 2008 was higher (86.6) that in 2006 (84).

• • •

To explore the background of all of this enthusiastic trashing of the Sands, I went back in time and looked at the history of the global warming scare, now about forty years old.[4] Originally, in the 1970s, the temperature trend was toward global cooling, and journalists and the U.N. whipped up terror stories about the coming of a new Ice Age, but there were a few maverick climatologists who claimed it could go the other way.

---

[4] See the Web Support Site, *Black Bonanza* Timeline—Environmental Movement. < * >

During the administration of George Bush senior, however, the U.S. thrust suddenly changed to warming, and funding available for climate science jumped from $170 million to $2 billion a year. Fueled by this cash, computers were bought, researchers hired, and data input, and soon their tweaked statistical models tended to confirm the theory of AGW—anthropogenic global warming.

Why this sudden interest in warming? Some have suggested the movement began in England, when Margaret Thatcher, whose husband was a British Petroleum executive, wanted to move Britons away from coal to cleaner North Sea gas and, at the same time, skewer her enemies, the Red-leaning coal miner unions. She too gave generous funding to climate scientists, and especially to the U.K. weather office at Hadley for supercomputers and climate modeling. The Americans followed suit, and soon well-funded scientists with supercomputers were busy building enormous models using data from weather stations, tree rings, and satellites.

Some critics of the movement feel that genuine environmentalism went into the ditch when the debate was gradually reframed along one obsessive line—global warming. By the late 1990s, a large El Niño and other heat events conspired to make global warming front and centre. An eager Al Gore, deprived of the U.S. presidency, turned his oratorical skills to the subject and the rest is public relations history.

• • •

In the 1990s, with the Sands up and running and SAGD promising an energy bonanza, two issues arose which had a direct bearing on the environmental impact of Athabasca operations and on world, especially North American, energy security:

AGW (Anthropogentic Global Warming)—the theory, promoted by the United Nations Intergovernmental Panel on Climate Change (IPCC), that man-made global warming through CO_2

emissions is causing desertification, polar melting, sea level rise, and all manner of other evils.

Peak Oil—this is the theory that world fossil fuel production has passed its peak and we are starting a terrifying slide that will severely impact our standard of living.

Let's look at the impact of the global warming movement on the Sands first. On the subject of AGW, let me get my opinions out in front right away.

You either trust that the global warming crisis is real or you do not. If you are a believer, your mantra is this: we cannot take the chance that the planet will overheat. We must spend billions to stop overheating and subsidize poorer nations who are suffering from climate change.

If you are a nonbeliever, you say that if global warming is real, it is occurring naturally, or the effects are not that serious. Your mantra is, if global warming is not real, why risk wrecking the economy by spending trillions of tax dollars on nothing.

Now, I have to say, I respect the opinions of my friends who truly believe that CO_2 is causing global warming, but as a natural-born skeptic and a historian, I am full of serious doubt. Ten years ago, Michael Mann's "hockey stick" graph seemed to have shown that, after 1,000 years of relative decline, global temperatures had shot up to their highest level in recorded history. The Mann graph provided Al Gore with the "money shot" in his controversial film, *An Inconvenient Truth,* as he used a hydraulic lifter to elevate himself to the top of the chart. Many people were shocked, and bought into the AGW theory. For some, the fight against global warming became an article of faith in a new religion.

To be sure, I totally agree with my friends that we must address environmental pollution of our air and water, and we should clean up the planet. But I believe we have to address all the many ways humanity is damaging our ecosystem without obsessing about a trace gas that helps plants grow. Goats have stripped vegetation from the Mediterranean and the Sahara for centuries, causing top-soil loss and desertification. This can be turned back. We have to do something about cars that release 75 percent of their fuel energy as heat. This is doable, especially with electric vehicles. Our cities are heat sinks; we can cool them with old and new technologies like green roofs. Soot from coal-fired power stations lands on ice and causes it to melt. Likewise, sulfur dioxide and other noxious gases from these power plants cause acid rain and all manner of illness. Polls show that most people are willing to pay more in energy bills for scrubbers to stop these substances from being released. But not billions of dollars more. People are known to rebel from too much taxation.

I have no doubt we can and will move to a clean energy economy (See Chapter 7, The Blue Shift). It's just that I do not buy the CO_2 argument. Not one little bit.

To explain why, I suggest that we must respect human history and despise anyone who tinkers and traffics with historical truth or warps history for political ends. So, when the historian in me looks at the history of climate change[5], he notes that we have had significant periods of naturally occurring heating (The Medieval Warm Period) and cooling (The Little Ice Age) in advance of the Industrial Revolution and the Oil Age. A thousand years ago, Britain was covered in vineyards and Viking farmers tended cows in Greenland. Less than 400 years ago, the sea froze between England and France, and you could drive a sleigh across the Baltic between Poland and Sweden. So when somebody comes along and shows me a chart that says that the climate shifts of 300 to 1,000 years ago never happened, I smell a rat.

To put it mildly, I have been increasingly appalled by the UN IPCC's politicization of both climate science and history.

In the months before this book went to press, the wheels seemingly fell off the AGW cart when a whistle blower released on the

---

[5] See the Web Support Site, *Black Bonanza* Timeline—Climate History. < * >

Internet more than 120 megabytes of e-mails and computer programs hacked from servers at the Climatic Research Unit (CRU) at the University of East Anglia, the world's pre-eminent AGW organization.[6] I, and many others, have been convinced after reading these documents that there has been a concerted attempt by some of the lead IPCC authors to "cook" data and fudge results in order to prove a phenomenon that simply does not exist—global warming caused by CO_2.

It gets worse; the dog ate their data. CRU head, Phil Jones, has now claimed that the researchers trashed their primary magnetic tape and paper files when they moved to new offices and only kept "the value-added (quality controlled and homogenized) data." So now their AGW conclusions and the prize data they gave to the UN can never be checked out properly. This is pathetic. Now, we have no idea how accidentally corrupt or fraudulently altered the CRU's current data might be. It is essentially worthless. And anyone trying to assemble a historical record of temperature changes will have to start from scratch.

Further computer analysis of the leaked CRU program code suggests we are looking at what may be the biggest scientific fraud since Piltdown Man. Either that, or the most astonishing procedural incompetence in the history of science. In their e-mails, the CRU statisticians and their friends in the U.S. describe how to manipulate the proxy data from tree rings and ice cores to minimize past climate variance such as the Medieval Warm Period and the Little Ice Age. Then they discuss re-jigging the proxy series and chopping off end years when it began to diverge from actual thermometer readings in the twentieth century, so they could exaggerate late twentieth century warming. Governments around the world bought their analysis. And why not? It seemed credible. The U.S Environmental Protection Agency used their analysis to build a whole regime of carbon regulations, and even declared the benign gas CO_2 to be an official poison.

---

[6] See www.climategate.org .

So what about the cooling trend we have seen so far in the twenty-first century, a trend still denied by the AGW alarmists? One e-mail writer complains that the earth has been cooling over the last decade and it is a "travesty" that they cannot do anything about it. Why? Because they had painted themselves into a corner; because their statistical tricks with proxy data would not stand up to the solid satellite numbers now coming onstream.

The real travesty is that these researchers largely succeeded in stifling transparent science and open debate over the past ten years and continued to maintain the position that the sky was falling when clearly it was not. In fact, NASA satellite data clearly puts us into a cooling trend for the next few decades.[7]

Looking back over a 10,000-year timescale and the historical record, I find no convincing case that the late twentieth century climate was particularly unusual. And nobody has come up with a way to predict the *actual measured* temperature going forwards, and do it consistently. The data is just not good enough yet.

The other crying shame is how much money and energy has been diverted from real environmental progress and science in pursuit of a foolish political agenda. And finally, the greatest travesty is that the influence of solar weather and the oceans on our climate has been shunted aside in attempting to push the CO_2 argument. To suggest that CO_2 is the only thing at work here is simply asinine.

How on earth did these people think they could get away with their behavior? Maybe they didn't, because their data was coming under heavier and heavier scrutiny. One frustrated AGW author complained to another about freedom of information requests, grumbling, "Man, will this crap ever end?"

So what does all this heat have to do with the Athabasca Sands? Well, it seems that the most radical high priests of the

---

[7] Craig Loehle, "Trend Analysis Of Satellite Global Temperature," *Energy & Environment*, Volume 20: No. 7, 2009; Web Support Site, *Black Bonanza* Footnotes—Chapter 6. < * >

AGW movement, James Hansen, the man who first alerted the U.S. Congress to global warming on June 23, 1988, targets the Athabasca Sands as the world's major incarnation of AGW excess. To solve the global warming problem, says Hansen, we have to "phase out global coal emissions within twenty years and prohibit emissions from unconventional fossil fuels such as tar sands and oil shale."[8] Since U.S. oil shale is impossible to exploit, unless you want to permanently destroy the Colorado River, that leaves the Athabasca Sands as the real demon that must be exorcised. The tar sands, says Hansen, must be shut down.

Hansen, by the way, considers cap and trade "an inefficient compromise, paying off numerous special interests. It must be replaced with an honest approach, raising the price of carbon emissions and leaving the dirtiest fossil fuels in the ground." He proposes a carbon fee at the mine head to drive offending polluters completely out of business.

Many disciples have taken their cues from Hansen's attacks on the Sands. Al Gore has commented that the "oil sands threaten our survival as a species," and "Junkies find veins in their toes when the ones in their arms and their legs collapse. Developing tar sands and coal shale is the equivalent." Canadian professor, Thomas Homer-Dixon, has also parroted Hansen and Gore, asserting that, "The rapacious exploitation of Canada's tar sands has distorted our economy, corrupted our politics, ruined our environment, and turned us, collectively, into a rogue nation of carbon polluters."

Al Gore is a fascinating character, particularly in his attitude toward fossil fuels. Few people realize that his family is intimately close to Occidental Petroleum, the once renegade oil company founded by Armand Hammer, a man who has been described as "the Godfather of American corporate corruption."

------

[8] James Hansen, "Copenhagen summit: Is there any real chance of averting the climate crisis?" *The Observer*, November 29, 2009; Web Support Site, *Black Bonanza* Footnotes—Chapter 6. < * >

Gore's late father, Senator Albert Gore Senior, made a great deal of his wealth while working for Oxy and Hammer. In 1968, he helped Hammer acquire most of the oil concessions in Libya from King Idris. When the elder Gore left the Senate in 1970, Hammer gave him a $500,000-a-year job as the chairman of Island Coal Creek Co., an Occidental subsidiary, and a seat on Occidental's board of directors, where he served for twenty-eight years.[9] So when Al Gore Junior starts up one of his barn-burner speeches about "big oil," it is wise for listeners to retain some sense of perspective.

In the first decade of the twenty-first century, spurred on by Al Gore and his masterful promotional abilities and seemingly unimpeachable statistics, a host of new AGW bureaucracies sprang up at the UN and in most countries of the West. At the same time, many foundations and most of the mainstream media happily went along for the ride on Gore's new green bandwagon.

But what is the payoff here and why has the focus of the AGW debate shifted almost entirely to the oil sands of the Athabasca? Why are they being singled out for demonization, when there are so many other worthy candidates? As the Latins used to say, *cui bono*? Who benefits? Another way of saying the same thing is what my old history professor once told me: Follow the money.

• • •

In essence, the roots of the demonization of the Sands lie in the politics of oil, the attempted polarization of the energy issue along party lines, and rent seeking by certain interest groups and corporations who want to benefit financially from government subsidies and tax breaks.

It also has to do with the weary acceptance by many business people, even in the oil industry, that if environmentalism leads to

---

[9] See for example, "Al Gore: The Other Oil Candidate" (http://corpwatch.org), and "How the Gores, Father and Son, Helped Their Patron Occidental Petroleum" (Center for Public Integrity); Web Support Site, *Black Bonanza* Footnotes—Chapter 6. < * >

taxation like cap and trade, they have to go along with the democratic will of the people, even though they may think it is wrong. If they are going to cope with carbon credits, the reasoning goes, they may as well plan for a cap-and-trade regime so at least they can get some stability by simply passing costs along to the customers. As it stands right now, there is too much instability.

One of the oilsands engineers I interviewed agreed, but he was still furious at what he regarded as unfair attacks by the "climate change mob." He strongly held the opinion that the assault on the Sands was rooted not in environmentalism, "Hell, I'm a dedicated environmentalist," he growled.

We can find clues to how this state of affairs developed by looking at the 2008 U.S. election and the rollercoaster ride of the last few years in the energy and banking industries.

During the 2008 election campaign, Barack Obama took the high green road, and the Democrats correctly bet that tapping into green concerns, harvesting green votes, and beating up on polluting industries could put Obama over the top. It was one of the cornerstones of his victory.

Obama's major campaign was against coal, not against the Athabasca Sands. In several campaign speeches in 2008, he told his adoring audiences that he wanted to "slow the rise of oceans and heal the planet." Both worthy goals, but privately, Obama was less flowery and let it be known that he was going to get tough on America's biggest polluters, especially the coal industry.

"Let me sort of describe my overall policy," he told a hall of San Francisco donors during the campaign.

What I've said is that we would put a cap-and-trade system in place that is as aggressive, if not more aggressive, than anybody else's out there.

I was the first to call for a 100 percent auction on the cap and trade system, which means that every unit of carbon or greenhouse gases emitted would be charged to the polluter. That will create a market in which whatever technologies are out there that are being presented, whatever power plants that are being built, that they would have to meet the rigors of that market and the ratcheted down caps that are being placed, imposed every year.

So if somebody wants to build a coal-powered plant, they can; it's just that it will bankrupt them because they're going to be charged a huge sum for all that greenhouse gas that's being emitted.

Obama's tough talk highlighted the fact that the "United States of Coal" has its own emissions problems. It is, without a doubt, far worse than Canada's. Just a few hundred miles (300 km) west of Washington, Appalachia has seen strip-mining's worst depredations. It's called MTR—mountain top removal. In the last twenty years, coal companies have cut almost 1 million acres of hardwood forests, stripped over 470 mountains, and despoiled 1,000 miles (1,600 km) of river in an area the size of Delaware. The explosive equivalent of several Hiroshima atomic bombs is set off every year in Appalachia, mostly to get out power station coal.

And yet, in 2008, the *National Geographic Magazine*, based in Washington DC, sent out a team of reporters and photographers whose mandate was clearly to blacken the Athabasca Sands. What is going on here, and why all this environmental anguish by Canada's southern neighbor?[10]

It surely begs the question, is the demonization of the Athabasca Sands one way of distracting Americans from the problems in their own backyard? Clearly, it doesn't hurt. Canada's oilsands operations are the world's biggest open-pit mining operation, and because they are far away from heavy population areas, they are a handy target for environmental critics everywhere. But the campaign against the Sands is a great deal more.

---

[10] To be fair to the *National Geographic Magazine*, they published a far more damning article on Appalachian mountaintop removal in March of 2006.

To be fair to Obama, when reporters asked him to comment on the oil sands during his visit to Stephen Harper in Ottawa, he pointed out that the U.S. faced similar environmental concerns with coal-fired electricity. Obama called his country "the Saudi Arabia of coal." The U.S. has 1,522 coal-powered generation plants representing 30.1 percent of world coal production. American coal-fired plants emit forty-four times more carbon than the entire oilsands operation. And America's "Holy Grail" of ethanol production is just as "dirty" as bitumen mining and upgrading; both require the same energy inputs per unit of energy produced.[11]

But U.S. politics is a complicated beast, and there are lots of reasons why Obama can't heal the planet just yet. Congress itself is supplied with life-giving air conditioning thanks to a couple of wheezing old coal power stations on Chesapeake Bay and the Atlantic coast, which spew their emissions out over the ocean. The coal companies won't open clean coal plants with technologies like flue gas treatment, carbon capture, and gasification, until they get major subsidies. There is another consideration for Obama—the U.S. coal unions are loyal supporters of the Democratic Party.

Congress is also a two-headed beast. It may come as a surprise to some people that Democrats are not all supporters of clean energy and Republicans are not all mouthpieces of big oil. In Opensecrets.org's list of major U.S. political donors, the electrical industry leans slightly more toward the Democrats, while the oil and gas sector leans more to the Republicans. Most major corporations fund both parties. There really isn't that much difference between the donkey and the elephant.[12]

---

[11] America also has the world's largest reserves of oil shale, a total to 2.6 trillion barrels. But currently, it takes massive amounts of water to extract oil from shale, and the shale expands 20 percent during production.

[12] See Open Secrets (www.opensecrets.org); Web Support Site, *Black Bonanza* Footnotes— Chapter 6. < * >

However, there are companies and groups that are dedicated to one party or another—"party pets" you might say. Goldman Sachs, for example, is a major backer of the Democrats, although there are a few partners who stubbornly vote Republican.

It may also come as a surprise to learn that many Americans support politicians hoping for some kind of financial benefit. This is not illegal. For example, some of Obama's friends and backers in Chicago, many of whom are enthusiastic supporters of the AGW crusade, have started a carbon exchange that they hope will make them all flush. And the Alberta Clipper pipeline now under construction and approved by Hillary Clinton in spite of protests from the greens, will deliver over 400,000 barrels a day of diluted Canadian bitumen directly to a number of thirsty Chicago refineries.

So is it any wonder that Obama can talk the talk—that's his job—but when reality intervenes, it is Congress that walks the walk?

If you look at U.S. politics from one perspective, the whole global warming crisis could be seen as a way to prepare the American brain for a major policy implant—much higher energy costs and taxes— so hundreds of billions of dollars a year can stay home and not end up in the hands of unfriendly dictators. No politician looking for re-election will raise taxes at the pump if there is a stealthy alternative. What is needed is a political operation to soften up the victim.

On the other hand, higher taxes on energy are appealing to some of us, but only if there are guarantees that the funds raised are not swallowed up into general government expenses, but put into tax credits for green and sustainable energy R&D.

But there is a third perspective, having to do with a sector of the U.S. business community who want not only to profit from green business, but also to profit from cap and trade legislation— the market makers.

• • •

The twin gurus behind the global warming crisis are two men who have been called "the obnoxious octogenarians," eighty-two-year-old billionaire hedge fund operator, George Soros, known as "The Daddy Warbucks of the Democratic Party," and the ubiquitous global character, Maurice Strong, the unlikely progenitor of the cult of green, who is eighty-three.

Strong chairs the Earth Council and is a senior advisor to both the UN and the World Bank. As we have seen, he was the founding CEO of Petro-Canada and is a former executive of Montreal's Power Corporation, owned by the Desmarais family, one of the major investors in French oil company Total, a major oilsands player. Strong began his UN green career in 1971 in the midst of a global cooling scare, when he commissioned a report on the state of the planet called *Only One Earth: The Care and Maintenance of a Small Planet*, co-authored by Barbara Ward and Rene Dubos. *Only One Earth* summarized the findings of 152 leading experts from fifty-eight countries in advance of the first UN meeting on the environment, held in Stockholm in 1972. This was the world's first "state of the environment" report.

In 1972, UN Secretary-General, U Thant, invited Strong to lead the first major UN Conference on the Human Environment in Stockholm, popularly known as "Stockholm" among dedicated greens. "Stockholm" put the green issue squarely on the international agenda and confirmed its close link with development. This led to the founding, in December 1972, of the UN Environment Program (UNEP), with headquarters in Nairobi, Kenya. Strong, of course, was chosen to lead UNEP, the first UN agency to be headquartered in a developing nation. As chief of UNEP, Strong convened the first international expert group meeting on climate change. In 1992, he served as Secretary-General of the fabulous UN Conference on Environment and Development in Rio de Janiero, popularly known as "Rio."

George Soros's major claim to fame is that he beat up the British Treasury, speculating the British pound would go one way, when the Bank of England said differently. He walked away from the casino a billion dollars richer.

Soros is a complex character. He and his Open Society Institute are the nexus of a new liberalism that funded and pulled together impressive forces against resurgent communism, global warming, and the Texas mafia of George W. Bush. Assembled on his side on his side are a band of "brothers and sisters" that include:

Politicians—the Clintons, John Kerry, Barack Obama, and Soros even funded John McCain!

Scientists—James Hansen of NASA and the UN Intergovernmental Panel on Climate Change (IPCC).

Journalists—Bill Moyers of PBS and NBC attack dogs; Chris Matthews and Keith Olbermann, who call rival Bill O'Reilly "the worst person in the world." And in England, there's voluble *Guardian* columnist, George Monbiot, affectionately known as "Moonbat." Monbiot is an eloquent and energetic spinner of apocalyptic visions, arguing that we are into "runaway global warming." His book, *Heat: Burning Planet*, is an earnest manifesto for a new world order.

Bloggers—Well scripted ones like Joe Romm of the Democratic Party's think tank, The Center for American Progress, and author of *Hell and High Water*, who argues that, "a twenty-foot sea level rise is all but inevitable."

Foundations—Pew and a raft of others. Yes, J. Howard Pew, the founder of Athabasca operator, Suncor Energy, is likely rolling in his grave. John F. Kennedy is probably doing the same. His nephew, Joseph Kennedy, runs a nonprofit foundation called Citizens' 877-JOE-4-OIL, that helps poor people heat their homes. Kennedy has run the nonprofit since 2005, which quickly ballooned from a Boston operation to a national one. Unfortunately, he has done this with the assistance of budding Venezuelan dictator Hugo Chavez, who donates nearly all of Kennedy's oil. Joe Kennedy's Chavez connection may turn out to be a severe liability if he ever ponders running for Congress.

Corporations—General Electric and Dupont are just two. Some argue that Dupont, which benefited from the Strong-engineered Montreal treaty limiting atmospheric ozone, already had a patented replacement in the wings and has subsequently made huge profits. GE, owner of NBC television, is also a major player in wind turbines. After GE Capital lost billions in the 2008 crash, they have had to look to other potential profit areas.

Al Gore—Gore's movement against global warming, as well as scores of outlying support foundations, have been heavily backed by Soros and Goldman Sachs. His private British company, staffed by three former Goldman Sachs partners, has just closed two "green funds" after collecting almost three billion dollars. After losing to Bush Junior, Gore set off to restore his finances and more. While he and his entourage of black Escalades generate enough GHG to power a small city, he buys his carbon credits and plows a good deal back into his foundations, particularly Repower America.

Soros has become more and more focused on global warming, and in October 2008 he told PBS commentator, Bill Moyers, that it was "the end of an era" and that the world needed "a whole new paradigm for the economic model of the country, of the world." The key to fixing the global financial meltdown, he said, was fixing the climate meltdown: "Global warming. It requires big investment. And that could be the motor of the world economy in the years to come."

• • •

The value proposition of the 21st century is air and water.
—Richard Sandor, Chairman and CEO,
Chicago Climate Exchange, Inc.

A major backer of Obama and the man who has put the whole cap-and-trade movement on the front burner of U.S. policy, is a brilliant and enigmatic Chicago economics professor, Richard Sandor.[13] Sandor, who has worked for the Chicago Mercantile Association and the Chicago Board of Trade, is the founding genius behind the Chicago Climate Exchange (CCX). Known as "Mr. Derivative," for his groundbreaking work in developing interest rate futures markets, Sandor first proposed the creation of the climate exchange in 2000, just before the signing of the Kyoto Accord on greenhouse gas reduction. Today, Sandor is also chairman of the Chicago Climate Futures Exchange (CCFE)[14] and head of a public company Climate Exchange plc, which owns CCX and CCFE as well as the European Climate Exchange, and is affiliated with the Tianjin Climate Exchange in China, the Montreal Climate Exchange in Canada, and Envex in Australia.

Sandor and his friends are a motley Chicago mob who want to make the Windy City the center of the kind of carbon trading market operation that Enron once considered. Wall Street banking survivor, Goldman Sachs, a major Democratic Party donor, also owns a 10 percent piece of the action. Initial CCX funding of almost $1 million came from the Chicago-based Joyce Foundation, whose board of directors included Barack Obama, then an Illinois state senator.

Current or former UN officials on the climate exchange's eighteen-member advisory board include: Maurice Strong (co-chair); Canadian Elizabeth Dowdeswell, former head of the UNEP;

---

[13] Chicago Climate Exchange; Web Support Site, *Black Bonanza* Footnotes—Chapter 6. < * >
[14] Chicago Climate Futures Exchange; Web Support Site, *Black Bonanza* Footnotes—Chapter 6. < * >

Rajendra Pachauri, head of the UN Intergovernmental Panel on Climate Change; Michael Jammit Cutajar, former executive director of the UN Framework Convention for Climate Change (UNFCCC); and Thomas Lovejoy, former science adviser to UNEP and currently senior adviser to the president of the UN Foundation, which was originally founded with a $1 billion gift from CNN founder, Ted Turner. The UN foundation calls itself "an advocate for the UN and a platform for connecting people, ideas, and resources to help the UN solve global problems." But it is also a political advocacy group for a cap-and-trade system that would be the basis of most of CCX's business. It's probable that if a U.S. cap-and-trade regime comes to pass, Canada will have to engineer or adopt a similar program to keep oilsands taxes and costs in sync with the American program.

CXX is a poor cousin of the much larger CME Group, the world's largest futures exchange founded in 2007 by the merger of the Chicago Mercantile Exchange (The Merc) and the Chicago Board of Trade (CBOT). In 2008, CME became the world's largest energy products exchange when it acquired NYMEX—the New York Mercantile Exchange (See Chapter 6, Peak Oil, for more on NYMEX). The three exchanges run separate operations, with NYMEX specializing in oil, metals, and other commodities.

Sandor theorizes that the way to control air and water pollution is to commoditize it. "If we can make them both commodities then we can both help the planet and help ourselves. These used to be seen as free goods but there isn't enough to go around and in the future these resources will take on precious value. The future may involve water markets in which businesses will trade." For example, "in China, one emissions problem is from smoldering fires in coal mines. If a business could earn emissions credits by putting out those fires they would have the incentive to fix this problem. In India, the methane from cow manure is a huge problem. Could there eventually be a business dealing in cleaning up the animal waste problem there?"

The Chicago and European climate exchanges run voluntary, but legally binding, pilot greenhouse gas reduction and trading programs for emission sources and offset projects.

Presumably, Sandor's vision for Athabasca Sands' operators involves them having to buy water and carbon credits in order to stay in business. The sellers of these credits would use the capital for sustainable and green energy projects.

Sandor may be too much on the bleeding edge. In the fall of 2009, with the recession deepening and Obama's cap-and-trade bill stalling in the Senate, values of carbon contracts on the CCX plunged to ten cents per metric ton, down from $7 a ton in May 2008.

Sandor may be able to salvage things if Congress adopts a modified cap-and-trade program, put the prospects are not good, because cap and trade is an $800 billion program, bigger than TARP (Troubled Asset Relief Program). And according to Declan McCullagh at CBS News Blogs:

> The Obama administration has privately concluded that a cap and trade law would cost American taxpayers up to $200 billion a year, the equivalent of hiking personal income taxes by about 15 percent.
>
> A previously unreleased analysis prepared by the U.S. Department of Treasury says the total in new taxes would be between $100 billion to $200 billion a year. At the upper end of the administration's estimate, the cost per American household would be an extra $1,761 a year.

So, while CCX may not be dead, it will most likely be dormant for several years to come, with the real action on the price of oil taking place on NYMEX.

• • •

Savaging the Sands has become big business and the major green groups, with revenues in the billions, happily tap both public sympathizers as well as rich companies and foundations like Pew, Hewlett, Ford, Tides, and Soros, which let them hire the world's best marketing gurus and ad agencies to tell them what to target to keep the funds flowing—guilt. Akin to the medieval practice of selling indulgences, these groups tap into religious emotions in people and sell redemption.

Since all North American taxpayers are directly and indirectly funding green groups through tax deductions and government programs, it is useful to look at these groups to see which ones have the most focus on the Athabasca Sands, and which are more or less keeping up an anti Athabasca portfolio for fundraising purposes.

The major Canadian groups are branch plants of the American or British behemoths—WWF, Sierra Club, Natural Resouces Defense Council (NRDC), and Greenpeace—and while they compete in the fundraising marketplace, their attack script is remarkably similar, predictably one-sided, and heavily weighted to CO_2 and global warming.

The best of the homegrown groups is the Pembina Institute in Alberta, which is staffed with biology nerds and happily holds the feet of both companies and the Alberta government to the fire. Pembina really cares—they do thorough research and never miss an opportunity to debate the companies. But they do it patiently and respectfully, and I say more power to them. Alberta's recent decision to push the companies to dry up and restore the tailing pond sites is due more than anything to Pembina's tireless lobbying. However, sometimes they can't help adopting extreme language and using the word "dirty" to describe bitumen.

The other major Canadian-based group is the David Suzuki Foundation (DSF). Suzuki is a guru to Canadian greens and produces a highly respected CBC television program, *The Nature of Things*. The DSF is now an elite Al Gore-trained global warming attack dog, run by Jim Hoggan's public relations company in Vancouver. Pro: Suzuki himself is not entirely obsessed by global warming. Con: Suzuki, originally a fruit fly geneticist, sometimes gives the impression he is Zeus on steroids. The DSF funded the Andrew Nikiforiuk book, *Tar Sands: Dirty Oil and the Future of the Continent* and, at the moment, is pretty obsessed with justifying AGW.

The two biggest foreign foundations are:

WWF—Who can argue with Prince Phillip, Duke of Edinburgh? Not me, that's for sure. Very slick marketing, hiring the best ad agencies on the planet and pushing half a billion in revenue a year. Pro: They do excellent mainstream research and conservation work and it's perhaps understandable that they have been tempted to push some of their cash toward demonizing the oil sands and its monstrous carbon footprint. Con: why do they try and copy Greenpeace?

Greenpeace—This gang has amazing survival instincts and still pulls over $200 million a year into their Washington headquarters. They too funded a damning Andrew Nikiforiuk report, and have unfurled their "dirty oil" banners several times on the property of oilsands producers. Pro: They have decent entertainment value and are a model on how to use Web 2.0 viral marketing. Con: These grizzled eco warriors do the same stunts over and over again, and still get on the nightly news, while actively recruiting young rock climbers to scale power plant chimneys.[15]

• • •

Yes, the leaders of the AGW movement are doing business in the marketplace of ideas and, in unguarded moments at the end of a hard bout of lobbying or a long day in meetings, they unwind and say what's really on their minds.

---

[15] A peripheral group is Nature Canada—The Polar Bear People. These people seem to be all marketing, and they won't leave you alone; their polar bear ad pops up on Google all the time, asking you to fill out their global warming petition.

Sometimes, cooling the planet is not the real point. The ultimate goal, and it is breathtaking, is remaking the human race in their own image.

Maurice Strong is quite up front about his aims, telling us that, "The overall goal of climate policy is to create a new economic basis for flows of money to the developing countries," and "We may get to the point where the only way of saving the world will be for industrial civilization to collapse, deliberately seek poverty, and set levels of mortality."[16] But Al Gore, the lead sled dog of the movement, is more guarded and cloaks his feelings in bureaucratic language. In May 2006, he opened up to readers of *Grist Magazine* about the wonders of sowing fear about global warming, and then bestowing redemption on the populace: "I believe it is appropriate to have an over-representation of factual presentations on how dangerous it is, as a predicate for opening up the audience to listen to what the solutions are, and how hopeful it is that we are going to solve this crisis."

Perhaps the most revealing comment comes from Stanford University's Steven Schneider, lead author of the UN's IPCC, who shows how tough it can sometimes be to maintain the AGW stance in public, and still retain a sense of balance:

> On the one hand, as scientists we are ethically bound to the scientific method, in effect promising to tell the truth, the whole truth, and nothing but—which means that we must include all the doubts, the caveats, the ifs, ands, and buts. On the other hand, we are not just scientists but human beings as well. And like most people we'd like to see the world a better place, which in this context translates into our working to reduce the risk of potentially disastrous climatic change. To do that we need to get some broad based support, to capture the public's imagination. That,

---

[16] See my collection of pro and con AGW quotations on the Web Support Site, *Black Bonanza* Quotations—Global Warming. < * >

of course, entails getting loads of media coverage. So we have to offer up scary scenarios, make simplified, dramatic statements, and make little mention of any doubts we might have. This "double ethical bind" we frequently find ourselves in cannot be solved by any formula. Each of us has to decide what the right balance is between being effective and being honest.[17]

Up in Canada, Environment Minister, Christine Stewart, caught off guard but not off camera in Calgary in 1998, put it a little more clearly: "No matter if the science of global warming is all phony... climate change provides the greatest opportunity to bring about justice and equality in the world."

And finally, a confused Steven Guilbeault of Greenpeace Canada, cornered by a reporter blurted out in a 2009 interview, "Global warming can mean colder; it can mean drier; it can mean wetter; that's what we are dealing with."

It is clear that for most participants in this crusade from Strong and Soros on down, the important thing is not really climate change. It is nothing less than global redemption. The tragic thing is, the public is being offered not science, but scary scenarios in a world of endless spin.

* * *

Let's look at the religious impulse behind the attacks on Sands development.

On the surface, the global warming creed seems essentially to be this: Global warming is out of control. When hydrocarbons are burned they release not only energy, but also CO_2. CO_2 traps the sun's heat and pushes up global temperatures. If left unchecked, it will keep warming the earth until: a) the polar icecaps melt; b) the

---

[17] Schneider twists himself into knots discussing this quote and the perils of what he calls "Mediarology." See also an older video of Stephen Schneider talking about global cooling; Web Support Site, *Black Bonanza* Footnotes—Chapter 6. < * >

oceans rise; and c) life as we know it becomes impossible. There is no doubt; the science is settled. The peer-reviewed papers prove this. Forget about the skeptics who are funded by the oil and coal industries. And deliver us from evil.

But for many in the world, fighting the green fight is not just helping out Al Gore and the UN. It is a crusade as mythical as the quest by Tolkein's hobbits to destroy the ring of power and clean up the earth.

Just as in ancient Mesopotamia, apocalyptic thinkers and doomsday cultists have often risen to attack human civilization and progress. They usually emerge from some deep human pessimism about technology or change. Today's environmental doomsday mentality looks at humanity from an extremely pessimistic position, as if it is almost too late to save the world.

Especially in a time of stress, some humans seem to require a simple explanation for sin and corruption, and look for ways to purify the world again in what Norman Mailer once called a "lust for apocalypse." Some of these people tend to see things increasingly in black and white, good and evil, and they tend to look for scapegoats. During the Middle Ages and the Little Ice Age, when Earth had cooled down considerably, people blamed witches for crop failures and burned them to death.

Many purists regard the human race as a pox or a plague on the planet, and like Gulliver's giant king, think humanity is "the worst race of odious little vermin that Nature ever suffered to crawl upon the face of the earth." Human sin and pride are the root causes of most of the world's woes, even the natural ones such as hurricanes, floods, drought, and fires. It's as if God is punishing us for our misdeeds.

Some are even looking for a final violent battle, where the forces of good will triumph over the forces of darkness. That's why the Sands of the Athabasca, which critics insist on calling the "tar sands," are such a strong symbol of darkness and evil. The Sands have it all; they're Tarmageddon.

But as writer Michael Crichton pointed out in 2003, environmentalism has become middle-of-the-road, and "the religion of choice for urban atheists." The carbon footprint symbolizes sinful behavior, and absolution can be gained through carbon-offset schemes. There are even some who want the Almighty to intervene on behalf of the climate.

Lord May, president of the British Association and a former chief scientist to the U.K. government, recently proposed that faith groups should take the lead in policing social behavior, and that religious leaders can play a frontline role in mobilizing people to take action against global warming in order to "save the planet." "The international reach of faith-based organizations and their authoritarian structures give religious groups an almost unrivalled ability to encourage a large proportion of the world's population to go green," he said.

"Maybe we could be clever enough artificially to engineer substitutes for these lost ecosystem services," says May, "although I fear this could see us living, at best, in the world of the cult movie, *Blade Runner*, and more likely *Mad Max*."[18]

For Lord May, the fear in going green and abandoning our oil guzzling habits is that we may enter a period where evil people battle over the last remaining hoards of gasoline.

●　●　●

THEY are the new generation of climate warriors. They are smart, politically savvy, idealistic, apparently indefatigable and very young. They have more technology in their mobiles and laptops than NASA had when it sent men to the moon, and they are "beginning to use them for tools, not toys.

—Australian Youth Climate Coalition Summit

---

[18] *The Guardian*. September 7, 2009; Web Support Site, *Black Bonanza* Footnotes—Chapter 6. < * >

Many organizations have tried to tap into youthful idealism about the fight against AGW. In the summer of 2009, about 1,500 Australians aged sixteen to twenty-six descended on the University of Western Sydney for Power Shift, a climate change camp. They learned about organizing and heard video-linked speeches from politicians—Rajendra Pachauri, chairman of the UN IPCC and former U.S. Vice President Al Gore, who was training an older generation of climate change campaigners in Melbourne.

According to their website:

Conference attendees will learn the best practices of climate organizing, including campaign and event planning, recruitment, media liaison, public speaking, lobbying, leadership development, coalition-building, campaign strategy, and community and campus organizing. The following sessions were available: Graphic design and climate change; Media training; Gender and climate change; Climate change and Hip Hop workshop. This workshop will ask participants to explore an issue around climate change using hip hop. The hip hop debate combines traditional debating with the MC Battle and is an interesting and challenging platform for exploring different sides of an issue.

In Canada, over five days in June 2007, a group of more than fifty young volunteers gathered at a rural site southwest of Edmonton to learn from veteran eco-activists and strategize about how to stage protests of oilsands developments. So far, says Alberta Venture, "this battle has not been joined, in the form of a blockade, boycott, political edict, or loss of business for a single oil producer. But it's coming. Bet on it."

The oilsands industry knows it has to clean up its act. It has been working on ways to reduce or capture its greenhouse-gas emissions and reclaim mine sites into viable wild lands. But it's nowhere near solving the riddle of what to do with the growing tailings ponds built to contain the toxic byproducts of heavy oil extraction, such as polycyclic aromatic hydrocarbons, naphthenic acids, heavy metals and ammonium. The Tar Island Dyke is the oldest, built by Suncor Energy on an island in the Athabasca River in the late 1960s to a height of 12 meters. But the tailings produced over the past 40 years turned out to be more voluminous than expected, and the Tar Island Dyke now rises 90 meters above the river.[19]

Yet in spite of a very real concern about pollution and the Sands, most people aren't buying into radical change. In fact, global warming hysteria and the mobilization of hip hop youth for social change have instead hardened the attitudes of many in the general public.

*   *   *

The oil sands is a massive resource, and undeniably presents some pretty hefty environmental challenges, but I think for Greenpeace it represents the low-hanging fruit of protest potential. Perhaps they should consider consumption-related action, with the understanding that riding bikes everywhere and ditching our jobs and lives to wander the world is simply not feasible (or desirable) for the vast majority of people. Diversifying energy sources is crucial, but it will happen slowly, and it will not happen by "stopping the tar sands."

—Deborah Jaremko, *Edmonton Journal*

In spite of cracks about "the dirtiest oil," and "the worst thing on the planet," polls still show that most people in Canada don't buy the demonization and support oilsands development. It's also

---

[19] *Alberta Venture.* December, 2007; Web Support Site, *Black Bonanza* Footnotes—Chapter 6.
< * >

clear that more and more people in the West are being turned off by radical environmentalism, whose bloated budgets and fundraising campaigns now require larger and larger doses of hysteria to have any effect.

In 2008 and 2009, a series of Gallup and Pew polls in the U.S. concluded that "green" was already slipping out of sight in the public's consciousness, and concern for "the economy" was on the rise. Jobs were far more important than saving the planet. A U.S. Bloomberg poll in September 2009, put climate change at only 2 percent in a list of important issues, after the economy (46 percent), health care (23 percent), the federal budget deficit (16 percent), and the wars in Afghanistan and Iraq (10 percent).[20]

In February of 2009, a Harris/Decima poll in Canada rolled out similar conclusions, that the risk of pollution from oilsands development was definitely a concern, but we had to put that problem aside and turn our attention to dealing with the recession.

The results:

- Some 57 percent of respondents believe that there were more benefits than drawbacks from oilsands development, while 35 percent saw more drawbacks. Regionally, a strong majority in all regions outside of Quebec saw more benefits overall for the country. Support was particularly strong in Alberta, where 70 percent saw more benefits, and in Ontario, where twice as many people saw more benefits (64 percent to 31 percent). In Quebec, a plurality (49 percent) saw more drawbacks and 39 percent saw more benefits.

The Quebec results doubtless stem from the fact that the province is a huge clean energy hydro producer and can afford to look down its nose at grubby western "maggot folk" who dig in the dirt.

---

[20] Bloomberg Poll conducted by Selzer and Co. September 10–14, 2009. N=1.004 adults nationwide. MoE plus or minus 3.1.

- Conservatives (76 percent to 18 percent) were overwhelmingly likely to see more benefits than drawbacks to oilsands development, while a majority of Liberals (57 percent) and Greens (53 percent) saw more benefits as well for Canada. Among NDP voters (49 percent) and Bloc Québecois voters (63 percent) the popular opinion was that there were more drawbacks than benefits to oilsands development.

A "Climate Confidence Monitor" survey released in November 2009 says support for urgent action on climate change is plummeting in Canada. Just 26 percent of Canadians now consider global warming among their chief concerns, down from 34 percent in 2008.

Concern in the U.S. has plunged even lower—to just 18 percent, down from 26 percent in 2008. The U.K.'s level of concern is the lowest of all, a mere 15 percent, down from 26 percent in 2008. Worldwide, the drop in concern over climate change has also dropped by eight percentage points, from 42 percent to 34 percent.[21]

In September 2009, the British Institute for Public Policy Research released a report entitled *Consumer Power: How the public thinks lower-carbon behavior could be made mainstream.*

The study found that climate change left most people unengaged and switched off. Many felt they were being "gamed" by the government and the media, and they didn't appreciate it. They were:

- tired and bored of hearing about climate change despite being aware of it;
- cynical about the government's motives in pushing for action on climate, viewing it as a simple excuse to increase taxes;

---

[21] The "Climate Confidence Monitor" is produced by the HSBC Climate Partnership, comprised of organizations such as World Wildlife Fund, Earthwatch Institute, and HSBC.

- appalled by government hypocrisy, for example, a recent decision to allow the building of a third runway at Heathrow Airport;
- doubtful about the effectiveness of adopting lower-carbon behaviors in Britain when other companies and countries are still emitting elsewhere;
- resentful of being made to feel guilty about their lifestyles;
- dismissive of environmentalists and "green" products as "smug" and "self-righteous"; and
- put off by the cost of choosing lower-carbon options.[22]

Most green groups are seriously worried by this downward trend in the polls, and are having to ramp up their fundraising efforts or let people go. It's tough times for the virtuous, but the most creative will survive. The biggest are continuing to enlist the aid of global ad agencies and top marketing specialists.

In the media, each side is backed by the usual suspects, who love disaster journalism because it gets people riled up and makes a useful frame for commercials. The U.S. warmists are led by most of the mainstream TV media, except perhaps John Stossel of ABC News and the Fox news brigade. The newspapers include the old reliables—*The New York Times* and *Washington Post*, except for George Will, who got into trouble by questioning the "settled science" of global warming.

The overall corporate response from the energy industry, I would argue, has been unengaging and unsophisticated. Some companies, exhausted by internal and external pressure, have resorted to "greenwashing" to clean up their image, as in BP's "Beyond Petroleum" campaign. The more cynical green activists call such corporate efforts "astroturfing"—throwing a green plastic

---

[22] Reg Platt and Simon Retallack, "Consumer Power: How the public thinks lower-carbon behavior could be made mainstream," September 2009, Institute for Public Policy Research; Web Support Site, *Black Bonanza* Footnotes—Chapter 6. < * >

blanket over their industrial activities. But others are finally taking the debate to the public.

• • •

Respect those who seek the truth, be wary of those who claim to have found it.

—Mark Twain

I find it refreshing that the green and black sides of the argument can have a respectful clash of arguments that look at both sides of the development issue without demonizing.

In February 2009, *Canadian Business Magazine* hosted a debate between David Collyer of the Canadian Association of Petroleum Producers (CAPP), and Simon Dyer of the Pembina Institute, an environmental group based in Alberta.

The topic, "Are Canada's Oil Sands Developing Too Quickly?" pretty much sums up the two sides of the argument.

Collyer began by looking at the global context. World demand is booming and will increase 30 percent by 2030, doubling by 2050. On the supply side, we need to meet demand from all sources, and develop responsibly. Hydrocarbons meet 85 percent of our energy needs today, dropping to 75 percent by 2080.

Canada, he said, is uniquely positioned to profit as conventional basins decline. Today, 500,000 Canadians depend on oilsands development, either directly or indirectly. Oilsands companies represent 25 percent of the value of the TSX, and paid $25 billion in taxes in 2007. In the next twenty years, from 2010–2030, they will generate $25 trillion in GDP.

Regarding the pace of development, Collyer said using market factors is the preferred route, since intervention hasn't worked in the past. Regarding regulation, he concluded the industry is among the most heavily regulated in Canada. The key is finding a balanced approach to development.

Simon Dyer argued that, in fact, the Sands symbolize unsustainable development around the world. He states that in Alberta, the rules to protect the environment are not good enough. Officials in both Ottawa and Edmonton agree that protection has not kept pace with the rapid pace of oilsands development, both environmentally and socially.

Dyer noted that a 1990s task force suggested production of 1 million barrels a day by 2020; the Sands reached that in 2004, sixteen years ahead of schedule. The regulators are overwhelmed; there are huge gaps in the management of this industry and a litany of environmental problems. He also notes that GHGs from the Sands will triple by 2017, amounting to half of Canada's growth; if the Sands were a country, they would emit as much GHG as New Zealand or Denmark.

Regarding health, he said there are concerns about rare cancers in the Fort Chipewyan area and there has been a sluggish response to find the root causes.

Other comments made by Dyer:

- An area of 25,000 square miles (65,000 square km) of land has been leased to oilsands developers with no follow-up environmental assessment; this is an area twice the size of Vancouver Island.
- Woodland caribou, an endangered species, have seen a 65 percent drop in the area in the past sixteen years.
- In forty years, only one-half square mile (1 square km) has been reclaimed out of 193 square miles (500 square km), while the mines have grown.
- The Athabasca River does not have a protective limit; in winter, in the so-called Red Zone, companies are still allowed to withdraw water; decisions to protect the river have been pushed back to 2011.
- Industry and government share speaking notes.

- Pricewaterhouse Coopers has told Alberta "without immediate action the gap between oilsands development and regional environmental management will continue to widen."
- The 2008 stock market and oil price crash has forced development to slow-Suncor has cut planned spending to $6 billion from $9 billion.
- Peter Lougheed urges slowing the pace of development, calling it "a major wrong."
- A majority of Albertans support a pause until we get these issues under control.

Collyer countered by arguing that we need to have a balance between development and the environment, and look at economic benefits, relative impact, and steps being taken.

On water use, he agreed with Dyer, but said the industry was making strides, for example at Cold Lake, where water use has diminished from three-and-a-half to half a barrel for every barrel of oil extracted. Industry has innovated so that it only uses 1 percent of the water from the Athabasca River, and there is a 5 percent cap during low flow.

Regarding health, Collyer said he has visited Fort Chipewyan. He noted a number of federal and provincial studies, but none has yet linked oilsands activities and health in Fort Chipewyan; a report is to be released soon.[23]

The oilsands area is 54,000 square miles (140,000 square km), with only about 2 percent amenable to mining. We are currently mining only 193 square miles (500 square km), the size of the city of Edmonton, and new reclamation processes are in place.

Collyer concluded by saying that only 0.1 percent of global emissions are from oilsands, so warming is not a reason to halt development. "This business is not about quick profits. We are

---

[23] The report, released in October 2009, found no evidence that Sands activities were causing the rare cancers that Dr. John O'Connor found and criticized his conclusions as being inaccurate.

going to be there a long time; it is in our interests to proceed responsibly."

Dyer then argued that the Alberta government sales material was downplaying environmental issues. He said it was hard to discuss the need for improvement when one side was in deep denial. He conceded that the industry was working hard to diminish their impact on a per-barrel basis, but in the context of rapid growth, the environmental situation is getting worse, not better. Small incremental improvements on a per-barrel basis are being washed away by massive increases in production.

Dyer posed the same central question that also concerns former Alberta Premier Peter Lougheed: What is the pace of oilsands development that is in the best interests of Albertans, Canadians, and North Americans?

Dyer reiterated that liquid tailing ponds currently cover 50 square miles (130 square km). Industry hasn't demonstrated they are able to deal with this waste; lagoons of toxic waste resulting from the extraction process are growing by 475 million gallons (1.8 billion l) every day. We know the ponds are leaking into the Athabasca River—we just don't know how much.

Canada, said Dyer, is littered with hundreds of abandoned mines where operators have decamped, in some cases leaving a poisonous heritage. The oilsands industry as a whole is only bonded for $13,000 per hectare; this is a ludicrous amount.

Regarding global warming, he said it was a common strategy to downplay the international importance of GHG emissions; the Sands emit three to five times more emissions than conventional oil, amounting to 5 percent of Canada's emissions and growing.

Our entire climate policy is being held hostage due to a timidity to protect expansion of the oil sands. The government and industry seem to see protecting the best interest of citizens as a low priority; the Sands belong to Albertans.

• • •

"I shan't call it the end, till we've cleared up the mess," said
Sam gloomily. "And that'll take a lot of time and work."
—J.R.R. Tolkien, *The Return of the King*

In spite of the urge to spin coming from their in-house public relations people, the mining companies, in particular, need to more seriously address the environmental problems lurking in the Sands. Pembina's Simon Dyer shakes his head ruefully and says that, "focusing on public relations instead of public policy is a strategy that backfires." He and others suggest that it will only take a couple of bucks a barrel to make a real impact against the pollution that threatens local communities with toxic clouds of ammonia and other noxious gases, and the whole Athabasca and Mackenzie Valley with a major spill. "Downplaying the risks is irresponsible. Responsible development can occur only if the governments of Alberta and Canada and the oilsands industry first acknowledge the issues and then implement policies, regulations, and approaches to address them."

Former Alberta Premier, Peter Lougheed, is pessimistic about avoiding a constitutional clash between the federal right to protect the environment and the provincial right to exploit natural resources. Former Imperial Oil scientist, Clement Bowman, agrees, warning that "the oil sands have almost hit a wall" until Ottawa takes seriously the need to clean up the mess, and hold Alberta's feet to the fire.

• • •

While the green criticism of Canada's dirty oil may be diminishing, the sands are shifting, and there are movements being made that will heal much of the damage done by overeager oilsands development.

Engineers are engineers, and they love a challenge. For the last thirty years they have been finding better and better methods to engineer different ways out of the dirty oil problem, by coming up with cheaper and cleaner technology.

What has changed after a decade of King Ralph and his successor Ed Stelmach, is that the Alberta government, stung by the environmentalists, finally decided to intervene before Ottawa's Department of the Environment beat them to it.

In February 2009, the Alberta Energy Resources Conservation Board issued *ERCB Directive 74: Tailings Performance Criteria and Requirements for Oil Sands Mining Schemes.* It gave oilsands mine operators a four-year deadline to stop accumulating fluid tailings and start "solidifying." They have to reduce fine particles by 20 percent by June 30, 2011; by 30 percent by June 30, 2012; and by 50 percent by 2013. They also must make tailing ponds ready for reclamation within five years after they are no long being used, and start to reclaim their mines to forest and fen.

The oilsands mining companies grumbled, but went ahead and registered their tailings pond plans and annual mine plans at the end of September 2009. They agreed to comply because they had no other choice. Most of the cleanup will involve dumping gypsum into the ponds and then burying the solid remains.

Presto, for about a buck a barrel, the ugly face of the oil sands, those nasty toxic lakes that you can see from space which threaten the whole Athabasca Mackenzie Valley ecosystems, will soon disappear. In their place will grow a home where the wood buffalo can roam.

The best thing these miners can do is set up a fund for the local aboriginal and Métis people, so they can start up a profitable buffalo business on top of the old oilsands mines.

Now *that* would be good public relations.

• • •

Over the longer term, Calgary economist Robert Mansell warns that the province of Alberta should take more steps to diversify its economy, because "substantial climate change, dramatic shifts in future U.S. energy policies, or the development of 'game-changing' energy technologies could quickly turn the province upside down."

I get the impression there is a lot of room for the energy companies to stop being the "meanest sons of bitches in the valley," and send a little more of their profits toward the people downstream and downwind, toward taxes and better social services for the Regional Municipality of Wood Buffalo.

●　●　●

The end of the Tar Wars is clearly in sight, as the global warming brigade are folding their tents and going home, perhaps fatally gored (pun intended) by the release of the damaging e-mails from the CRU. Thermageddon is clearly not happening; the seas are not rising, and the poles are stubbornly refusing to melt, despite the efforts of thousands of climate change bureaucrats and climate modelers to make it so.

Frustrated by a cooling sun and a decade of dropping temperatures, the hot air is starting to hiss out of the balloon. The movement was given its death knell by none other than Barack Obama, who, while playing lip service during his election campaign to "healing the planet and stopping the rise of the oceans," stopped short of raising taxes to pay to stop the warming when he found out that climate change was an albatross around his administration's neck, and in the nicest possible way, dumped it. Polls showed that climate fatigue was setting in, and reforming health care and fixing the economy were a much higher priority.

In Britain, at least 20 percent of the people have remained bloody-minded climate change skeptics, and no amount of unrelenting spin could change the minds of the broad middle, who just didn't want to believe any more. Perhaps three years of hilariously erroneous forecasts, "barbecue weather!" by the weather office at Hadley, played a part.

Britons also discovered, to their horror, that with North Sea oil on the decline, if they didn't build some new coal-fired power stations pronto, they would soon be shivering in the dark. No amount of banner hanging or nude campaigning during the morning rush hour could persuade them otherwise.

Still, while climate fatigue is starting to afflict the mainstream, the beat goes on, and many respected institutions have joined the battle against oilsands development. In January of 2009, the revered Washington-based National Geographic Society published an article highly critical of the Athabasca Sands.[24] The magazine article shocked many Canadians, and some Albertans saw it as sensational drive-by journalism.

• • •

The article also sparked an important religious discussion about the Athabasca Sands, shortly after its release in the *National Geographic*.

In Pope Benedict's pastoral letter for the celebration of the World Day of Peace 2007, "The Human Person, the Heart of Peace," the Pontiff suggested that, "humanity must be increasingly conscious of the links between natural ecology, or respect for nature, and human ecology." His words soon struck a chord in the communities of Fort McMurray and Fort Chipewyan, Alberta, and a respectful debate arose between clashing moralities, represented by the comments of the Catholic and Anglican bishops of the territory, who held strikingly different views.

Bishop Luc Bouchard of the Roman Catholic Diocese of St. Paul led off the debate with a pastoral letter opposing a careless approach toward the natural environment:

---

[24] *National Geographic*, in 2007, suggested that "the Arctic Ocean could be nearly ice-free at the end of summer by 2012, much faster than previous predictions," and in 2008 that, "Arctic warming has become so dramatic that the North Pole may melt this summer."

I am forced to conclude that the integrity of creation in the Athabasca Oil Sands is clearly being sacrificed for economic gain. The proposed future development of the oil sands constitutes a serious moral problem. Environmentalists and members of First Nations and Métis communities who are challenging government and industry to adequately safeguard the air, water, and boreal forest eco-systems of the Athabasca oil sands region present a very strong moral argument, which I support. The present pace and scale of development in the Athabasca oil sands cannot be morally justified. Active steps to alleviate this environmental damage must be undertaken.[25]

Taking a more conciliatory stance, Archbishop John Clarke of the Anglican Diocese of Athabasca wrote:

There is no question that when you view the mining process it gives a very devastating picture, which is what we have all seen in the reporting of the National Geographic article. Nowhere did I see any reference to the reclamation area complete with lakes, fish, birds, and buffalo. The buffalo herd in this area is being managed by the Fort McKay band and I do believe there is hope to replace the diseased buffalo in Wood Buffalo National Park with this herd. The important point is that there are honest, and very expensive, efforts to deal with returning the landscape to something like or better than before the mining process began. This point needs to be acknowledged in the present dismissal of the Oil Sands as an environmental failure.

There is no question that there needs to be a fair assessment of the approach that is presently being taken. The former Premier of this Province, Peter Lougheed has made this very point. However I do believe that there needs to be some balance in that

---

[25] "Pastoral Letter" opposing development; Web Support Site, *Black Bonanza* Footnotes— Chapter 6. < * >

assessment and less judgment through the media. Under current atmosphere it is so easy to dismiss the commitment of those many, many people who have made Fort McMurray their home and have used their God given talents and work to benefit the whole of Canadian society. It is so easy to forget that the real resource of the north is not found in its minerals, forest, or water but in the caliber of its people. From what I have witnessed over the past twenty-five years we are blessed in that category.

It is time for all of us across the Diocese of Athabasca and the Canadian Church to support the good work of the people of the City of Fort McMurray and not allow the agenda to be driven by the sensationalism of the National Geographic approach. It is time for all of us to be proud of what people have accomplished and, by the grace of God will accomplish in the future of Fort McMurray.[26]

For many, the argument simply mirrored the debate raging in their own souls, between the green of the earth and their black bonanza.

While this debate was raging, there was another oil sands-related issue emerging to take the focus off pollution and global warming. It was an issue that threatened human civilization itself–the phenomenon of peak oil.

---

[26] "Pastoral Letter" supporting development (PDF). See also the article, "Canadian Anglican and Catholic bishops battle over oil"; Web Support Site, *Black Bonanza* Footnotes—Chapter 6. < * >

7

Peak Oil Terror and the Athabasca Answer

Peak Oil is a potential Black Swan event, where the conse-
quences are so great that after it we spend most of our time
justifying why we didn't anticipate it... It is a global issue and
global bodies need the clout and courage to address them.
—Chris Holtom, former head of British military intelligence

It's a windy October day in the mid-1980s. I'm sitting at the kitchen
table of Dave Mitchell, president of Alberta Energy Company (AEC),
at his ranch south of Calgary. To the west, the golden foothills
roll away toward the green slopes and snowy peaks of the Rocky
Mountains.

Mitchell had engaged me to research and write a history of AEC's
early years. I had driven out from Calgary after checking out the company's archives and various operations—from the gas wells at Suffield
military range, to the refinery and pipeline facilities at Edmonton, to
the mammoth Syncrude plant north of Fort McMurray.

We had tromped around the ranch where he proudly showed
me a new cattle pen he had developed that was "easier on the
animals." Back in the ranch kitchen, we warmed our hands with
a cup of instant coffee. "You know," he said, with what I thought

was a twinkle in his eye, "there's more crude oil in the tar sands than there is in the entire Middle East."

At the time I was talking with Mitchell, whose company then owned a big hunk of Syncrude, experts reckoned that we could get about 100 billion barrels out of the Sands using strip mining. The rest was simply too deep to get at. But while Mitchell and I were talking, he didn't let me in on a secret—a Calgary geochemist named Roger Butler had just figured out a potential way to extract hundreds of billions more barrels from deep in the Sands by pumping down steam and pumping up crude. Mitchell, an oilman's oilman, who had spent his life drilling a decent percentage of dry holes, could hardly believe what he was hearing about Butler's experiments and the number of barrels that could be extracted using this new method.

Even today there are unbelievers, despite evidence that we can tap at least one trillion barrels from the Athabasca Sands. The good news is being virtually ignored by analysts at the International Energy Agency and the prophets of peak oil. Peak oilers, those who subscribe to the theory that we are not discovering enough new oil to meet our future needs, are particularly blind to Canada's black bonanza. To them, it's "unconventional."

So what is the premise of peak oil and does it holds water? How serious is the threat of decline and what are the grounds for action—essentially rationing our remaining reserves?

• • •

A big fear is that the largest oil field in the world, Saudi Arabia's Gowar, which brings us just above 4 million barrels a day—5 percent of global oil—is being depleted.
     —Eric Sprott, CEO, Sprott Asset Management

After 9/11, the U.S. government developed a core policy to wind down oil imports from the Middle East, Venezuela, and other less secure nations, and lock-in friendly North American supplies, particularly from the rich oil-soaked Sands of the Athabasca. As Bush's Secretary of State, Condoleeza Rice,[1] a former Conoco oil executive, put it, the U.S. wanted to diversify and integrate its energy supply, "increasing the number of energy suppliers, expanding the market, and reducing supply disruption." In fact, it was not just supply disruption that was the problem. More and more Americans were starting to subscribe to Hubbert's peak oil theory, that their seemingly insatiable demand was now permanently outstripping supply. For many Americans, that was a terrifying prospect and one that could rock their whole way of life.[2]

Today, Hubbert's many disciples say we have probably passed the peak of global production already. Some even say we went over the hump in 2004.

According to the peak oil tribe, unless we do something radical, the incontrovertible fact of decline from the peak will send our economies and our western civilization spinning into a hellish future, ending our comfortable, urban lifestyles. As it did in the *Mad Max* movie, society will collapse and gangs will prowl the roads stealing any gasoline they can find.

❋   ❋   ❋

Happily ensconced in the snug of an Irish pub, retired petroleum geologist Colin Campbell opines that our remaining crude oil supply is like a pint of Guinness stout, pumped up from the basement, and we are now halfway down the glass. It's been more than a quarter century since we discovered more oil than we used, he says. "Since then, discoveries have been falling relentlessly, despite amazing technological and geological advances. There is no reason to expect this downward trend to change."

---

[1] In her honor, Conoco named one of its oil tankers "The Condoleeza Rice."
[2] See my selection of peak oil videos on the Web Support Site, *Black Bonanza* Video—Peak Oil. < * >

The real terror that grabs peak oilers like Campbell and his friend, Houston energy analyst and Hubbert apostle Matthew Simmons, is the fact there are 3 billion new consumers in the marketplace—the Chinese and the Indians. While the Saudi Oil Minister Ali Al Naimi says, "We have more than sufficient reserves to increase production in line with demand," the peak oil crowd doesn't buy it. Writer and analyst, Robert Hirsh, says it's impossible to know the extent of Saudi reserves since the Kingdom took over all oil production and expelled the major oil companies in the 1970s. "And frankly, on something that's the lifeblood of our civilization and the way we live, to trust someone who won't allow any audits is extremely risky... If we get this wrong, we are all in very serious trouble".[3]

But Hirsh is an old-time doomsayer, and he reckons without the trillion barrels now being made available in the Athabasca Sands via SAGD, and possibly almost as much in heavy oil and oilsands deposits in the rest of the world, particularly Venezuela and Russia. Peak oilers reckon without the ability of a free market to deliver the goods, and they are finding their theory hard to justify with the recent natural gas glut produced by innovations like horizontal drilling.

* * *

We are headed into a social and economic maelstrom so severe, as the people on this earth contest over the remaining oil and gas supplies, that everything about contemporary life in America will have to be rearranged, reorganized, reformed, and re-scaled. The infrastructure of suburbia just won't work without utterly dependable supplies of reliably

---

[3] Journeyman Pictures, from an ABC Australia Interview; Web Support Site, *Black Bonanza* Footnotes—Chapter 7. < * >

cheap oil and natural gas. No combination of alternative fuels or energy systems will permit us to run what we are currently running, or even close to it. The vaunted hydrogen economy is, at this stage, a complete fantasy, and at the very least there is going to be an interlude of severe disorder and economic discontinuity between the unwinding of the cheap oil age and anything that might plausibly follow it.

—James Howard Kunstler

Is the growing global terror about peak oil for nothing?

Some petro-pessimists, those who also buy into global warming, tell us with the utmost confidence that the crunch is already here and we're entering a real age of scarcity on the road to ruin. They say our fossil fuel civilization is toast, because world crude oil production has peaked and we're not finding enough oil to replace what we are consuming.

Peak oilers say that demand is still skyrocketing from new customers in China and India, and prices will rise into the hundreds again, burdening industries with job-killing energy costs. For those with a lust for the apocalypse, it's going to get so bad many of us will have to return to hunting and gathering. (Some gentle green souls even think that maybe that's not a bad idea.)

Unfortunately, they say, the Athabasca Sands and recent discoveries like BP's in the Gulf of Mexico will just slow down the decline and do nothing to stop it. Some even say these new discoveries will make things worse, by keeping us addicted longer when we should be going cold turkey. "The greatest threat to our future," intones Canadian political scientist Thomas Homer-Dixon, is not "that our fossil fuel economy will disappear but that it will endure."

Welcome to the wacky world of peak oil, where doomsday scenarios abound and all agree that it's only a matter of accelerating time before Nature's bounty runs dry.

The peak oil movement has become its own industry, churning out new hand-wringing documentaries, articles, and books every other month. Indeed, peak oil clearly threatens to dethrone global warming as the *cause célèbre* of our new decade. This is because when it comes to our pocketbooks, climate change can't compete against energy insecurity. Thermageddon can't beat Carmageddon—the end of the automobile as we know it. What's a 0.1 percent rise in CO_2 in the atmosphere compared to the end of suburban civilization?

The peak oil crusade is attracting many former global warmists, exhausted by "climate fatigue" and the stress of keeping up their increasingly ragged dogma that the earth is warming when, in fact, it is cooling. Some hard-core anthropogenic global warming (AGW) activists are even adapting the peak oil theory to bolster their climate change arguments, because higher prices will be one more reason to butt out of petroleum, which is what they really want us to do. With peak oil, they say, winter produce will be too expensive to ship, commuting by car will become too expensive, we'll have to relocate, change jobs, abandon the suburbs, go vegetarian, tele-commute, and all those good things.

What these activists don't realize is that without petroleum-based fertilizers and diesel fuel, or a close substitute, world agriculture could decline to third-world conditions, and mass starvation could be the result. In the eyes of some radical warmists, that might not be a bad thing, because the world is far too populated anyway.

• • •

My father rode a camel, I drive a car, my son flies a jet plane, his son will ride a camel.

—Saudi saying

If we apply our "Where's the money?" rule to peak oil hysteria, we unearth many of the same suspects that we found with the global warming neurosis, with the addition of the Kingdom of Saudi Arabia. Since peak oil means scarcity, higher prices, and government management, I believe that a growing terror about peak oil will benefit Saudi Arabia, because American insecurity and thirst for oil will ensure that Washington keeps on protecting the Kingdom.

American global warming leaders, George Soros and Al Gore, have peripheral but key links to the Saudis. Soros' Open Society Institute is represented by Qorvis Communications Inc., the major public relations advisor to the Saudis, who have spent millions since 9/11 on focus groups, print, radio, television ads, and so on, to shore up the Kingdom's reputation. Qorvis' strategic partner, Washington law firm Patton Boggs LLP, is the second-largest lobby shop in Washington, and performs major lobbying for the Saudis. Many of its partners have worked on Al Gore's campaigns.

So, to make some sense of the peak oil issue and how it relates to the Athabasca Sands, we should start by looking more closely at the Kingdom of Saudi Arabia, and America's long-standing relationship with the House of Saud.

For sixty years, the Kingdom of Saudi Arabia has enjoyed privileged access to U.S. oil markets and to the very highest levels of American power. And the Saudis have rewarded their American friends handsomely.

In spite of stresses and strains, U.S. ties with Saudi Arabia have been strong since 1945, when a dying Franklin D. Roosevelt met an aging King Ibn Saud on a U.S. battleship in the Persian Gulf. They forged an enduring bargain in which Riyadh provides oil to the U.S. and helps maintain the supply-demand balance in the world. In return, Washington provides military security to the Kingdom.

This bargain has always been more important to Saudi princes than American politicians, because it involves the very survival of their family business: the country is the personal property of one ruling dynasty.

Due to internal fighting and shifting foreign relations with its neighbors Egypt, Israel, Iraq, and Iran, the Saudis have not always been happy with their arrangement with America, and the U.S.–Saudi friendship has shown signs of slipping, in spite of the best efforts of the friends of the Kingdom in Washington.

Back in 1972, two years after the U.S. reached peak oil production and following the Arab–Israeli "Yom Kippur" War, the Organization of Petroleum Exporting Countries (OPEC), following a meeting on oil prices in Vienna, raised their price by 70 percent, from $3.01 a barrel to $5.11, and also declared an embargo on all oil sales to the U.S. and the Netherlands—the major oil port of Western Europe. Crude prices surged to over $11 a barrel by January 1974, causing the worst economic decline since the Great Depression.

World prices then collapsed in the mid-1980s, and by 1998, reached the lowest price in real terms that they have ever been. Record lows led to U.S. over-consumption, an era of monster trucks and SUVs, and then to the collapse of an unprepared U.S. auto industry when crude prices recovered and shot up in the first decade of the twenty-first century.

The oil shocks of the seventies and eighties were a major wakeup call to the West, and declared that the era of easy energy was ending. U.S. Presidents from Nixon to Clinton played up "energy independence" to reassure citizens that their country could serve its own needs with the help of its allies. But it was not until the tragic events of 9/11 that the shattered American psyche woke up to the global problem of "energy security." When it became apparent that a rogue son of the Saudi Arabian Bin Laden clan had masterminded the attacks, and fourteen of the hijackers were Saudis, the U.S. was deeply shaken and lost some confidence in its ability to control the global energy environment. The wars to liberate Iraq and Afghanistan followed to shore up and protect the embattled Kingdom of Saudi Arabia, but also to counterbalance Iran and control a new secure supply.

Big changes have occurred since Sheik Ahmed Zaki Yamani was the Saudi oil minister, and Saudi Arabia governed the price of oil for OPEC. Today, veteran Saudi oil minister, Ali al-Naimi, laments that OPEC has lost control over prices to the New York Mercantile Exchange (NYMEX) who deal in "paper oil." "Despite our best efforts, Saudi Arabia and OPEC have had little ability to curb the rapid rise in prices," he says. When pressed about who is to blame for high oil prices, Al-Naimi says it's not Saudi Arabia, it's "unwarranted pessimism"—Saudi Arabia has oceans of oil. He blames "speculators" on the one hand and "Canada's high-cost oilsands industry" on the other.

Al-Naimi estimates that there are 7 trillion barrels of oil left on the planet. What he doesn't say is that almost half of that is in Canada.

• • •

All in all, I wish we had discovered water.
    —Sheik Ahmed Zaki Yamani, Saudi Oil Minister

The tragedy of 9/11 also led the U.S. Congress to put America's historic relationship with the Kingdom under the microscope and examine how the Kingdom's tolerance of a radical wing of its state religion, Wahhabi Islam, could lead to terrorism and jihadism. Some argued that the relationship had to end, and this led to considerable stresses and strains within the Washington power establishment and between Washington and Riyadh.

The fact remains that since 9/11, the percentage of Saudi oil that has made it to U.S. refineries has trended lower, and not because of peak oil and scarcity. In 2004, Canada surpassed the Saudis as America's number one supplier of crude.[4]

---

[4] See U.S. Imports by Country of Origin; Web Support Site, *Black Bonanza* Footnotes— Chapter 7. < * >

The election of President Barack Obama restored some sense of balance with the Saudis—the new president had a Muslim father and was schooled by Muslim teachers during his boyhood in Indonesia. At his first meeting with King Abdullah Bin Abdul Aziz, President Obama bowed from the waist, a gesture he did not accord to the Queen of England hours earlier.

There is a greater fear haunting the Saudis than losing the U.S. military umbrella. It's the fear of progress and change, not necessarily in their society, but in the kind of innovative technology now being developed in Canadian labs that has given Canada more accessible oil than the entire Middle East. Saudi leaders have publicly expressed these worries for the past twenty years. In February 2009, Saudi oil minister, Ali al-Naimi, predicted a "nightmare scenario" for the Kingdom if client countries started developing cheaper alternative fuels. As far back as 1990, Sheikh Ahmed Zaki Yamani said the same thing, calling technology "the real enemy for OPEC."

In private, the Saudis are gnawing their nails about their own looming peak oil problem—how long their oil will last and whether they will go back to riding camels in one generation. They are still fretting about American loyalty to the Kingdom after 9/11, and about the famous sixty-year-old blood brotherhood signed by Franklin D. Roosevelt and King Ibn Saud. Some even question whether the ruling family will survive or be overthrown like the Shah of Iran, and whether the streets of their proud country will descend into hell and become like the streets of Baghdad.[5]

The Saudis are concerned about the rise of flex fuels, fuel replacement, unconventional oil, and all manner of energy innovation, but most of all, they are losing sleep over the growing glut of natural gas in the world and especially the trillion barrels of new petroleum coming onstream in the oil sands of not only Canada, but also in Russia and Venezuela as they adopt steam assisted

---

[5] Some theorize that renegade Saudi Osama bin Laden's major goal is to accomplish just that, by driving a wedge between Washington and the ruling princes of the Kingdom.

gravity drainage (SAGD) technology for their own oil sands and heavy oil deposits.

The Saudis can still manage the world price and produce crude more cheaply than anyone else, but since it won't last forever, some of them argue, why not husband the remaining resources, even if the U.S. asks them to open the spigots to bring down world prices? They are no longer America's favored oil supplier; they don't even share that honor with Canada, who now sells the U.S. 50 percent more crude than they do. And if the Saudis lose their special influence in Washington and become just another commodity supplier, they are in danger of losing the most precious benefit of all for a nation that belongs to one ruling clan—trust, and the military protection Washington has always given them.

Many modern Saudis now realize they are living in a new world and must adapt, but many are still U.S. obsessed, even though they can easily replace some of the American market with customers in Europe or China. And instead of wringing their hands about technology, they can bring their formidable capital north and start investing in the Canadian oil sands, before the thirsty Chinese snap up some of the more attractive properties, as PetroChina has started to do.[6]

Saudi frustration showed itself clearly in early 2009, when Prince Turki al-Faisal, Saudi ambassador to the U.S., was yanked back home by Riyadh. His parting shot before leaving was to advise American politicians to drop their energy independence fetish, calling it, "about as essential as baby-kissing." He accused them of "demagoguery," and "political posturing at its worst—a concept that is unrealistic, misguided, and ultimately harmful to energy-producing and consuming countries alike." "Like it or not," said the exasperated Turki, "the fates of the United States

---

[6] In late August 2009, PetroChina International Investment Co. Ltd. struck a deal to buy a 60 percent interest in the MacKay River and Dover SAGD projects of privately-owned Athabasca Oil Sands Corp. for $1.9-billion, as well as other financing arrangements. PetroChina is the world's most valuable oil and gas company.

and Saudi Arabia are connected and will remain so for decades to come."[7]

The Saudi prince is, of course, correct. The Kingdom is still awash with oil costing $3 a barrel to extract, and when pressed or prompted to help moderate the world price, it can temporarily open the floodgates until supply meets demand, or until prices reach some rational level. But they can also drive prices down too low, and this power definitely affects the ability of Canada's oilsands producers to make a profit or invest in new mines or SAGD operations.

After a lot of pushing from George W. Bush, the Saudis did open the floodgates to lower prices in the summer of 2008, but they were too late. The market crashed of its own weight and, once more, oilsands operators in the Athabasca had to cope with bust conditions.

In many ways, prosperity in the Sands relates directly to Saudi security. The Sunni Saudis, above all, fear a stronger and bolder Shiite Iran, and they know that keeping the price low hurts the Iranian mullahs. The Saudis don't want a nuclear-armed Iran, but more importantly, they fear the potential for an *intifada* in the oil fields in the Eastern Province of the Kingdom, home to most of Saudi Arabia's downtrodden Shiites. They want to keep the U.S. onside on the one hand, but seem increasingly jealous of Canada on the other hand.

● ● ●

Strange to say, few peak oilers consider the trillion-barrel bonanza of "dirty oil" in Canada. Hubbert apostle, Matthew Simmons, simply dismisses it as "an atrocious resource." Is that because the Sands of the Athabasca mess up his math?

---

[7] Prince Turki al-Faisal, "Don't Be Crude: Why Barack Obama's energy-dependence talk is just demagoguery," *Foreign Policy Magazine*, Sept/Oct., 2009; *Black Bonanza* Footnotes— Chapter 7. < * >

Even most oil analysts still maintain the strange fiction that the Athabasca Sands are second only to Saudi Arabia in recoverable oil reserves. This fiction persists in the face of evidence that the Athabasca Sands are far larger. A trillion barrels of synthetic crude is four times greater than Saudi Arabia's 250 billion odd barrels, and the 175 billion barrels that the International Energy Agency estimates for Canada as a whole.

The long-term threat to Saudi interests posed by the rush to alternative fuels is compounded by Canada having a larger store of black gold than the Kingdom itself.

When Ahmed Zaki Yamani uttered his famous line, "The Stone Age didn't end because we ran out of stone, and the Oil Age won't end because we run out of oil," he meant that the time is coming, and maybe soon, when we will power our vehicles with electricity. Too bad for Saudi Arabia, but it is also too bad for Canada. So why speed up the day it happens?

Maybe we should speed up the day when crude oil becomes simply a commodity like all the others, not a magical talisman of power. The world will be a better place if crude oil loses its strategic importance—being crucial for national and global security.

True energy independence means we'll finally be free of the peak oil threat, free of price manipulation by dictators and scoundrels, free of soaring and crashing oil prices, and free from the roller-coaster ride of booms and recessions. The U.S., in particular, will free itself of having to spend up to $2 billion each and every working day to buy imported crude.

Energy independence will come sooner than most people think and, as Yamani correctly suspected, it will come from technology and alternative fuels. If U.S. futurist Ray Kurzweil and others are correct, and I believe they are, it will come before 2020, when solar cells engineered with nanotechnology deliver the energy equivalent of oil at a lower price.

●　●　●

According to oil expert, Daniel Yergin, Canada's oil sands represent the future of North American energy. In the next five years, production should double, and the producers are counting on the U.S. market to absorb it all, says Greg Stringham, a vice president at the Canadian Association of Petroleum Producers.

I had a talk about the potential of Sands development with Neil Camarta, vice president of gas at Suncor, in his Calgary office. Camarta was in charge of building the Shell Albian Sands mine from scratch, and he explained the true value of the Sands in an era of declining discoveries. "Oil sands are not the same as oil," said Camarta. "With oil drilling, the time of discovery is the best time, when pressure and flow are high. The oil sands do not act this way, and never deplete like oil wells."

Unlike most deposits in the world that have to be hunted down, the Sands are just lying there for the taking, some of them up to 140-feet (43 m) thick. All you have to do is build a giant washing machine or underground pressure cooker, pay the friendly government a royalty, and promise to clean up when you leave. You don't have to explore for the oil. You know the deposits have a very long life—Suncor, for example, has access to oil that could support its current production for one hundred years. All you have to do is steam the bitumen off the sand or melt it underground, and then thin it with solvents so it flows to your upgrader or refinery. But many critics feel that is the problem. They say that making light synthetic crude oil from heavy bitumen costs money, up to ten times more money than pumping sweet crude up from pools under the Saudi desert. It's so big a problem that the "unconventional" oil sands are regarded by the International Energy Agency as merely a "fallback" energy source. Some fallback.

A closer look at the facts tells a different story. To take oil from the Athabasca Sands, you don't have astronomical drilling costs—like BP's $100-million-plus offshore well in the Gulf of Mexico that is as deep as Mount Everest is high. You don't have to pay the danger premium or subsidize local potentates. Canada is stable, and you could say Alberta is even more stable. After capital costs, you can extract a barrel of bitumen from the Sands today for about $35, far less than it cost back in the 1960s.

For oil companies interested in a stable business model, the Sands deliver. And that's why the world's major energy companies are getting deep into the Athabasca. One-third of multinational giant Shell's reserves are now there. Until the 2008 downturn, institutional investors were flocking to buy a piece of the action, and all of this action made Alberta second only to China in its growth rate. The growth will continue.

● ● ●

Many rational economists and policy experts are now warning against proceeding with policy based on AGW or peak oil alarmism, and trying to negate the alarmists' warning that doing nothing may be too dangerous, and the consequences could be serious.

If we do have a problem with global warming and peak oil, the jury is still out on the seriousness of these twin problems. We have had major warming and cooling periods in history, and the current temperature is stable, if not dropping. We have suffered peak oil predictions before, but when prices have risen, the market has usually delivered the goods.

Many argue that there are very real dangers in acting too rashly, giving in to climate change or peak oil hysteria and bankrupting our economies.

To illustrate the risk of acting rashly, some point to the tragic story of the Xhosa tribe in South Africa, whose way of life was being encroached upon by Boer and English settlers. One day in April or May of 1856, a young girl named Nongqawuse went down to the river to fetch water. When she got back, she told people that she had met the spirits of three of her ancestors. They warned her that her people must destroy their crops and kill their cattle. If they did this, the sun would rise red on February 18, 1857, and the ancestors would sweep the foreign settlers from their land and bring them fresh, healthier cattle.

Of course, this didn't happen, but the people killed 400,000 of their cattle, and in the resulting famine, the tribe's numbers dropped from 105,000 to less than 27,000. Some Xhosa people even resorted to cannibalism. All because of the fantasy of a teenager.

Some historians believe the Great Cattle Killing was, in part, motivated by class animosity. The Xhosa people had been losing ground to white settlers, and some blamed their more prosperous members. Cattle were a status symbol, in effect, the SUVs of their day. Killing the cattle put most of the burden of their destruction on the tribal leaders.[8]

Are we in a similar situation today? And have we developed better ways to handle the social and cultural stress caused by growth, technology, and the use of energy, than by killing our cattle to placate the gods?

• • •

More people, and increased income, cause resources to become more scarce in the short run. Heightened scarcity causes prices to rise. The higher prices present opportunity, and prompt inventors and entrepreneurs to search for solutions. Many fail in the search, at cost to themselves. But in a free society, solutions are eventually found. And in the long run the new developments leave us better off than if the problems had not arisen. That is, prices eventually become lower than before the increased scarcity occurred.

—Julian Simon

---

[8] The Great Cattle Killing; Web Support Site, *Black Bonanza* Footnotes—Chapter 7. < * >

A good way out of our boom and bust fossil-fuel fix is to rely, as much as possible, on transparent markets to sort out supply and demand and prevent gouging by the world's petro-kleptocrats.

NYMEX was founded as the Butter and Cheese Exchange of New York in 1872. NYMEX has the single most important impact on world oil prices and supply, in some ways making OPEC irrelevant. While most of the oil majors offer supply and price insurance to their best customers, this New York exchange is used today by major oil users such as airlines, shippers, and retailers who want to lock in prices and bet on trends by buying futures and options. Financial firms speculating for their clients or for themselves, account for about 80 percent of the oil contracts on NYMEX.

The exchange lets real-world fundamentals determine the real cost of oil, while speculators grease the wheels. In the past, NYMEX has provided an expensive learning experience for arrogant producers like the OPEC countries and the old Soviet Union, who thought they could push prices higher, or it has humbled speculators who thought they could ride a bubble and get out in time.

By late 1985, NYMEX was trading paper oil by the tanker-load. At that point, Saudi Arabia got greedy and opened the taps, rebelling against its role as the "swing" producer, refusing to slow down production to prop up world prices. In one year, prices fell by two-thirds to under US$10 per barrel on some tanker loads and averaged barely half the level of 1985. Months of low prices—in 1998, gas prices were the lowest in real terms than they have ever been—finally made the Saudis see reason. They too had started to lose revenue, and the value of their oil had plunged. So the NYMEX oil market did its job, nudging the Saudis back into their necessary role, and restoring a better balance between supply and demand by calming price swings.

The original NYMEX trading floor was located within the World Trade Center complex. Its location may be one reason the WTC was attacked on 9/11. On February 26, 2003, NYMEX moved into the World Financial Center nearby, and also built a secure $12 million-trading floor backup facility outside New York, with 700 traders' booths, 2,000 telephones, and a backup computer system. On March 17, 2008, NYMEX was bought out by CME Group, the parent of the Chicago Mercantile Exchange and the Chicago Board of Trade.

From 2003–2009, world oil demand rose by 8 million barrels a day with the entry of China and India into the market. Only thirteen years ago, China was a net oil exporter; today it is the second-biggest importer in the world, after the U.S. This and other "above ground demand factors" have recently conspired to drive up the price of oil. As well, underinvestment in the 1990s, when oil was cheap, has resulted in too few tankers and refineries in places like Iran, Iraq, and Nigeria, which are surrounded by turmoil.

In the recent run-up to $140 a barrel and the subsequent crash, producing governments failed to predict skyrocketing demand and consumers were afraid that there wouldn't be enough supply to cope. But that is where NYMEX comes in, giving the world future price signals so that investments could be made where they were most needed. The energy business did not collapse, but the price crash sure went a long way toward damping down irrational exuberance. Its likely effect on production from the Athabasca Sands will be to keep prices moderate, but stable, and that is what the industry needs to avoid cycles of boom and bust.

• • •

Perhaps trumping all other factors against the peak oil argument is the very real security that a stable supply of Athabasca oil gives to North America and the world.

Having a trillion barrels of supply in a friendly location and available at $60 a barrel and up, means that no dictatorial regime will be able to hold the world to ransom.

Such a supply can also be used as a weapon, in conjunction with other suppliers like Saudi Arabia. If Venezuela's Chavez or the Iranian theocracy decides to hold hostage developing countries such as China or India, or even stable oil-poor areas like Europe, by tightening supply to exercise leverage, then Saudi and Canadian oil can ride to the rescue.

The stability this state of affairs gives to the world is incalculable. And the power it gives to those in control is paramount. Some argue that the collapse of the Soviet Union in the 1980s was due, more than anything, to the collapse in the world price of crude, engineered by Saudi overproduction.

Current low prices are clearly useful in bringing lunatics and bullies to heel. The International Monetary Fund recently determined that oil prices must rise to $90–$95 a barrel; for Iran and Venezuela to balance their books. With the price at $75–$80 a barrel, the Iranian economy alone will lose $50 billion a year. Current Sands producers can live with a price of $65 a barrel.

Bearing all of this in mind, it would seem very much to the geopolitical advantage of democratic nations to keep fossil fuel prices low.

* * *

All media exist to invest our lives with artificial perceptions and arbitrary values.

—Marshall McLuhan

If the truth be told, many in "Big Oil" have tended to regard the whole green and peak oil movements as a bit of an annoyance. Some are still living in the past, when the "Seven Sisters" ruled the world. Now these oil companies are running only 25 percent of the world's oil business—the national oil companies (NOCs) like Saudi Aramco or Mexico's Pemex or Petroleos Venezuela run the rest.

In the last decade, Big Oil has had to scramble for a response to the green and peak oil movements. Their public relations departments have attempted all manner of greenwashing and astroturfing to portray themselves as good corporate citizens. To great hilarity, BP even reinvented itself as "Beyond Petroleum" for a while. Nobody believed them, and the campaign was quietly shelved. But now, Big Oil is playing hardball, and they are determined to engineer themselves out of this political predicament. And it looks as if they are succeeding, with the help of recession economics.

When Obama's cap-and-trade scheme came up against the reality of the U.S. Congress—the world's largest lobby bazaar—it squeaked through in the House, but it was gutted and delayed, perhaps fatally, in the Senate. A recession was no time to be tinkering with an $800 million cap-and-trade scheme that could lead to massive tax increases that would, in turn, delay the U.S. recovery.

It's not easy being green, said Kermit the Frog on *Sesame Street*, and the consumption of fossil fuels goes on regardless, even in the most progressive hives of green consciousness. On the U.S. West Coast, while the Governator and his fellow Californians turn up their noses at "dirty" Canadian oil, they gratefully grab all the Canadian gas they can burn. And while excited alarmist groups urged Hilary Clinton to shut down the Alberta Clipper pipeline bringing "dirty" Canadian oil to Obama's hometown of Chicago, in the end, security trumped redemption, and the dirty deed was done.

With a stoke of Clinton's pen and an Obama speech at the UN downplaying the Copenhagen climate change meetings, the release of the damning Climatic Research Unit (CRU) papers and the U.S. gas glut, the air seemed to go out of the AGW and peak oil balloons altogether. But did anybody hear the escaping hot air?

• • •

In the fall of 2009, a group of industry and government stakeholders in the Sands came together at Alberta's Global Business

Forum at the Banff Springs Hotel in Alberta. There they were informed that the problem was not their industry or its attitude to air or water pollution, but the problem was, they were not poking, blogging, or twittering enough.

"The world has changed," warned Richard Edelman, CEO of Edelman, the world's largest independent public relations company, and the lead public relations firm for Microsoft. "You have a big problem and it is going to get worse unless you get your story out there," said Edelman. "Once the facts are understood, there's acceptance of the need for oil sands oil."[9]

The *Financial Post's* Diane Francis agreed with Edelman, saying that:

> Alberta and Canada have an image problem and it's called the oil sands. Non-government organizations such as Greenpeace and others have made these gigantic open-pit mining operations their current whipping boy. And by deploying hyperbole or inaccuracies, these organizations are winning the public relations game in the U.S. where the lion's share of this oil is destined. For instance, California's environmentalists are calling for an outright ban on oil from Alberta's oil sands on the basis that it is unacceptably "dirty" even though most of California's crude oil is identical in terms of its environmental "footprint" or its emissions when refined or used.[10]

Edelman told that gathering that unless they got out there and corrected these inaccuracies, they would spread uncorrected across the blogosphere and other sites. He then quoted Benjamin Franklin: "A lie spreads around the world overnight before the truth even gets out of bed."

---

[9] Edelman's London office is a favorite target of the green activists who are protesting Edelman's consulting work for the company building a new coal-fired power station, without which, Britain will freeze in the dark.

[10] Diane Francis, "Canada's oil sands PR train wreck"; Web Support Site, *Black Bonanza* Footnotes—Chapter 7. < * >

Edelman told the stakeholders they had to proactively communicate their message on new media platforms: "You have to go to where the conversation is and this means posting on influential blogs, social sites like Facebook, Twitter, YouTube, and creating your own online websites where the debate, pro and con, can be posted plus research." He said this was how, with his help, the American Petroleum Institute convinced the American public to support offshore drilling, which went from 75 percent opposed to offshore drilling in 2008, to 75 percent of polled Americans in favor in 2009.

"You have to inform the conversation; act and tell; engage with influencers of all stripes; create and co-create content," he said. "You have to tell your story multiple times in multiple places."

I'm not sure whether I buy Edelman's prescription. Groups like the Canadian Association of Petroleum Producers (CAPP) are already doing a lot of Internet work.

But is getting acceptance for your story the point at all? Do those Greenpeace eco-warriors who chained themselves to a Shell heavy hauler give a damn about "acceptance of the need for oil sands oil?" Of course not, because you're not trying to convince them. They're just trying to steal the show. You're trying to shore up your middle ground.

A number of people that I have talked to in the industry feel like they have been cornered by a green lynch mob. "What went wrong?" I asked. "Why didn't you see this coming? What are you going to do about it?"

One experienced observer told me that the reason the industry hasn't stood up for itself is that engineers are, by nature, inward looking, and don't have great communications skills. They just like to get on with their job. In this case, building advanced new SAGD operations, making the Sands cleaner, and delivering bitumen and synthetic crude oil at a lower price to a grateful public.

Another agreed with Edelman, but noted that you can tell the story all you want, but if nobody's listening maybe you have a problem. Then again, maybe not. The more likely conclusion is that the public relations crisis is already over, snuffed out by the recession.

Maybe there's something these Athabasca oil people are missing. Instead of whining and complaining about negative attacks, and blogging and twittering to justify themselves like Richard Edelman recommends, why not clean up the environmental mess and then proudly trumpet the black bonanza that delivers a huge helping of energy security to North America and the world?

• • •

So, where does all this endless "spin doctoring" leave us, the ordinary car-driving North American, stuck in traffic or hauling our kids to soccer practice?

Some new UN-sponsored panic will undoubtedly come along to excite fresh platoons of whiners and wailers. But for the moment, we have the gift of time, because nature has given us another trillion barrels to burn just as we were thinking our entire civilization was toast.

Northern countries will need this energy boost if we start to enter a cold shift—which we may be in already—or even another Little Ice Age. So, in the meantime, as Danish astrophysicist Henrik Svensmark says, "enjoy global warming while it lasts."

We now have the time and even the luxury to concentrate on the major change that is before us—transition to a new energy era I call the Blue Shift.

With energy shortfalls or global cooling, the biggest risk we face is food supply and famine, because the Green Revolution was built on energy and petrochemicals. So energy security means food security, and if oil reserves in parts of the world start to decline, then remaining supplies have to be allocated to food production. To feed the population of the planet, we need time to assemble reliable sources of energy, and that will include cleaner-burning natural gas and biofuels, and eventually solar energy. But how do we get to there from here?

After the oil shocks of the past thirty years, the Sands are a last chance to make what I describe as the Blue Shift, to adopt new power technologies and get to the other side of any energy security minefield that the world may have to cross.

Roger Butler's SAGD invention has given the citizens of the planet a hundred or so years of energy security that we never thought we had. The Sands of the Athabasca will help insulate us from the shock of temporarily higher prices, while we make the Blue Shift toward solar power. The Sands are a lifeline for North America and the world, until we engineer technology that can better tap the blessed radiation of the sun.

8

Blue Shift

A New Frontier in Energy

We are like tenant farmers chopping down the fence around our house for fuel when we should be using Nature's inexhaustible sources of energy sun, wind, and tide. I'd put my money on the sun and solar energy. What a source of power! I hope we don't have to wait until oil and coal run out before we tackle that.

—Thomas Edison, 1931

Blue is the new green.

I was mildly outraged the other day to see a plastic bottle of lemon vitamin water in my local supermarket with the phrase, "Green is the new black," and "Please recycle responsibly" emblazoned on the label. As if drinking this stuff was the coolest thing you could do in the eyes of your friends.

If you Google "green is the new black," you'll come up with pages and pages of websites proclaiming this same message. Apparently it started in 2006, when *Vanity Fair* editor, Graydon Carter, proclaimed the mantra putting Julia Roberts up as a cover goddess wrapped in a laurel wreath of green leaves, with Al Gore, George Clooney, and Robert Kennedy Jr. fawning at her feet.

Bono gets it too, and so does the *New York Times*: "When Earth Day reaches its 35th anniversary Saturday," the paper wrote in 2009, "it will have one small success to celebrate. The fashion industry, built on constant change and quick turnover, is taking a longer view. You no longer have to be an eco-warrior or a hippie to grasp the message. For the cool and stylish, green is the new black."

It's been getting worse, except for the patent lawyers. Over 300,000 "green" trademarks were filed with the U.S. Patent and Trademark Office in 2007.

I'm sorry people, but this bandwagon of green group thinking has already gone down the road. It's become obsolete. Green is no longer the new black.

"**Blue** is the new green," and blue is where the future lives.

• • •

Blue is the color of clear sky and deep oceans, the color of clean flame and the electric spark. Blue is the color of our energy future, a future that is clean, pure, and unlimited, like the sky.

The word "blue" comes from the old German *blao*, which means "shining." Blue is the color of the light from our sun as it scatters through the gassy prism that is our sky.

Blue is the color of cool clear ice and the color of a cloudless sky. Blue is heavenly—the big blue yonder. Blue is Environmental-ism 2.0, covering far more scope than green environmentalism. Blue allows you to get on board the environmental train without having to handle all that green guilt.

Tastemakers are already making the shift from green to blue. France awards the *Pavillon Bleu* (a blue flag with a blue wave) to towns and harbors that meet blue ribbon environmental standards. The Plan Bleu is an environmental project to build a sustainable future for the people around the Mediterranean Sea, while protecting its biodiversity. Even the car business is getting it. Mercedes-Benz has trademarked the name "Bluetec" for its latest clean diesel technology. In the U.K., Level Blue Limited, provides sustainability and environmental management services.

Above all, blue denotes clean, clear water. We call Earth "The Blue Planet" because the oceans cover two-thirds of it. The problem is, just 3 percent of that water is fit for human consumption. So blue is a challenge waiting to be mastered.

Finally, blue offers a more calming individualistic color preference, a clearer more joyous vision of innovation, discovery and inspiration, curiosity and real change.

So how do we get to blue?

●　●　●

I expect Ray Kurzweil has the answer. Kurzweil is a futurist with a track record. He's the inventor of the first practical optical character recognition system, the CCD flatbed scanner, the text-to-speech synthesizer, the first practical speech recognition system and reader for the blind, and the first popular music synthesizer. In his 1989 book, *The Age of Intelligent Machines*, Kurzweil forecast the demise of the Soviet Union due to cellular phones and fax machines taking power away from authoritarian governments by removing state control over the flow of information. Of course, as we have seen, the plunging price of oil was also a contributing factor.

In his 1999 book, *The Age of Spiritual Machines*, Kurzweil predicted that computers would one day prove superior to the best human financial minds at making profitable investment decisions. Okay Wall Street, game over.

Kurzweil has recently turned his attention and his formidable intelligence to the problem of energy, and just in time. Kurzweil calmly predicts that solar power innovation is on an exponentially rising curve, and will scale up to produce all the energy needs of

Earth's people in just twenty years. Repeat, *all the energy needs of Earth's people in just twenty years.* Ray Kurzweil is enchanted by the future of solar energy, which he describes as a form of information technology. He says that solar power capture technology is advancing in accordance with his "Law of Accelerating Returns." That law yields a doubling of price performance in information technologies every year.

At the 2005 TED (technology, entertainment, design) conference, Kurzweil predicted that, "if we could convert 0.03 percent of the sunlight that falls on the earth into energy, we would meet all of our projected needs for 2030."

> We can't do that today because solar panels are heavy, expensive, and very inefficient. There are nano engineered designs that have been analyzed theoretically that show the potential to be very lightweight, very inexpensive, very efficient, and would be able to provide all our energy needs in this renewable way. Nano engineered fuel cells could provide the energy where it is needed. That's a key trend which is decentralization—moving away from centralized nuclear power plants and liquid natural gas tankers to decentralized resources that are environmentally more friendly and a lot more efficient, capable and safe from disruption.[1]

Kurzweil is now working with Google co-founder, Larry Page, to make that a reality, and he thinks the tipping point is near— when solar energy will be more effective and less expensive than the alternatives. The ascending curve suggests we will start to see real results in about 2015.

"Even people who don't care about the environment will adopt it," he says, simply because it will be cheaper. "Solar energy has the

---

[1] See Kurzweil's chart of the exponential growth in the effectiveness of solar panels; Web Support Site, *Black Bonanza* Gallery—Chapter 8. < * >

added benefits that it's renewable, it's friendly to the environment, and we have plenty of it. We have 10,000 times more sunlight than we need to meet all of our energy needs."

Using older silicon panels, the energy per watt is three or four times more expensive than fossil fuels. The tipping point where solar energy will be cheaper than fossil fuels is definitely within five years, maybe sooner, Kurzweil predicts.[2]

• • •

Okay oil sands, the game is over. Or is it?

Not so fast. What's happening now is the spread of heavily subsidized "utility grade solar." The first use of solar panels to power the grid came with big feed-in tariffs in Germany and Spain, where shifting the tax policy towards blue created predictable profits and lower prices, even though motorists suffered from higher prices at the gas pump. This policy kick started utility scale purchases of solar panels and large-scale solar projects. But the recession and competition from cheaper and more efficient Chinese panels has hit these programs very hard.

The key metric is **grid parity**—when it's as cheap to harvest power at home as it is to buy it off the grid. Italy has lots of sunny weather and relatively high electricity prices, and the country should reach grid parity in 2010 or 2011. More northerly nations with cheap electrical power will take longer to reach grid parity, but subsidies and mortgages for solar panels that last forty years could speed things up. Of course, says Kurzweil, nanotech will change the equation much faster than that.

Right now, the solar industry worldwide is heating up and it's all about "big solar" or large-scale plants. The first solar company recently announced a ten-year project to build a two-gigawatt facility

---

[2] See Ray Kurzweil, "Powering the Singularity"; Web Support Site, *Black Bonanza* Footnotes—Chapter 8.

in China, which will be 50 percent bigger than the entire U.S. solar capacity today.

You think solar only works only when the sun shines? No, solar plants can power boilers to provide power during low input hours. They could even be used to extract bitumen from the Athabasca Sands, but here, natural gas still has the edge.

• • •

Natural gas is also a major part of the Blue Shift and is the major fuel that powers oilsands extraction. This abundant fuel burns with a clear blue flame and North America still has huge natural gas reserves. The same horizontal drilling used in SAGD is also making a big difference in the hunt for gas, unlocking massive new shale reserves. Some say there is enough gas in North America to last for another century at least.

Energy leaders like Encana's Randy Eresman says that natural gas deserves to play a major role in transportation. He suggests tax policies to promote conversions to natural-gas vehicles and the creation of a network of filling stations, starting in the major highway corridors. "In the U.S.," he says, "T. Boone Pickens' plan encourages using tax breaks, the conversion of long-haul vehicles to compressed natural gas or liquefied natural gas with accelerated tax writeoffs... That alone can displace about half of the imported oil in the U.S., so it is a huge, huge market."

> By reducing imported foreign oil and replacing [it] with natural gas, you get three or four benefits: You increase energy security for North America; you increase jobs because you have the development of the natural gas business in North America; you improve trade balances because the money is not going off the continent; and you have the environmental benefit because if you use natural gas in vehicles, it emits about one-third less carbon dioxide into the atmosphere.

EnCana is making itself into a major gas player, spinning off its Cenovus Energy Inc. as an integrated oilsands company, with a focus on SAGD bitumen recovery.

There is also the matter of 6 trillion tons of natural gas hydrates, methane clathrate molecules trapped inside crystals of frozen water on the deep ocean floor and in permafrost such as the Mallik gas hydrate field in the Mackenzie Delta of the Canadian Arctic. These deposits are a potentially vast energy resource, but nobody knows how to get them safely out of the ground and to market. The technology to extract this energy may be a major part of the Blue Shift.

The only knock against natural gas is that it may become *too* popular. If we make the shift to natural gas transportation and generate more electricity with the stuff, the reserves may be gone in less than fifty years. Right now, America has about 1 million megawatts of installed electric generation capacity. Forty percent of that capacity already runs on natural gas—about 400,000 megawatts, compared to just 312,000 megawatts of coal capacity.

The Athabasca Sands is a major consumer of natural gas, both above ground and in SAGD sites. Unless the engineers can design closed-loop systems that use their own energy, the Sands will definitely consume a lot more natural gas as demand rises for Athabasca synthetic crude.

• • •

The world's biggest bank, HSBC, says the global clean energy and environmental sector has already surpassed aerospace and defense, and is on track to become a $2 trillion sector by 2020. This sector includes: companies that make low-emission energy gear; energy-efficiency; and water and pollution management.

Whether or not you believe in global warming, renewable energy has a huge future. While some green-tinged souls in the West yearn for a return to hunting and gathering in the Garden of

Eden, millions in developing countries long for, and are actively building, high-energy lifestyles. That means cars, but it also means better food, refrigerators, air conditioners, and of course Internet access.

Of the major emitters, China and India are now realizing they cannot pollute their way to prosperity, because they will choke to death from dirty air. They see that clean technology and cracking the solar energy puzzle is the next great global industry.

We are beginning this blue revolution with high hopes and a new focus. Environmental concerns about energy are no longer driven by a desire to adhere to various UN protocols. On the contrary, climate change is turning into a mere distraction. With potentially higher energy prices, we're finding a very good business case for producing cleaner energy from the Athabasca Sands. That's why the engineers in companies and research institutes are working so hard to get rid of foul tailings, eliminate petrochemical pollution, create closed-loop water and heating systems, and restore the mined landscape on an ongoing staged basis.

It's perhaps ironic that solar energy will eventually replace crude oil and natural gas as the fuel that powers the world, but we should be thankful that plentiful hydrocarbon resources such as those found in the Sands will let us make the transition without stress and violence, without the risk of an apocalypse, and without the collapse of liberal democracy.

• • •

The major danger in the shift to blue is having enough petroleum to keep fueling the agricultural revolution so we can avoid the specter of large-scale famine.

Few people realize the crucial role played by petroleum energy in keeping the planet fed. Global security depends on food, because an insecure world breeds panic and apocalyptic movements that can lead to anti-democratic and dictatorial solutions.

Indeed, balancing the price and supply of energy is key to keeping the world at peace.

In the 1960s and 1970s, the non-Communist world was afflicted by famines, revolutionary movements, and lunatic doomsday predictions. In 1968, a year after Suncor's GCOS plant went into operation, Paul Ehrlich published an influential best seller called *The Population Bomb*. In it, he terrified a large sector of the populace by hysterically suggesting that 60 million Americans might be starving to death by the year 2000, and we would be watching great famines on television starting in 1975.

Back then, it wasn't the rise of the oceans that was the big fear; it was mass starvation caused by too many people. "The battle to feed humanity is over." Ehrlich wrote in tones eerily similar to those used by global warming alarmists today, "In the 1970s, the world will undergo famines. Hundreds of millions of people are going to starve to death in spite of any crash programs embarked upon now... The operation will demand many apparently brutal and heartless decisions. The pain may be intense. But the disease is so far advanced that only with radical surgery does the patient have a chance of survival."

Ehrlich also said the earth was cooling, because: "The greenhouse effect is being enhanced now by the greatly increased level of carbon dioxide in the atmosphere. In the last century our burning of fossil fuels raised the level some 15 percent. The greenhouse effect today is being countered by low-level clouds generated by contrails, dust, and other contaminants, that tend to keep the energy of the sun from warming the earth in the first place. At the moment we cannot predict what the overall climatic results will be of our using the atmosphere as a garbage dump." Ehrlich also predicted that half of all species would be extinct by the year 2000, the death rate would quickly increase due to pollution, we would run out of natural gas in about 1980, and rising prices of increasingly scarce raw materials would lead to a reversal in the past centuries' progress in the standard of living.

Most of the structure of the green movement took hold at the same time Ehrlich's book was released. In September 1969, U.S. Senator Gaylord Nelson of Wisconsin announced a nationwide grassroots demonstration on the environment and "Zero Population Growth," to be held in the spring of 1970. Nelson viewed the stabilization of the nation's population as an important aspect of environmentalism and later said: "The bigger the population gets, the more serious the problems become...." Nelson proposed a nationwide environmental protest to thrust the environment onto the national agenda. "It was a gamble," he recalled, "but it worked."

A few months later, an article in the *New York Times* reported on the hysteria of "global cooling," saying, "Rising concern about the environmental crisis is sweeping the nation's campuses with an intensity that may be on its way to eclipsing student discontent over the war in Vietnam... a national day of observance of environmental problems is being planned for next spring, when a nationwide environmental 'teach-in,' coordinated from the office of Senator Gaylord Nelson is planned."

Senator Gaylord Nelson's first Earth Day was held as an environmental teach-in across the U.S. on April 22, 1970 and about 20 million people participated. Some felt that the date was chosen by anti-Vietnam War activist, Ira Einhorn, an Earth Day organizer in San Francisco, because it was the 100th anniversary of Vladimir Lenin's birthday, an event celebrated in the Soviet Union.

Nelson wanted a grassroots demonstration that, "would shake the political establishment out of its lethargy and, finally, force this issue permanently onto the national political agenda." Denis Hayes, the national coordinator, organized massive rallies, and thousands of colleges and universities protested for population control and against the deterioration of the environment.

Paul Ehrlich happily whipped up the hysteria, telling one rally, "In ten years all important animal life in the sea will be extinct. Large areas of coastline will have to be evacuated because of the stench of dead fish." University of California, Davis ecologist, Kenneth Watt, jumped on the bandwagon, predicting, "If present trends continue, the world will be about four degrees colder in 1990, but eleven degrees colder by the year 2000. This is about twice what it would take to put us in an ice age." International Wildlife warned that, "a new ice age must now stand alongside nuclear war" as a threat to mankind. *Science Digest* maintained that, "we must prepare for the next ice age." The *Christian Science Monitor* announced that armadillos had moved out of Nebraska because it was too cold, glaciers had begun to advance, and growing seasons had shortened around the world. *Newsweek* reported, "ominous signs" of a "fundamental change in the world's weather."

Later that year, the U.S. Congress passed the Clean Air Act and a bill creating the U.S. Environmental Protection Agency (EPA). In 1971, the movement went international with Maurice Strong and Stockholm, the founding of Greenpeace, and U.S. biologist Barry Commoner publishing *The Closing Circle*, suggesting an eco-socialist response to the limits-to-growth thesis and arguing that capitalist technologies were chiefly responsible for environmental degradation, not population pressures. In 1972, The Club of Rome, an association of scientists and political leaders, including Maurice Strong, published *The Limits to Growth*, to draw attention to the growing pressure on natural resources from human activities. They predicted the world could run out of raw materials such as oil and copper by 1990.

Of course, none of this Malthusian foolishness happened because of two things. First, market forces delivered the goods that people needed, and Norman Borlaug's Green Revolution happened. Borlaug was a plant scientist from Minnesota who moved to Mexico, where he developed semi-dwarf, high-yield, disease-resistant wheat varieties that soon spread around the world. It's been estimated that these plants, along with dwarf rice, saved billions of lives.

At the same time, particularly in the West, there was a revolution in agricultural technology, as farmers used better machinery and more and more petroleum-based or energy -intensive fertilizers, insecticides, herbicides, and fungicides. U.S. corn yields, which were twenty-five bushels per acre in 1900 and forty bushels per acre in 1950 at the start of the Green Revolution, are now an astounding 152 bushels per acre. But the amount of energy used to produce these yields is thirty to fifty times more than that used in 1950.

So food today is heavily linked to fossil fuels and inorganic fertilizer. The biggest risk right now is not peak oil; it's maintaining the equilibrium, and we must do it by maintaining secure energy supplies and food at a reasonable price and by ramping up solar technology. This is no time to be taxing energy and shoving people into poverty.

A second risk is our ability to respond quickly to cyclical drought, plant disease, and global cooling. A return to conditions like the "Little Ice Age" in late medieval times would severely impact growing seasons.[3] One risk that is diminishing is the production of cereal-based biofuels, which promised to reduce America's dependence on foreign oil. These biofuels have been a bit of a bust. It is currently a highly subsidized business, which needs roughly one calorie of energy to produce around one calorie of fuel. At its height, one-third of the U.S. corn crop was used for ethanol or alternative fuel production, but today, almost 70 percent of U.S. biodiesel production capacity sits idle, hit hard by the recession and falling oil prices. But technology is riding to the rescue, and the industry is moving to less costly non-food biomass extraction from weed plants, wood pulp, and garbage. One start-up company, Joule Biotechnologies, says it can make 20,000 gallons of biofuel per acre per year, at prices competitive with fossil fuels.

---

[3] See my climate history timeline on the Web Support Site; *Black Bonanza* Timeline—Climate History. < * >

As for Norman Borlaug, he stated that his work has been "a change in the right direction, but it has not transformed the world into a Utopia." On the "green movement," he noted that, "some of the environmental lobbyists of the Western nations are the salt of the earth, but many of them are elitists. They've never experienced the physical sensation of hunger. They do their lobbying from comfortable office suites in Washington or Brussels. If they lived just one month amid the misery of the developing world, as I have for fifty years, they'd be crying out for tractors and fertilizer and irrigation canals and be outraged that fashionable elitists back home were trying to deny them these things."

*   *   *

We must all obey the great law of change. It is the most powerful law of nature, and the means perhaps of its conservation.

—Edmund Burke

Fossil fuels are a one-time gift from nature that has lifted us from subsistence to civilization. We have a responsibility to wisely use this gift from God and/or Gaia, depending on your deity. Let's not blow it.

It won't happen overnight, but we clearly need to replace fossil fuels as our dominant energy source as soon as we can. We should also move away from relying on nineteenth century technologies such as the internal combustion engine; in a standard fossil-fuel car, only 25 percent of the energy is used for pushing, roughly 75 percent of the energy is lost in making the engine and radiator hot. This is no longer acceptable and will soon bankrupt nations who insist on tolerating this level of waste.[4] We have to think

---

[4] See this chart showing how the U.S. loses over half of the energy it uses; Web Support Site, *Black Bonanza* Gallery—Chapter 8. < * >

long and hard about our energy future and how to ease the move towards solar energy—the gift that will keep on giving. When we could cover all of our current energy needs by covering just 2 percent of the Sahara Desert with solar cells, why are we delaying?

We will, of course, need fossil fuels during this adaption period, while we rework our energy systems or we risk global conflict and economic cataclysm.

Let's go beyond the either-or debate and the fruitless global warming sideshow and get moving on change—global warming is just a diversion. We have to deal with the reality of where we get our energy and focus on efficiency and technology. We need to smooth out the highs and lows of energy production and take demand pressure out of the market.

Skillful international energy diplomacy is also required to stop the violence and instability in other oil producing regions. We must get Russia onside and moderate the demands of the petro-dictators.

To get to blue, we must invest in our good fortune—for example, the trillion barrels of oil that have turned up under the boreal forest of Canada—with cleaner and more innovative technologies.

We also have to be more realistic and less romantic. George W. Bush's quip that we are addicted to oil is beside the point—we currently don't have any practical alternatives to petroleum. Wind power, tidal power, and biofuels are all secondary to the continuing use of fossil fuels, and will remain so until the Blue Shift is made. But there is one more massive energy resource—human ingenuity.

●　●　●·

Driven by higher prices and sheer bloody mindedness, many smart people are attacking energy use with a passion, using the best renewable energy resource of all—conservation.

Energy conservation is cheap, abundant, and clean, and it can be implemented immediately. Forget carbon emissions, ozone pollution, roller-coaster prices, and peak oil. Don't worry about the risk of terrorist attacks or the growing dependence on foreign crude that threatens national security.

By wasting less energy, the U.S. could easily rid itself of imports from outside North America. Efficiency doesn't require sacrifice, it makes money, and it's the fastest way to shift to new energy sources that can't be cut off.

In terms of vehicle technology alone, if the U.S. moved to having half hybrid and half plug-in electric vehicles, this would save the country an estimated 8 million barrels a day. Half of U.S. cars are driven less than twenty miles (32 km) a day, so a plug-in electric car with that range would cut fuel consumption by, on average, 85 percent. Plug-in hybrid electric cars can now get 100 miles (161 km) per gallon of gasoline. If the U.S. went over to these and other flex-fuel vehicles, the country could cut imports by 13 million barrels a day.

You would think that one major energy incremental discovery, say in nanosolar technology, could put Canada's synthetic crude on the road to obsolescence as a vehicle fuel. But changes never happen that quickly. Synthetic crude from the Sands is just a great insurance policy for North America.

Canada currently supplies about 20 percent of America's oil, primarily from the Sands, and this will increase with a few more open-pit mines and a spreading collection of SAGD underground sites. Production is ramping up, and depending on prices and demand, will likely settle at about 5 million barrels a day, about 40 percent of projected U.S. imports. But if pressed, the Sands could supply more, and for the next couple of hundred years. It can be done—at about $10 billion each for a mine and $1 billion and change for a SAGD operation.

The Sands offer lots of advantages for oil companies. New technology has gradually ratcheted down the cost of stripping oil from sand. You don't have to go out there and explore. The supply and, therefore, the price are pretty secure, and you don't have to deal with bad guys—let the Europeans, Chinese, and Indians do that. The only downside for oilsands strip miners is that, after a decade of laissez faire under King Ralph, they are facing a hefty clean-up bill.

The biggest risk to Canada is that it will become a petro state afflicted with "Dutch Disease." In the 1970s, the Netherlands experienced a gutting of its manufacturing industry when the guilder rose so high with North Sea oil wealth that nobody could afford Dutch exports. Norway's response, when faced with the same bonanza of riches, was to create a sovereign wealth fund where a large percentage of oil royalties were put into a pool for investment abroad. Because the money was untouchable by the Norwegian government and people, the Norwegian krone was prevented from skyrocketing like the Dutch guilder. If Canada can keep its government small, its tax policy smart, and its savings rate high, it can prosper too, and avoid gutting its manufacturing industry, even without a sovereign wealth fund like Norway's.

Instead of a *Mad Max* scenario of war and decline, the Sands can be a big part of a transition game plan to make the best use of the planet's remaining oil riches.

The future of the Sands is intimately tied to energy security and the Blue Shift. Canada's black bonanza gives North Americans plenty of time to undertake the shift—from black to green to blue.

The Blue Shift is no mirage. We are presently on the cusp of one of the great epics in human history—the age of unlimited energy—and the plentiful, secure fuel from the Athabasca frontier will help us get to this big blue yonder.

It's clear we still have a massive amount of fossil energy left in the earth, but it will get more and more expensive to burn. Whether or not we are halfway through the Oil Age or not, we have to invest a large portion of this bottled sunshine in moving toward solar capture, electric storage, and transport. When we get there, and we will, our civilization will shine like the sun.

Index